AF597800

Salzburg European Union Studies

edited by

Prof. Dr. Klaus Gretschmann
Prof. Dr. Stefan Griller
Prof. Dr. Sonja Puntscher Riekmann
Dr. Doris Wydra

Volume 2

Sandra Sonnleitner

Bilateral Diplomacy and EU Membership

Case Study on Austria

© Titel: Blick auf die Edmundsburg, Salzburg fotografiert von Magdalena Lepka

Gedruckt mit Unterstützung der Österreichischen Forschungsgemeinschaft

The Deutsche Nationalbibliothek lists this publication in the Deutsche Nationalbibliografie; detailed bibliographic data are available on the Internet at http://dnb.d-nb.de

a.t.: Wien, Univ., Diss., 2016

ISBN 978-3-8487-4701-6 (Print Nomos)
978-3-8452-8931-1 (ePDF Nomos)

ISBN 978-3-7089-1687-3 (facultas Verlag, Wien)

British Library Cataloguing-in-Publication Data
A catalogue record for this book is available from the British Library.

ISBN 978-3-8487-4701-6 (Print)
978-3-8452-8931-1 (ePDF)

Library of Congress Cataloging-in-Publication Data
Sonnleitner, Sandra
Bilateral Diplomacy and EU Membership
Case Study on Austria
Sandra Sonnleitner
274 p.
Includes bibliographic references.

ISBN 978-3-8487-4701-6 (Print)
978-3-8452-8931-1 (ePDF)

1st Edition 2018

Introduction: Challenges of the Europeanization of Foreign Policy

How does the process of European integration impact the traditional roles, functions and institutions of the member states? This question is especially relevant when it comes to the sensitive areas of "high politics", in this case foreign policy, concerning vital issues of security and defining the state's position in the international order. The process of creating a "deeper union" and thus the development of greater interconnectedness between the member states of the union in a number of policy areas has driven the demand for the Union to speak with a "single voice" and to shape the image of the European Union (EU) as a global player. Common interests and normative visions, as also expressed in the founding treaties of the EU, add a policy layer to the traditional national foreign policies of the member states. As a consequence coherence became increasingly regarded as key challenge for European foreign policy, also because of the unique structure of the EU polity. In a communication of the year 2006 the European Commission stresses the importance of the coherence of EU and national actions in the area of foreign policy, as increasingly internal policies like environment, agriculture or the fight against terrorism impact on internal relationships and the *"reaching of internal policy goals depends on the effective use of external policies"*[1]. How does the "one voice" of the EU affect the voices of the member states, who traditionally have their own (and often diverging) foreign policy priorities?

The creation of the European External Action Service (EEAS) with the Treaty of Lisbon now was to address the problem of coherence, efficiency and visibility of the Union's foreign policy. The strengths of the newly created service, as pointed out by the then High Representative of the Union for Foreign Affairs and Security Policy, Catherine Ashton, in the review of the service in the year 2013, were the effective and timely delivery of European Foreign Policy, the coordination of EU external policies (trade, development, but also energy security and climate change) and the close partnership with the national diplomatic services of the member states to

1 Communication from the Commission to the European Council of June 2006, Europe in the World - Some Practical Proposals for Greater Coherence, Effectiveness and Visibility, Com(2006) 278 final, 8.6.2006

guarantee an effective division of labour and an efficient use of resources. This raises the question in how far the newly established service was to transform the institution of diplomacy.

Already before the creation of the EEAS in 2005 Jozef Bátora raised the question whether the established notion of what diplomacy is changed as a consequence of the increasing involvement of the EU in diplomatic activities, but also as the logics, norms and structures of the Westphalian system of diplomacy become more ambiguous by the new dynamics the European order introduces to the bi- and multilateral relationships of the member states, not only among themselves, but also with regard to third states. Several studies have been conducted since then to analyse how (and whether) the work of diplomats changed as a result of these European dynamics. These analyses point to a changing role for bilateral diplomacy when it comes to the coordination of "European domestic policy" (policy making within the EU), but also the emergence of new tasks, as diplomats no longer solely communicate their traditional foreign policy interests, but also national positions on EU policies, thus perceiving a trend to the development of a unique "European diplomacy".

This book provides an in-depth study on the changes of bilateral diplomacy in the context of European integration, illustrated by the case study of the Austrian Ministry of Foreign Affairs (MFA), analysing the level of inner-EU bilateral diplomacy as well as bilateral relations to third states. It covers the first 20 years of Austria's EU membership (1995-2015) and contributes in an innovative way to the discussion of the international challenges and the role of the EU in international relations particularly on four aspects:

First, it raises the question of the *Europeanization* of bilateral diplomacy and shows how the participation in the evolving European system of foreign policy making and diplomacy creates the need for member states to adapt their individual forms of foreign policy making to European dynamics. An EU-oriented approach is added to national foreign policy priorities and increasingly collective action of the EU and its member states is required. This has an effect on the bilateral relations between member states, as security concerns no longer rank first, but other tasks gain prominence, mainly related to communicating and representing specific national positions on EU policies. When it comes to the relation with third states the question has to be addressed what effect the interaction between foreign policy priorities and EU foreign policy generates, not only on the formulation of national policy positions, but also on the structure of ministries, the working relation and information share between the EEAS and national ministries and the European diplomatic culture. New forms of socialisation take place, new logics of appropriateness arise and it has to be analysed how this leads to a merging of national interests and the creation of new identities as diplomats assume a dual role as representatives of sovereign nation states and the EU at the same time.

Secondly the book focuses on a *small member state* of the EU, in this case Austria. This is of particular interest as usually the analysis of foreign policy is geared towards "great powers" and their national and strategic priorities. But especially within the context of the EU it is of particular interest how smaller states adjust to the new circumstances of inner-EU bilateral diplomacy and to the system of common European foreign policy making. Do smaller member states adapt differently to the new European structures, as they are more willing to cooperate in a European framework as it saves resources and increases influence and the possibility for alliances? What kind of patterns can small member states develop to find their role within the system of European diplomacy? This leads to the third important aspect, the issue of *identity*. States engage in constructing an "international identity", defining who they are on the international arena (their political self). For Austria this is essentially the status of permanent neutrality, but also its image as "bridge-builder" between East and West, and nowadays to the Western Balkan. This identity is communicated in international relations and forms the background of interaction with other states. But as Manners and Whitman[2] show, also the EU has developed an international identity, based on norms, values, consensus and principles, which has an effect on how the EU is constituted, constructed and represented internationally. How does the European integration shape the "political self" of its member states? Are identities reshaped and how? This book addresses these questions by showing how already becoming a member of the EU had an impact on the rather ambivalent foreign policy identity of the Austrian republic, how especially neutrality had to be redefined after the accession to the EU, but also how this accession redefined the scope for action for Austrian diplomacy.

Fourth, but equally important, the book contributes to a better understanding of the development, the role and the impact of the *European External Action Service*. The studies on the EEAS so far have mainly concentrated on the difficulties of its formation, the changes it brought to

2 Manners, I.; Whitman, R.G. (2003), The 'Difference Engine': Constructing and Representing the International Identity of the European Union. Journal of European Public Policy, 10(3), pp. 380-40

the institutional order of the EU when it comes to the formulation of foreign policy priorities and an assessment whether it is indeed able to deliver a more coherent approach to foreign policy. The novel perspective presented in this publication is that it addresses the effects of the newly established service on the diplomatic relations of the member states as it changes the form of interaction among member state representatives, leads to the emergence of new working modes, brings to the fore new questions of competence, but also provides new possibilities to act. How does the new service influence national foreign policy activity? Can it serve as a kind of central hub of the EU foreign policy making system and thus contribute to the common achievement of mutual foreign policy goals?

By investigating the Austrian MFA and the Austrian diplomatic service within this European setting in detail, the book provides new insights into the contemporary changes in and challenges for European diplomacy. It thus also contributes to the aim of the Salzburg European Union Studies series to discuss current challenges for the EU, and defining the role of the Union in the international arena is one of the urgent challenges the EU faces at the moment. The recent global strategy of the European Union stresses the need for a stronger Europe to face the existential crisis for the European project, as new threats like terrorism, but also violations of the European security order emerge and question the existence of the EU itself. This demands for greater unity, a more joined–up Union is regarded as key priority and thus more coherence across the external policies of the member states and the Union. The EEAS is ascribed a special role to guarantee for this coherence, and new fields of external action have to be opened, including energy diplomacy, cultural diplomacy and economic diplomacy. This publication therefore is a timely contribution to the debate on diplomacy in the European context as a core aspect of foreign policy formulation and implementation. The study is an outcome of the interdisciplinary research project EUFORPOL (2011-2014), conducted at the Comenius University in Bratislava, focussing on the role of small member states in the emerging system of EU foreign policy making.

The first section of this book concentrates on how diplomacy can be embedded in theoretical contexts, offering different perspectives on the practices of diplomacy. It introduces the concept of diplomacy as an institution and shows that modern diplomacy and the Westphalian state system evolved as mutually reinforcing concepts. The EU here acts as a driver for change, introducing new actors to the system, but also challenging the Westphalian system of states as such and thus having an impact on the institution of diplomacy as well.

This actual impact of European integration on bilateral diplomacy is addressed in the second section. It introduces the notion of Europeanization as adaptation of national and regional norms to EU-wide norms. It presents the state-of-the–art in this field of research and illustrates theoretical assumptions on the future of Ministries of Foreign Affairs in the EU, also concerning the likely developments in the professional identity and occupation image of diplomats, also in their engagement with the EEAS.

In the third section the methodological approach is set out that will then enable the analysis of the effect of European integration on the Austrian MFA and the Austrian bilateral diplomacy. Austria is chosen as a case study, as it represents a small and neutral member state. The 20 year history of EU membership investigated, allows for conclusions on the transformative power of European integration on national diplomacy, as it can be brought in contrast with pre-EU developments. In an embedded-case-study design, the inner-EU bilateral relations and the relations to third states will be analysed, investigating changes in structure, practices and tasks, but also analysing symbolic elements, ideation and meaning when it comes to the occupational image of Austrian diplomats. This section also outlines predicted development patterns, informed by preliminary observations, previous studies and theoretical assumptions, which should indicate the overall direction of change and serve as a comparative framework for empirical data.

In the fourth section the foundations of Austrian foreign policy are defined, assessing that they also define the Austrian relationship to the surrounding world. This draws on aspects of nation-building in the second republic, stresses the importance of permanent neutrality (albeit with a particular Austrian interpretation of its content), its small state status and the effect it has on resources, but also relevant aspects of Austrian domestic policy, referring to the influence of the Bundesländer on the formulation of foreign policy, the special status of the social partnership within the Austrian political system, but also the dominance (at least until recently) of grand coalitions.

These different elements have a huge impact on the Austrian foreign policy identity formation, which is discussed in greater detail in the fifth section of this book. Here it is stressed the professional conduct of diplomats is influenced by several sources of appropriateness, a particular Austrian diplomatic identity, having developed over time and having been shaped by specific events and personalities. It draws on the "Kreisky era" and its globalisation of Austrian policy, also successfully positioning itself in the international system with its concept of positive neutrality, but also discusses the effects of the "Waldheim affair" on the construction of the thesis, that Austria was a victim of Nazi-Germany. This explains the ambivalent foreign policy identity, with a focus on the cultural heritage of the Habsburg monarchy and the neutrality status as a central component of the republic's self-perception.

The accession to the EU in 1995 fundamentally changed the basis for foreign policy making and also the framework in which Austrian bilateral diplomacy is conducted. Not only the concept of neutrality had to be reformulated in the context of increasing efforts of the EU to proceed with the project of a Common Foreign and Security Policy, but foreign policy priorities in general had to be brought in line with European objectives. Section six provides detailed insights into the dramatic changes of the Austrian foreign policy identity after 1995.

Section seven analyses the Austrian MFA as a diplomatic actor, provides an overview over the historical development, the legal framework, strategic focus and the organizational set-up of the Austrian MFA. It depicts how the priorities of foreign policy were also reflected in structural and organizational changes, adjusting to new functions, now also in the context of being part of a broader European environment.

In the eighth section on Europeanization tendencies in Austrian bilateral diplomacy, research results from the case study are displayed concerning the fields of structural developments in the Austrian MFA, changes in the conduct of Austrian bilateral diplomacy inside and outside the EU as well as adaptations in the occupational image and professional identity of Austrian diplomats. It also provides information on the role definition of Austria within the EU foreign policy framework, but also the effects of the Europeanization of diplomacy on resources and tasks of diplomatic representations. Here the case study draws on the interviews from three generations of Austrian diplomats to offer a multi-dimensional perspective on the changing processes of the professional identity and occupational images before and after EU accession.

In the last section, results are reflected against the study's theoretical background. Conclusions thereby are drawn on the basis of the predicted development patterns, drawing attention to new forms of bilateral diplomacy, changing role definitions and the Europeanization of diplomatic processes. It concludes that with the increasing role of the EU in foreign policy processes, member states are not only simply confronted with a new actor that adjusts to their form of interaction in diplomacy, but a new actor that challenges their framework of interaction by introducing new logics in a post-Westphalian system.

This publication is supported by *Österreichische Forschungsgemeinschaft* (ÖFG) and *Österreichische Gesellschaft für Politikwissenschaft* (ÖGPW).

Doris Wydra *Salzburg, 2017*

Table of Contents

Theorizing Diplomacy and its Change in the Context of the EU 21

Diplomacy in Theory 21
Diplomacy as an Institution 25
The Evolvement and Interrelations of the Westphalian State System and Modern Diplomacy 30
Institutional Change of Diplomacy 33
The European Union within the Institution of Diplomacy 38
The European External Action Service as Diplomatic Actor 41

The Impact of European Integration on Bilateral Diplomacy 47

Bilateral Diplomatic Relations within the EU 48
Bilateral Diplomatic Relations to Third States 52
The Future of Foreign Ministries in the European Union 55
Professional Identity in the Organizational Field of Diplomacy 57

The Case of the Austrian Ministry of Foreign Affairs 61

Methodology and Development Patterns 61
Data Collection and Evaluation 66

Foundations of Austrian Foreign Policy 71

Nation-building in the Second Republic of Austria 71
Permanent Neutrality as Foundation for Austrian Foreign Policy 72
Small State Status 76
Relevant Aspects of Austrian Domestic Policy 77

Identity-building in Austria's Foreign Policy and Diplomacy 81

Period of Occupation and the Issue of South Tyrol 83
State Treaty and Western Orientation 85
Hungarian Uprising as Touchstone of Neutrality 87
The Kreisky Era 89
Waldheim Affair and Victim Thesis 95
Middle East Policy 99
An Ambivalent Foreign Policy Identity 103

Austrian Foreign Policy in the European Union 105

Accession Negotiations against the Background of Neutrality 105
Implications on Austrian Foreign Policy Making and Diplomacy 109

The Austrian Ministry of Foreign Affairs as Diplomatic Actor 119

Historical Development 119
Legal Framework 131
Strategic Focus 133
Organizational Set-up 137

Europeanization Tendencies in Austrian Bilateral Diplomacy 145

Structural Developments and Changes 145
Austrian Bilateral Diplomacy inside the EU 163
  Bilateral Diplomacy as Supporter of Multilateral Cooperation 166
  New Actors in the Diplomatic Framework 174
  Impacts on the Diplomatic Corps 177
Austrian Bilateral Diplomacy in Third States 180
  A New Framework for Cooperation 182
  Effects on the Austrian Ministry of Foreign Affairs 191
  Austrian Diplomats in the EEAS 196
  Austrian Expertise in the EEAS 198

Cultural Heritage in Austrian Bilateral Diplomacy 203
Consular Services in Austrian Bilateral Diplomacy 205
Economy in Austrian Bilateral Diplomacy 206
Impacts on the Profession of Diplomacy 209
From Neutrality to European Identity 209
Different Preconditions for Conducting Diplomacy 211
New Professional Roles in Bilateral Diplomacy 215

Discussion and Conclusion 231

Direct and Indirect Effects on the Structural Level 232
Between Traditional and New Forms of Bilateral Diplomacy inside the EU 235
Role Negotiation in the European Foreign Policy Making System 239
From National to Europeanized Diplomatic Processes 242
A Third Dimension in the Professional Identity 245
Results related to the Institution of Diplomacy 247

Bibliography 249

Empirical Sources 273

Table of Figures

Figure 1: Organizational Chart of the Austrian MFA 1983 123
Figure 2: Organizational Chart of the Austrian MFA 2017 139
Figure 3: Budget Distribution in the Austrian MFA 2015 141
Figure 4: Distribution of Staff in the Austrian MFA 2015 142
Figure 5: Number of Austrian Representations 1995-2015 149
Figure 6: Geographical Display of Openings of Closures of Austrian Representations 1995-2015 151
Figure 7: Graphical Display of Openings and Closures of Austrian Representations 1995-2015 154
Figure 8: Budget Development in the Austrian MFA 1995-2015 156
Figure 9: The MFA's Share of the Federal Budget 1999-2015 157
Figure 10: Staff Development 1995-2015 158

List of Abbreviations

CFSP	Common Foreign and Security Policy
COREPER	Committee of Permanent Representatives
CSDP	Common Security and Defence Policy
EEAS	European External Action Service
EEC	European Economic Community
EC	European Community
ECFR	European Council on Foreign Relations
EFTA	European Free Trade Association
EPU	European Payment Union
ERP	European Recovery Program
EU	European Union
FRG	Federal Republic of Germany
IAEO	International Atomic Energy Organization
MFA	Ministry of Foreign Affairs
MSA	Mutual Security Agency
ICRC	International Committee of the Red Cross
IMF	International Monetary Fund
IR	International Relations
OECD	Organization for Economic Co-operation and Development
OEEC	Organization for European Economic Cooperation
OSCE	Organization for Security and Co-operation in Europe
ORF	Austrian Broadcasting Company
PLO	Palestine Liberation Organization
SI	Socialist International
UNHCR	United Nations High Commissioner for Refugees
UNIDO	United Nations Industrial Development Organization
VIC	Vienna International Centre
WEU	Western European Union
WJC	World Jewish Congress
WTO	World Trade Organization

Theorizing Diplomacy and its Change in the Context of the EU

Bilateral diplomacy had to face multiple challenges and changes in its recent history. The breakdown of the bipolar world order, the information revolution and ongoing economization have influenced bilateral diplomacy during the last decades. The European experience, however, is of a special kind, as it affects the basic foundations of the contemporary conduct of bilateral diplomacy. Studies on bilateral diplomacy inside the EU give first insights on how diplomacy and the work done by diplomats is about to change in EU member states in the context of European integration. Outside the EU, the establishment of the European External Action Service (EEAS) brought a new actor to the diplomatic system that operates beside the member states. This book focuses on how these two dimensions of nation state diplomacy – inner-EU bilateral diplomacy and bilateral relations to third states – are influenced and transformed by EU membership. Analysing diplomacy and its change beforehand requires an intense consideration of the underlying concept of diplomacy in analytical as well as in historical terms.

Diplomacy in Theory

The growing field of literature on diplomacy conveys the impression that theorization on this topic is at an advanced stage. However, in social sciences, diplomacy is a rarely analysed or explored field yet (Der Derian, 1987; Sharp, 1999; Neumann, 2003; Jönsson & Hall, 2005; Der Derian, 2009). A major part of the existing literature on diplomacy outlines practitioners' experiences and their notions on how to conduct diplomacy (Jönsson & Hall, 2005, pp. 7-9). Some literature has emerged from the research area of diplomatic history, an old sub-discipline that cannot really be linked to international relations (IR).

Examinations on the theoretical level are distinguished by Sharp (2013, pp. 51, 59-60) into theories of diplomacy and diplomatic theory, whereby theories of diplomacy are to be found in international and in social theory. In the field of social theory, diplomacy is investigated by anthropologists as well as by social theorists. The former concentrate solely on potential origins of diplomacy in relations of early societies, while the latter focus rather on the embeddedness of diplomats into their professional environment.

For his exposition of diplomacy in international theory, Sharp (2003, 2013) orients himself towards the English School of IR, which ascribes special importance to diplomacy. The *British Committee on the Theory of International Politics* came to the conclusion that diplomacy lies in the centre of IR and is central to what happens in IR. Nevertheless, Sharp (2003, p. 856) is of the opinion that neither scholars of the English School, nor others *"were able to do much with this insight"*. The English School encompasses a *realist*, a *rationalist* and a *revolutionary* tradition, whereby all three offer different understandings of diplomacy. Sharp (2013, p. 55) points at the fact that there are dangers in this distinction, which can be reduced by not interpreting them as mutually exclusive or competing. In the realist tradition, two theoretical directions offer different views on diplomacy. Classical realist approaches define diplomacy and diplomats as *"instruments of foreign policy and elements of state power"*, while latter realist approaches focus on communication in the international system as the main task of diplomats and diplomacy. Rationalists accredit an ordering function to diplomacy and diplomats in IR. Sharp (2013, p. 56) hints at the fact that rationalism is a highly diversified theoretical tradition and therefore every formation has its particular view of this ordering function. In the revolutionary tradition, diplomacy is seen as an instrument to cover the discrepancy between the self-representation of states, their underlying realities and the desire for peace and justice in an environment where systems of social relations, containing exploitation and domination, are in competition (Sharp, 2013, p. 57) .

Diplomatic theory, in a conventional perception, is primarily linked to professional diplomatic conduct, including rights and duties of diplomats as well as rules of professional interaction. Some scholars investigate this field on the supposition that *"diplomacy is what diplomats do"* (Sharp, 2013, p. 61). Berridge (2002, p. 1) for example defines diplomacy as an *"essentially political activity"* that *"consists of communication between officials designed to promote foreign policy"*. These perspectives ascribe an instrumental or functional character to diplomacy, but the question concerning the diplomatic element of diplomacy remains unanswered. Scholars also tried to identify specific features in order to answer this particular question. Berridge (2002) follows Nicolson (1988) and defines negotiation as the central category for determining diplomacy in political activity, while others offer broader views. Sharp, (1999, pp. 34-35) for example, criticizes the narrow perspective of diplomacy only being a communication tool in foreign policy. From his point of view, diplomacy would not be as central in IR, if it would merely act as a way of communicating. He instead names representation as the central feature of diplomacy and concentrates on diplomats representing interests and identities of their sending unit. He argues that historically, representatives of political leaders endeavoured to stabilize their represented identity and the terms and modalities of representation. Within a thin social context where identities are less apparent, stabilization needs more diplomacy than in social contexts where identities are obvious and rules and roles are clearly defined (Sharp, 1999, pp. 48-50). The question is whether representation, as a central feature of diplomacy, can exist without communication being a core element. The comprehensive concept of communication may also cover representation, especially concerning the aspect of identity-building, which is central in Sharp's approach. It is of interest that Sharp (1999, pp. 50-51) does not classify diplomacy as an institution of the modern state system. He instead perceives diplomacy as a reaction to the need to maintain relations, while living purposely apart from each other. This point of view is related to Der Derian's (1987, pp. 5-6; 2009, p. 9) perception of diplomacy, who refers to the theory of alienation, developed by Hegel, Feuerbach, Marx, Satre and others. Alienation can be seen as a spiritual, religious or social process, which had always been part of humankind. Applied to diplomacy, alienation theory provides a theoretical and historical foundation for the study of its origins. Mediation was required, as the primeval alienation of men from other men led to estranged relations. In modern terms, this means to investigate diplomacy as the mediation of estranged people, organized in states, who interact in a specific system (Der Derian, 1987, p. 42).

Thus, two representatives of the latest generation of English School scholars, Sharp (2009, 2013) and Der Derian (1987), do offer comprehensive approaches on diplomacy with links to social theory. They do also to some extent mark the exception to Neumann's (2003, p. 356) as well as Bátora and Hynek's (2014, p. 11) assessment that the English school was not able to create a profound connection to social science in its approach on diplomacy. Neumann (2003, p. 364) however argues that his book *On Diplomacy* led Der Derian away from the English School.

This exposition of different perspectives on diplomacy is by no means complete, but it is able to demonstrate that diplomacy is a multifaceted phenomenon, which can be perceived and interpreted from various angles. Depending on the underlying conditions, elements such as communication, negotiation, representation or mediation are defined as features of diplomacy.

However, concentrating on individual aspects of diplomacy will not lead to a sufficient picture. Situating diplomacy in a social science context offers the possibility to get deeper insights to diplomacy and to the character and dimension of its change.

Bátora and Hynek (2014, p. 11) outline three existing, *"yet incomplete"*, social scientific approaches on diplomacy: *the environmental fitness explanation, the actor and practices explanation* as well as *the structural explanation.*

Regarding the *environmental fitness explanation*, Bátora and Hynek (2014, p. 11) concentrate on its key representative Hendrik Spruyt (1994), who argues that the efficiency of the modern territorial state in taxation, standardizing measures and warfare was the foundation for its triumphal march. Concerning environmental fitness, Spruyt (1994) states that as soon as the environment of political governance changed in a way such that the sovereign state became standard, other forms of governance were gradually selected in a sense of the survival of the fittest. He outlines clear evolutionary breaks, where the survival of an exogenous shock is not dependent on the circumstances before the shock, but on the new environment and the simultaneously existing forms after an exogenous shock. Hence Spruyt uses a social evolutionary approach to explain the predominance of the sovereign state over other forms of organizing polities. Bátora and Hynek (2014, p. 24) hint at the incompleteness of this social scientific approach when focusing on diplomacy. The incompleteness lies in the fact that diplomacy rather is seen as a *"centralized gatekeeping tool of newly formed political units"* and is not really linked to the debate on social evolutionary change.

The *actor and practices explanation* outlined by Bátora and Hynek (2014, pp. 39-41) concentrates on the micro-level of diplomatic interaction, where discourses and practices are central. They mainly focus on the work of Neumann (2003), Pouliot (2010) and Seabrooke (2011), who detect a chance to determine the changing nature of diplomacy by studying practices and the practical conduct of diplomacy. Thereby, Neumann's (2003) approach derives from the assumption that diplomats act according to a certain professional habitus which can be analysed by micro-level investigations. Pouliot (2010) follows a similar approach and argues for the investigation of changes in daily routines in diplomatic missions, as they are built upon a set of local rules, norms and routines. Seabrooke (2011) instead focuses on a certain aspect of the diplomatic practice. He argues for the investigation of work content of diplomats in order to detect change, with special attention to the growing importance of the economic agenda in the daily working life. Bátora and Hynek (2014, p. 41) criticize these approaches for their one-sided reduction to the micro-level and to actions of individuals. Similarly, they also criticize approaches which mainly focus on the structural level.

Structural explanations *"tend to elevate – and thus essentialize – the territorial sovereignty structure to the level of an all-encompassing phenomenon"*. Here they mainly focus on the work of John Ruggie (1983, 1993), who argues that actorness in the modern state order cannot be understood without taking the constitution of this order into account. From his point of view, the modern state order is constructed as a "*homonomy*". In using this rather biological term, Ruggie (1993, p. 151) wishes to illustrate that all states within this system are *"functionally alike"*, while past systems, like in the medieval period, were heteronom, what means that the acting parties in this system were *"functionally different"*. According to Bátora and Hynek (2014, p. 34), from this point of view, diplomacy can be seen as *"a function of the territorial, state-based system, effectively emerging as a result of state sovereignty replacing heteronomy"*.

All three approaches outlined above, *the environmental fitness explanation, the actor and practices explanation* as well as *the structural explanation*, do indeed focus on a certain aspect of the evolvement and development of the international system. Each approach has certain implications on the process of research on diplomacy. However, for an in-depth conceptualization of diplomacy, all three approaches are too narrow, as they do not make sufficient consideration of the respective other side. Bátora and Hynek (2014) therefore plead for an approach on diplomacy that considers all three perspectives: environments, structures and practices. They suggest focusing on diplomacy as an institution.

Diplomacy as an Institution

Understanding diplomacy as an institution opens up a broad field of options, which includes several approaches and definitions. The term institution is linked to a variety of expectations, based on different ideas. In the English School diplomacy is classified as one of five institutions constituting the international society. Wight (1977, p. 53) considers diplomacy to be the master institution within this system, while Bull (1977, pp. 171-172) lists it alongside the balance of power, international law, war and great power. Watson (1984, p. 4) argues that diplomacy emerged as an organizing institution in the European society of states. Sharp (1999, p. 51) uses the term institution to explain that diplomacy is a response to the phenomenon of people living separated from each other, while maintaining relations. This means that diplomacy as an institution had already evolved, even before the development of the modern state system.

This outline represents only a brief extract of the multiple use of the term institution in the context of diplomacy. Bátora and Hynek (2014, p. vi) argue that if diplomacy is perceived as key institution of the international political order, it should be studied against the backdrop of institutionalist approaches. Such a practice had already been implemented by Bátora (2005a), followed by Jönsson and Hall (2005). The latter classify diplomacy as a perennial international institution that *"expresses a human condition that precedes and transcends the experience of living in the sovereign, territorial states of the past few hundred years"* (Jönsson & Hall, 2005, p. 3). Jönsson and Hall build upon the work of March and Olsen (1989; 1998), who pose the question of how social order develops and how it stabilises or falls apart. Routinized action is a normal status in political institutions, people do what they are expected to do and every institution has a repertoire of routinized action or procedures. Rules are the ordering element to select among them. Thereby rules can, on the one hand, be imposed from outside in a coercive manner by organizational authority, or they can, on the other hand, be internalized through socialization or education, what leads to appropriate and rule-bound behaviour in a certain situation. March and Olsen (1989, pp. 22-23) state that action is more often guided by norms and the need to act in an appropriate way according to these norms than by rational choice. Actors are aware of their social role and act based on their duties and obligations rather than based on consequential decision making. Appropriate action in a certain situation is determined by institutions and mediated through socialization.

Inspired by these assumptions, Jönsson and Hall (2005, p. 25) define institutions as

> "a relatively stable collection of social practices consisting of easily recognized roles coupled with underlying norms and a set of rules or conventions defining appropriate behaviour for, and governing relations among, occupants of these roles".

Jönsson and Hall (2005, p. 28) classify diplomacy as a hybrid institution because it does not fit into traditional classifications of institutions. One of these classifications is the distinction between *evolved* institutions, which develop spontaneously, and *designed* institutions, based on planning. Diplomacy, according to Jönsson and Hall (2005, p. 27), features both elements, whereby the spontaneous ones were more obvious in the early development of diplomacy, while designed elements became evident in the formation of organizational structures. Institutions are further distinguished by being *primary* institutions, which constitute polities and international society, or *secondary* institutions, which are in charge of regulating practices among polities as soon as actors and rules are established and legitimated. Jönsson and Hall (2005, p. 27) argue for diplomacy rather being a *primary* institution, but also hint at the fact that in practice this distinction often is difficult to sustain. Because of this, they turn to another classification made by Holsti (2004, p. 25), who distinguishes between *foundational* and *procedural* institutions. *Foundational* institutions legitimize certain actors in awarding them a privileged status, and these institutions as well determine principles, rules and values for interaction. *Procedural* institutions are less concerned with elementary issues and more with instrumental ones. They are assembled of repeated practices, ideas and norms, which regulate interaction. Holsti (2004, p. 22) labels *"free and unfettered communication"* as most significant norm of diplomacy. In general he chooses a rather narrow approach to it. In his view diplomacy rather is a *procedural* than a *foundational* institution (Jönsson & Hall, 2005, p. 28). Jönsson and Hall (2005, p. 28) however describe diplomacy as a hybrid phenomenon, with *foundational* and *procedural* elements as well as with features of *primary* and *secondary* institutions. Thereby, institutions are not to be equated with organizations. In contrast to institutions, organizations are mostly tangible and physically represented. Diplomacy, for example, is described by Jönsson and Hall (2005, pp. 25-26) as institution, while MFAs are organizations involved in this institution. The differentiation becomes clear if one has in mind that *"diplomacy as an institution (...) has quite a long history, the organization we today associate with diplomacy, the foreign ministry with its diplomatic corps, is of recent origin"*. According to neo-institutional organizational theory, organizations are dependent on material resources and information that support them in conducting their tasks. Beyond that, an organization's legitimacy, represented by its credibility and the acceptance it gets, is crucial for its existence (Meyer & Scott, 1992; Walgenbach & Meyer, 2008, p. 63). Legitimacy thereby appears in diverse forms. Acting in accordance with rules and regulations represents a form of pragmatic legitimacy. Moral legitimacy can be achieved by orienting towards accepted norms and values. Cognitive legitimacy is gained when organizations pursue aims which are accepted as appropriate and desirable. Legitimacy is not a stable factor and organizations are able to influence their respective status of legitimacy. Thereby, different strategies are used for different situations because organizations might be in the position to establish, maintain or reestablish their legitimacy (Suchmann, 1995; Scott, 2014, p. 74).

Bátora and Hynek (2014) argue for an approach that focuses on institutions as an intermeshing of environments, actors and structures, since stability and processes of change are almost never linked to only one of these dimensions (March & Olsen, 1989). Therefore, *"the individual, the institution and the collection of institutions that constitute the environment"* have to be considered when studying institutional stability and change because it is likely that the requirements for change are different on each of these levels (Bátora & Hynek, 2014, p. 48). Their view on diplomacy as an institution is based on the assumption that diplomacy is a social phenomenon, which is currently related to the sovereign state, but already existed in several variations long before the emergence of the modern state system. *"In principle, any form of regularized mediation between two human collectives, be they organized as tribes, cities, duchies or states can be considered diplomatic"* (Bátora & Hynek, 2014, p. 49).

Thus, the institutionalist approaches of Jönsson and Hall (2005) as well as Bátora and Hynek (2014) do not limit the existence of diplomacy as an institution to the modern state system, consisting of sovereign nation states.

In particular, Bátora and Hynek offer a broad view on diplomacy, which serves as the basis for this piece of work. However, the concept of diplomacy as an institution has to be further limited for this investigation, because a pre-EU status-quo has to be determined when analysing change in bilateral diplomacy in the context of European integration.

In his article from 2005, Bátora focusses on the transformation of the institution of diplomacy in the context of the EU and therefore concentrates on modern diplomacy conducted between sovereign states in the Westphalian state system. His view on diplomacy is grounded on two new-institutionalist perspectives, the work of March and Olsen (1989) as well as the work of DiMaggio and Powell (1991a). Bátora uses both approaches complementary, as the previous one concentrates primarily on the emergence of homogeneity in structures, while the latter one conceptualizes the emergence of shared meanings, identities and expectations (Bátora, 2005a, p. 45). The new institutionalism in organization theory and sociology offers alternative explanations to rational-actor models. It regards institutions as independent variables and turns toward cognitive and cultural explanations. Sociological institutionalists are off the opinion that individuals are not able to choose freely among institutions, customs, social norms or legal procedures. Individuals have to decide between different options in all areas of their lives all the time, and they make these decisions against the background of their socialization. Hence, individual choices and preferences cannot be understood outside their cultural and historical frameworks (DiMaggio & Powell, 1991a, pp. 8-10).

March and Olsen (1998, p. 948) describe institutions as *"a relatively stable collection of practices and rules defining appropriate behaviour for specific groups of actors in specific situations"*. According to DiMaggio (1997), such rules and practices are enclosed in structures of meaning and schemes of interpretation, which explain and legitimize certain identities and the rules and practices related to these identities. March and Olsen (1998, p. 948) add that

> *"practices and rules are also embedded in resources and the principles of their allocation that make it possible for individuals to enact roles in an appropriate way and for a collectivity to socialize individuals and sanction those who wander from proper behaviour".*

March and Olsen (1998, p. 948) refer to Weber and Giddens when they explain the process of institutionalization as the development of practices and rules within their related context, the context in which they are used. Central in the approach of March and Olsen (1989, pp. 949-952) is the basic logic of action by which human behaviour is interpreted. Action can be seen as driven by a logic of anticipated consequences and prior preferences. In this sense, actors are choosing among alternatives by evaluating their likely consequences concerning personal or collective objectives. This point of view however seems to disregard the significant role of identities, rules and institutions in shaping human behaviour. From a different perspective, human behaviour can also be seen as driven by a logic of appropriateness as well as by senses of identity. Within this context, action is rule-based. Rules relate particular identities to particular situations. Here, the pursuit of purpose is linked with identities more than with interests and with the selection of rules more than with individual rational expectations. Appropriateness also concerns consequences, but on a different level, as it considers ethical dimensions, targets and aspirations. March and Olsen, however, (1998, pp. 949-952) allude to the fact that these two logics are not mutually exclusive.

Bátora (2005a, p. 44) applies the approaches outlined to diplomacy and its constitution within the Westphalian state system and defines the institution of diplomacy as "*a constitutive framework of principles, rules and organized patterns of behaviour in interstate relations*". Bátora (2005a, p. 46) follows Der Derian (1987, pp. 106-107) and states that *"modern diplomacy and the Westphalian state system evolved as mutually reinforcing concepts*". Bátora and Hynek (2014, p. 75) describe this evolvement as a *"story of gradual interpenetration and co-institutionalization of two orders with dissimilar origins and natures"*. Conceptualizing modern diplomacy in the context of the Westphalian state system offers a pre-EU-perspective as starting point for investigating influences of contemporary developments, especially when it comes to the determination of change, as later chapters will show. Before this, a brief outline of the discussion on the emergence and development of the Westphalian state system and modern diplomacy shall demonstrate their interconnectedness in order to outline the foundation of the pre-EU-status of diplomacy.

The Evolvement and Interrelations of the Westphalian State System and Modern Diplomacy

Modern diplomacy is classified as a European phenomenon in its origins and is closely related to past developments on the European continent. Within these developments, the Peace of Westphalia of 1648 is seen either as the basis of the European state system or as the myth of its origin. Some scholars are about to de-construct the myth of 1648, while others state that the Peace of Westphalia signals a crucial point in the historical development of Europe.

Scholars of IR mainly assume the connection between the Peace of Westphalia and the development of the sovereign territorial state. Osiander (2001, p. 264) traces this back to an article of Leo Gross (1948, p. 20), who marks the Peace of Westphalia, together with others, as *"being the first of several attempts to establish something resembling world unity on the basis of states exercising untrammeled sovereignty over certain territories and subordinated to no earthly authority"*. Osiander (2001, p. 265) states that in this article Gross *"expresses or at least adumbrates"* nearly all components the Westphalian myth is created of, and which are reproduced until today. Osiander (2001, p. 265) further points out that he is aware of only one IR scholar who, at least in his earlier works, had chosen a critical approach to the Peace of Westphalia, but alleviated it a few years later. He refers to Stephen D. Krasner. By 1993, Krasner (1993, p. 235) stated that the Peace of Westphalia does not mark a clear break or turning point in the development of the modern state system. But a few years later, in 1999, Krasner (1999, p. 82) describes the Peace of Westphalia as a *"break point with the past"*, though not in the way most students of IR and international law would understand it, but as *"transition from Christendom to reason of state and balance of power as the basic cognitive conceptualization informing the actual behaviour of European rulers"*. To Osiander (2001, p. 265) this appears like a *"nod to conventional wisdom"*, also because in his treatise on sovereignty, Krasner (1999, pp. 3-4) develops the term Westphalian sovereignty in order to distinguish it from international legal, domestic and interdependence sovereignty. According to Krasner, international legal sovereignty refers to mutual recognition, while domestic sovereignty refers to the formal organization of political authority within the state. Interdependence sovereignty refers to the ability of public authorities to regulate flows across the borders of their states, like information, people, capital and so on. Westphalian sovereignty refers to political organization based on the exclusion of external actors from authority structures within a given authority. These authorities are not mutually exclusive. In Krasner's (1999, p. 4) approach, one form of sovereignty is able to undermine another one. He gives the example of international legal sovereignty undermining Westphalian sovereignty in the system of the European Union. Bátora and Hynek (2014, p. 170) contradict this idea when arguing that these two kinds of sovereignty are able to co-exist. Nevertheless, there are doubts on the existence of an immediate link between the Peace of Westphalia and sovereignty. Schilling (1998, p. 25) points out that the peace treaties were fundamental for the development of the European state society, because the contracting parties had equal rights. However, Osiander (2001, p. 266) argues that the treaties do not contain elements dealing with the balance of power and also do not contain a reference to sovereignty as a principle, like non-intervention. Moreover, he doubts the pan-European attempt of the treaties, because they were only agreed between three parties.

The assertion that the state system came into existence completely in 1648 has been under constant criticism. On the one hand, it is believed that the growth of nations and nationalism is rather a phenomenon of the eighteenth and nineteenth and not of the seventeenth century. On the other hand, it was noted by many that the developments allocated in the seventeenth century took place much earlier (Caporaso, 2000, pp. 2-3). Therefore, the impact of the Peace of Westphalia on the development of the international system is controversial. Some years after Osiander's (2001) criticism of the uncritical approach of most IR scholars to the Peace of Westphalia, Teschke (2003, 2006) argues in favour of a social and historical approach in analysing the consequences of the Peace of Westphalia. To him, 1648 does not mark a turning point towards modern interstate relations, but an alignment towards absolutist, dynastic polities. He is of the opinion that analysing this issue requires going beyond the visible characteristics of political phenomena like sovereignty, territoriality and anarchy, in order to unpack the *"social relations of sovereignty that underwrote the Westphalian state order"* (Teschke, 2003, p. 3). He therefore suggests different research programmes concerning *"country-specific co-developments of capitalism, revolution and state formation"* in order to overcome inside-out and outside-in explanations (Teschke, 2006, pp. 8-10).

Nevertheless, and independent of the impact of the Peace of Westphalia for the development of the international state system, the so-called Westphalian state system is considered to be based on the principles of territoriality, authority, sovereignty, legal equality and balance of power. The modern understanding of society and politics, citizenship, nationalism and political development is closely related to the territorial state (Caporaso, 2000, p. 22). Caporaso (2000, p. 5) is of the opinion that the Westphalian state system in its entity is more than the sum of its individual parts and constantly develops through the interaction of these individual parts.

Although the role of the Peace of Westphalia in the development of the modern state system remains somewhat controversial, its importance for the development of modern diplomacy is generally uncontested. According to Schilling (1998, p. 26), the Peace of Westphalia was the foundation of international law and initiated peace diplomacy and the institutionalization of congresses. Diplomacy had a long tradition in different forms, even before the Peace of Westphalia (Der Derian, 1987; Bátora & Hynek, 2014), but after 1648 the system of officially accredited state agents, permanent missions and diplomatic immunities spread over Europe (Held, McGrew, Goldblatt, & Perraton, 1999, p. 38). Certainly, the conduct of diplomacy of that time is not comparable with today's conduct. Nicolson (1988, p. 32) calls it an "*ill-balanced and undignified system*", full of poorly informed ambassadors and corrupt semi-official agents.

At this point, the complexity of pre-Westphalian medieval diplomacy should not be disregarded. Mattingly (1955, p. 18) argues that towards the last century of the Middle Ages, a kind of common body of law was established, which also included regulations on diplomatic conduct, like recognition and status of diplomatic principles, behaviour and immunities of diplomatic agents, negotiations as well as validity and observance of diplomatic agreements. He also highlights the fact that medieval law was constructed in a different way than through systematic codification, formal acts or treaties. Diplomatic conduct was instead organized by generally accepted principles and old-established customs. The rise of modernity led to the development from medieval diplomatic conduct to modern diplomacy. This process was closely connected to new forms of sovereignty, as Bátora and Hynek (2014, p. 54) demonstrate:

> *"The object of mediation was gradually shifting from mediation between personal representatives of various kinds of principals towards mediation exclusively between sovereign rulers of sovereign territories and later between sovereign states".*

By 1815, the Congress of Vienna, and by 1818, the Congress of Aix-la-Chapelle established the diplomatic service upon an agreed basis. The categories of representatives were defined as well as the precedence in each category. It was no longer the status of the sending state that defined the rank of the ambassador within the diplomatic corps, but the priority of his or her appointment, in order to avoid disputes. From 1815, diplomatic services were recognized as a distinct branch of the public service in the respective country, and diplomacy as a profession started to emerge (Nicolson, 1988, pp. 31-33). In 1961, the Vienna Convention on Diplomatic Relations formed the legal basis for diplomatic immunity, which defines the rights and obligations of sending and receiving states.

The Peace of Westphalia was a landmark for solving inner-European conflicts by means short of war. Beyond that, it is often attributed a greater significance than it may have indeed had, especially if one is aware of the possibility that not only the Peace of Westphalia led to following developments, but also that previous developments led to the Peace of Westphalia. Thus, it marks one event within a long-term development that created the modern, so-called Westphalian state system, which builds the environment for conducting diplomacy between sovereign states. Therefore, the transition from medieval diplomacy to modern diplomacy is not marked by one clear break. Bátora and Hynek (2014, p. 56) perceive a *"co-existence of old and new organization structures of diplomacy"*. This finding opens a wider perspective to the discussion on change in and of the institution of diplomacy, which is represented in the following section.

Institutional Change of Diplomacy

In Bátora and Hynek's (2014, p. 50) conceptualization of diplomacy, the institution can be examined from two different perspectives, as they differentiate between *"the core purpose or function of diplomacy"* and *"the organizational basis of diplomacy"*. Here, *"mediation of difference while respecting a common set of rules and norms"* is defined as the core purpose or function of diplomacy. In analysing the transformation process from medieval diplomacy to modern diplomacy, Bátora and Hynek (2014, pp. 54-55) perceived continuity concerning the core function of diplomacy, while the organizational basis changed. In medieval times, the core function of diplomacy, mediation, was conducted in an environment consisting of individual sovereigns, while modern diplomacy is conducted in a modified environment consisting of sovereign nation states. This process of transformation caused a shift in the organizational structure of the institution as well as in the underlying concept of professional identity of persons, who conduct diplomacy.

Before the rise of the modern state, a variety of forms of organization of foreign affairs administrations existed. The growing interconnectedness of foreign services of nation states and finally the standardization of diplomatic conduct in the course of the Congress of Vienna harmonized the forms of organization of foreign services among nation states. Within this process, the existing structures of diplomacy, which developed before the rise of the nation state, were integrated to the new form of conducting diplomacy, which is related to the concept of the nation state (Bátora & Hynek, 2014, pp. 57-58). According to Bátora and Hynek (2014, p. 57), this was the basis for the formation of an organizational field in the sense DiMaggio and Powell (1991b). Beyond the structural basis, the transformation from diplomacy conducted between individual sovereigns to diplomacy conducted between sovereign states also changed the guiding principle for persons who conduct diplomacy. The diplomatic environment of individual sovereigns was a cosmopolitan one. With the rise of the nation state, the cosmopolitan environment of diplomacy gradually became a nationally informed environment and nationalism became a central part of the professional identity of modern diplomats (Bátora & Hynek, 2014, p. 58).

This organizational field, consisting of old and new structural elements, but also consisting of old and new diplomatic practices (Bátora & Hynek, 2014, pp. 59-63), developed in the nineteenth century through increasing interaction between MFAs of various European countries. In particular, the mutual recognition of diplomatic agents and their rights promoted the institutionalization of diplomacy. The Western cognitive frameworks and meaning systems of diplomacy had been spread around the world, as isomorphic pressures occurred (Bátora, 2005a, pp. 45-47; Bátora & Hynek, 2014, p. 59).

According to Anderson (1993, p. ix), the mutual interaction over time in conducting diplomacy led to unity and to an underlying intellectual structure among diplomats. A definite profession with its own hierarchy and rules had been constituted (Nicolson, 1988, p. 26). As a result, a shared professional identity gradually developed. Now, professional norms, rules and values are imparted through standardized socialization procedures at MFAs. Therefore, professional diplomats from different countries become a group of professionals with a joint feeling created by the diplomatic service (Bátora, 2005a, p. 47). From this point, Bátora (2005a, p. 48) turns to March and Olsen's (March & Olsen, 1998, p. 951; 2004) concept of the logic of appropriateness and argues that diplomats structure their actions against the background of diplomatic rules, norms and principles, which designate legitimate actors and participants as well as actions and situations. Therefore, diplomacy decreases complexity in interstate relations. Despite the differences between cultures, political regimes and interests, a common institutional identity is shared by states, predominantly constituted by the institutional framework of diplomacy. Diplomats from around the globe are enabled to classify events similarly against the background of a common logic of appropriateness. According to Bátora (2005a, p. 46), diplomacy can not only be seen as organizational field (DiMaggio & Powell, 1991b) that distributes shared structures to all states, but it can also be seen as an expression of a transnationally shared logic of appropriateness (March & Olsen, 1998, p. 951), shaping actions and identities of states. In this regard, Bátora (2005a, p. 44) focuses on diplomacy as *"a framework of principles, rules and organized patterns of behaviour regulating interstate relations in the Westphalian system of states"*. Although states around the world differ from each other concerning culture, political regimes and national interests, they do have diplomacy in common, as it provides a common organizational platform for their interaction. One of the central preconditions for the functioning of diplomacy, in the sense of a system of norms and rules regulating interstate relations, is the existence of a common basis shared by all states. Currently this framework is challenged by multi-layered transformations and disruptions in its environment. Several aspects of the globalization process influence the institution of diplomacy and cause changes and adaptations. The breakdown of the bipolar-system led to a transformation of international relations, and the spread of capitalism throughout the world strengthened the economic side of diplomacy. MFAs are more and more confronted with other governmental actors working in the field of diplomacy and they are also confronted with non-state actors handling issues of international policies. Information and communication technology (ICT) changes processes of interaction in foreign policy and diplomacy (Rana, 2011, pp. 13-18).

Regional diplomacy thereby takes on a life of its own. Rana (2011, p. 14) alleges the EU to be the most successful example of regional diplomacy, although the degrees of success are varying (Rana, 2011, p. 38). Fossum (2002, p. 9) even argues that the EU is the most radical peaceful challenge to the Westphalian system of states:

> *"The EU is no doubt the most radical current peaceful attempt to depart from the prevailing doctrine of state sovereignty and national identity. As a novel system of binding interstate interaction it poses a direct challenge to the still prevailing conception of the international system, the Westphalian one."*

When following the reasoning of Bátora (2005a, p. 46) as well as Bátora and Hynek (2014, p. 75), this implies that the EU also means a challenge for the institution of diplomacy, because the Westphalian state system and the institution of diplomacy mutually influence each other in a process of *"gradual interpenetration and co-institutionalization"*.

The question rises in which way transformation processes in the environment of the institution of diplomacy will influence diplomacy. According to Eisenstadt (1964, p. 240), there are two effects an institution can experience, when being confronted with change within its environment. On the one hand, change can be absorbed by the institutional structure, while on the other hand, the institutional structure can be undermined by processes of change. Fundamental change appears in situations where social arrangements, which supported institutional regimes, become problematic (DiMaggio & Powell, 1991a, p. 11). Diplomacy has experienced a range of adjustments and changes throughout its history. Strong institutions like diplomacy perceive and accommodate changes in their environment with regard to the established logic of appropriateness (Bátora, 2005a, p. 50). Bátora (2005a, p. 50) states that diplomacy *"provides 'institutional lenses' for interpretations of events in its environment, facilitates the creation of shared accounts of history, and hence produces a protective belt of ideas and meanings around its own existence"*.

Hence, changes in the institution's environment, like the process of European integration, are *"reflected in a path-dependent adaptation of the organizational basis of diplomacy"*. The result is that structures, procedures and agenda at MFAs are continuously adapted, while the principle concept of diplomacy and the role of MFAs remain unchallenged. Bátora (2005a, p. 50) terms such an adaptation congruent with the institutional identity as change in diplomacy. However, if a situation occurs *"that cannot be met with established practices, rules and behavioural patterns by organizations or a society"* the institution turns into a crisis (Bátora, 2005a, p. 50). Schütz (1964, p. 231) defines the term crisis as a situation where the environment, usually taken for granted, becomes doubtful. Thus, if the environment of an institution changes in a way that the institutional identity is not able to perceive and accommodate, the institution is exposed to a performance crisis according to its own criteria of success (Olsen, 1996, p. 253). Such a radical sort of institutional change is labelled by Bátora (2005a, p. 50) as change of diplomacy.

As mentioned before, to Fossum, (2002, p. 9) the EU is the most radical peaceful challenge to the Westphalian system of states. But is it also a radical challenge to the institution of diplomacy?

Jönsson and Hall (2005, p. 31) describe diplomacy as an institution that structures relations among polities, not among states. They use Ferguson and Mansbach's (1996, p. 34) definition of polity, in which it is characterized as a political authority that *"has a distinct identity; a capacity to mobilize persons and their resources for political purposes, that is, for value satisfaction; and a degree of institutionalization and hierarchy".*

Jönsson and Hall (2005, p. 31) argue that the connection between state sovereignty and diplomacy is not inevitable, but historically contingent. They hint at the fact that a trans-historical perspective on diplomacy demonstrates that

> *"diplomacy may involve all sorts of polities, be they territorial or not, sovereign or not (...) the international system can be conceptualized as being constituted by something other than the consequences of interacting self-constituted actors. Indeed, the international system becomes analytically and ontologically prior to the individual units populating it".*

With regard to the question of what will happen to the institution of diplomacy if existing polities are challenged by new emerging ones, they consider the impact of developments on the levels of communication, representation and reproduction of international society. Regarding the influence of the EU on the institution of diplomacy, they detect tighter communication networks and far-reaching innovation in terms of representation, apparently in the form of EU delegations. They see hardly any influence from the EU on the reproduction of international society, as the territorial state still remains to be the central actor in the diplomatic world. To them, the absorption of the exception of the rule, represented by the EU, proofs the flexibility and adaptability of the institution of diplomacy (Jönsson & Hall, 2005, pp. 160-162).

To Bátora and Hynek (2014, p. 64) diplomacy is a *"highly robust and well-entrenched institution anchored in layers of historically contingent rules, structures and norms"*. Although new actors evolved in its environment and the institution has to deal with new practices, it gradually adapts to the new circumstances, while elements of medieval origin remain intact. The possibility for participation of a non-state diplomatic actor in the diplomatic system, like the EU, is ascribed to the ontological elasticity of the institution, what means that different interpretations of appropriate standards and norms in the diplomatic order are possible. This is not an exclusive feature of the institution of diplomacy. Generally, participants in institutions differ from each other and perceive the institution in different ways. This circumstance is a source for different interpretations and potential conflict, which might lead to institutional change (Eisenstadt, 1964, p. 246; Bátora & Hynek, 2014, p. 76). The EU is one such actor, that interprets appropriate standards and norms, used within the institution, in different ways.

The European Union within the Institution of Diplomacy

Considering the EU in the context of diplomacy offers a variety of perspectives on two levels, the level of multilateral and the level of bilateral diplomacy. The EU and its member states established an own framework for conducting multilateral diplomacy. The states operating within this framework are not only affected on the multilateral level by growing interconnectedness, but also on the bilateral level, because EU membership creates new conditions for conducting bilateral relations inside and outside the EU. Furthermore, the EU itself conducts external relations and is represented in third countries as well as in international organizations. The EU thereby combines two kinds of diplomatic actors: its members being sovereign states, as well as the intergovernmental and supranational institutions of the EU. Hence, the EU is represented by sovereign and non-sovereign actors in the diplomatic system (Bátora & Hynek, 2014, p. 138).

In its external relations, the EU adopts a two-sided approach. On the one hand, its diplomatic conduct contains traditional elements of diplomatic actorness, like promoting interests in relations to states. On the other hand, it contains normative- and cosmopolitan-oriented elements, like promoting democracy, human rights and good governance, in the sense of soft power (Bátora & Hynek, 2014, pp. 139, 144). With regard to the EU within the institution of diplomacy, Bátora and Hynek (2014, p. 155) perceive *"a combination of conformism with established standards and stretching of these standards"*. The EU's neighbourhood policy is an illustrative example for this condition. In relation to states which are interested in becoming EU members or in relation to states which are interested in intensifying their ties with the EU, the EU is able to interfere in domestic policies. Thereby, a fundamental feature of the Westphalian state order and the institution of diplomacy, territorial sovereignty, is challenged. Hence, the EU has established practices within the institution of diplomacy, which are non-conform to Westphalian principles. These practices are, however, accepted by other actors, even if they are unable to use them. Enlargement efforts of nation states for example are usually not accepted in the diplomatic world. Still, the enlargement efforts of the EU are accepted by many nation states. This indicates growing heteronomy, as actors are valued differently in the institution of diplomacy (Bátora & Hynek, 2014, pp. 142-145).

Also interesting in this regard is the role of the EU in international organizations. With the implementation of the Lisbon Treaty and the establishment of the EEAS, the role of EU delegations in international organizations did change, due to their new character in representing the EU as such (Comelli & Matarazzo, 2011, p. 5). Concerning the legal set-up, Comelli and Matarazzo (2011, p. 6) see EU delegations in international organizations in an evolutionary role, because the EU and the member states now divide competences, which had originally been only assigned to sovereign states. The term international indicates that the structural frameworks of international organizations were originally designed for the cooperation between states. Hence, supranational organizations are not matched by these frameworks and every international organization had to find a solution for the implementation of the EU to its existing framework. These solutions differ from organization to organization and even differ within organizations. If exclusive EU competences are covered by the mandate of an international organization, the EU is the main actor to cooperate with this organization. If shared competences are included in the mandate of an international organization, the EU generally has the status of *observer*, *enhanced observer* or *virtual member*. The last two possibilities offer the full functional rights to participate, but without the right to vote. In the case of parallel competences, the EU acts as *observer* or *virtual member* (Comelli & Matarazzo, 2011, p. 6). In the World Trade Organization (WTO), the EU is accepted as a full member beside its member states. Trade is one of the main competences of the EU, and its member states agreed on a negotiating mandate that makes the EU the exclusive negotiating actor in this constellation. In the Organization for Economic Co-operation and Development (OECD), the EU was granted the status of a *quasi member*. Thereby, different committees of the OECD treat the EU and its member states in different ways. In the Organization for Security and Co-operation in Europe (OSCE), the EU is a *virtual member* and has full operational rights to participate, but is not allowed to vote (Comelli & Matarazzo, 2011, pp. 7-10). The situation of the EU in the United Nations (UN) is a special one. Before the implementation of the Lisbon Treaty, the European Commission represented the EU in concerns falling under Community competences in the UN General Assembly, while the member state holding the EU presidency represented the EU in issues of Common Foreign and Security Policy (CFSP) as a full UN member. Now the EU delegation represents the European Union in its entirety, but the EU is no longer able to act upon the basis of a full UN membership, as it is not represented by a nation state. The EU was granted the status of *observer* within the UN framework. In this status, the EU was able to take the floor, but only after all state representatives, who wanted to do so, took the chance to speak. This way it is more difficult to address issues of importance for the EU than it was when the holder of the EU presidency was able to take the floor at an early stage of discussion (Bátora & Hynek, 2014, p. 148). However, the EU was able to win the majority of votes on a resolution that granted some of the most important rights of participation and representation of full members to it. This includes presenting proposals and amendments as well as being able to reply on statements concerning EU positions. Yet, the EU is not able to vote or to field candidates. Still, the EU is the first regional organization that gained such acceptance in the UN General Assembly (Comelli & Matarazzo, 2011, pp. 7-8).

This shift caused serious discussions on the nature of the UN as an organization. The question arose whether the UN charter has to be changed, in order to integrate the EU into a framework consisting of rights and privileges reserved for nation states. This in turn led the discussion to the origin and essence of the UN. For many states, especially post-colonial and smaller ones, UN-membership is an important feature of their statehood and diplomatic identity, as at least the General Assembly provides equal rights to all states. Beyond that, it represents the most important forum for the international community. Therefore, the topic of opening up for other actors than nation states is controversially discussed against the backdrop of the UN being an organization of states or becoming *"an organization of organizations*" (Serrano de Haro, 2012, pp. 20-23). Such developments are labelled by Bátora and Hynek (2014, p. 150) with the term *"new heteronomy"*:

> *"By maintaining its fringe position as a systematically different player on the inside of the Westphalian diplomatic order, the EU is endogenously contributing to its gradual transformation":*

Hence, the EU functions as *"a driver of change"* in the Westphalian diplomatic order (Bátora & Hynek, 2014, p. 156). The implementation of the Lisbon Treaty, and in this context, the establishment of an EU foreign policy personality in form of the High Representative, as well as the EEAS and its delegations, have particularly supported this development. The following chapter will briefly outline the character of this new form of organizing intergovernmental and supranational foreign policy elements.

The European External Action Service as Diplomatic Actor

The EEAS is labelled as the EU's diplomatic service and supports the High Representative for Foreign Affairs and Security Policy in conducting his or her duties. This organization functions autonomously from other EU bodies, but has to ensure the consistency of its policies with EU policies. Beyond that, the EEAS also supports the High Representative in his or her function as Vice-President of the European Commission and President of the Foreign Affairs Council. The service was established in 2010, after the Lisbon Treaty entered into force. Thereby, the High Representative took over the functions in foreign affairs which were previously held by the rotating presidency. He or she exercises authority over EU delegations in third countries and in international organizations. The EU is represented by about 140 delegations and offices around the world. However, the EU's external representation already had a long tradition before the establishment of the EEAS. The first external office had been opened in 1954, but with the implementation of the Lisbon Treaty and the creation of the EEAS, the focus of EU delegations changed. During the period of representing the European Commission, the main fields of operation of EU delegations were trade and aid policies. They were predominantly dealing with technical and financial cooperation programmes and trade as well as cooperation agreements. Political officials in EU delegations were rare, because political and security issues were handled by the respective embassy of the member state holding the EU presidency (Comelli & Matarazzo, 2011, p. 3). If a member state had not been represented in a third country, the embassy of the member state holding the previous or next presidency was in charge. With the Lisbon Treaty the EU received legal personality and EU delegations now also deal with foreign and security policy. Regarding this matter, Comelli and Matarazzo (2011, p. 3) point out the fact that CFSP remains essentially intergovernmental and the Lisbon Treaty does not provide a transfer of foreign policy competences from member states to the European Union, thus not from member states' embassies to EU delegations. Therefore, EU delegations do not overtake the position of member states' embassies in the diplomatic system, but represent a new actor within the system (Comelli & Matarazzo, 2011, p. 5). This new actor still needs to find a balanced role in the system and finding this role is complicated by the multi-layered structure in which EU delegations do operate (Maurer & Raik, 2014, pp. 16-17). The constitution of this new actor is described by Bátora (2013) as interstitial, which means that the organization emerges in interstices between organizational fields. Thereby, interstitial organizations use facilities and resources from different organizational fields. These facilities can be physical, informational, financial or legal resources, or facilities and resources of legitimacy from other institutions. They are used to establish the interstitial organization within certain organizational fields.

The status of interstitiality entails that principles and practices from different institutions are implemented to the EEAS. As a result, the EEAS is confronted with different expectations from actors within the organization and from outside. Thereby, the variety of expectations as well as principles and practices may cause conflicts. In his depiction of the EEAS as interstitial organization, Bátora (2013) focuses on three organizational fields, from which the EEAS receives resources: EU institutions, EU member state governments and institutionalized models of proper organizing. One example for drawing from resources of other organizational fields is EEAS-staffing. The body of personnel of the EEAS consists of individuals from the European Commission, the Council of the EU and the member states. Thereby, at least 60% of the positions should be occupied with EU officials and at least one third should be recruited from national diplomatic services (European Council, 2010, Article 6/9). Onestini (2015) and Spence (2015) depict the challenges of this hybrid constitution. Bátora and Hynek (2014, p. 153) argue that within this set-up, traditional diplomatic cultures meet new forms of organization. This applies to the assignment of the EEAS and its delegations and also applies to the professional identity of the staff working within the EEAS. So far, EU delegations do not have military, consular or cultural sections, but they do already have political, information and communication sections, alongside the already long since existing trade and aid sections. On request from member states, EU delegations are able to undertake consular duties for EU citizens. Beyond that, political reporting as a traditional diplomatic task is increasingly undertaken by EU delegations (Comelli & Matarazzo, 2011, p. 5). It remains to be seen whether delegations are able to further expand their field of operation, probably against the resistance of member states, which perceive a lack of expertise among the staff of EU delegations (Comelli & Matarazzo, 2011, p. 5). The fact that EU officials working in the EEAS were mainly dealing with big cooperation programmes so far and are not as experienced as national diplomats in foreign and security policy issues is deemed as problematic because they may not be ready to undertake assignments that demand fine diplomatic skills. On the contrary, temporary agents from national diplomatic services may not be ready to handle large assistance programmes (Comelli & Matarazzo, 2011, p. 5). This problem could be solved by the establishment of a European diplomatic academy. Until then, two working cultures will collide and it has to be noted whether EU officials assimilate into the working procedures of the existing diplomatic system, or if the minority of temporary agents takes over working procedures from the majority of EU officials, or if a new EEAS-specific working culture develops. Creating a common set of values and goals, an *esprit de corps*, however, seemed to be difficult in the EEAS at the beginning, as shown in a study by Juncos and Pomorska (2015), based on interviews conducted between 2010 and 2014.

With regard to the professional identity of diplomats, Bátora (2005a, p. 45) suggests that modern diplomacy, as traditionally conducted in the Westphalian state order, is of a *"Janus-faced character"*. Diplomats do have to promote national interests, but they are also part of a transnational group of professionals. This group shares a *"corporate culture, professional language, behavioural codes, entry procedures, socialization patterns, norms and standards"*. Bátora (2005a, p. 45) perceives an *"elementary tension within the institution of diplomacy"*, because diplomats on the one hand have to represent the interests of the respective state towards other states, and on the other hand have to interact with representatives of other states in an organized system of transnationally shared principles, norms and rules. According to Bátora (2005a, p. 45), the professionalization of diplomacy accommodates this tension through recruiting and socialization procedures, which are aligned to this dual role. However, the EU is a challenging factor to this dual system, whereby the human resources policy of the EEAS is a good example for this challenging momentum. As mentioned before, the EEAS will be staffed with one third of national diplomats from member states' diplomatic services and with 60% of EU officials, after it reached its full capacity (European Council, 2010, Article 6/9). Juncos and Pomorska (2006) have shown that working in an EU institution promotes European conduct to the disadvantage of national conduct through socialization processes. This implies that the institution of diplomacy faces new actors in the form of EEAS representatives, who have not been socialized into the dual role of diplomats promoting national interests in a transnational environment, but bring an EU focus to diplomacy. Moreover, Murdoch and Trondal (2015, p. 106) state that the hiring procedures of the EEAS "*are intrinsically geared towards the selection of candidates that are not necessarily diplomats in the traditional Westphalian sense*". Member states have to guarantee immediate reinstatement of national diplomats, who have worked for the EEAS, after their period has ended. This period lasts up to eight years, but can be extended for a maximum term of two years (European Council, 2010, Article 6/11). During this time temporary agents undergo a process of socialization and by the time these temporary agents return to their home MFAs, a shift in the organizational culture of these MFAs is possible, as new working methods and procedures and probably also new networks are implemented. This could bring a Europeanization effect to national MFAs.

Apart from personnel resources, the EEAS also draws from resources of further organizational fields. The organizational structure of the EEAS and its procedures and routines follow the model of the European Commission. It also orients itself towards other established forms of organization. MFAs were a main reference group, beside the field of new public management. Due to the fact that the EEAS deals with different competences than conventional foreign services, ministries of defence and agencies specialized in the field of crisis management also served as role-models for the set-up of the EEAS' organizational structure (Bátora, 2013).

Resources of member states are drawn from when the EEAS reaches its limits within the diplomatic system. The Vienna Convention on Diplomatic Relations from 1961 regulates the functions of diplomatic missions, defines diplomatic ranks and regulates rights and obligations of the sending and the receiving state. Originating with the UN, the convention only regards sovereign states as actors within the international system. The Council tried to position the EEAS at an equal rank as nation states. The Council Decision establishing the organization and functioning of the EEAS determines that the High Representative has to ensure that EU delegations are treated like national diplomatic actors:

> "*In particular, the High Representative shall take the necessary measures to ensure that host States grand the Union delegations, their staff and their property, privileges and immunities equivalent to those referred to in the Vienna Convention on Diplomatic Relations of 18 April 1961.*" (European Council, 2010, Article 5/6)

The situation of demanding a certain status without a legal basis causes problems in several situations. The EU for example, is not able to issue diplomatic passports to EEAS staff members. In order to guarantee the same rights and protection to EU-diplomats as to national diplomats when travelling, the EEAS provides its diplomats with diplomatic passports from the member states they originate from. Bátora (2013) draws attention to the fact that this is not a standardized method and the EEAS is dependent on the willingness of the respective MFA. This is a good example for how the EEAS operates in interstices, while *"bending the rules to fit in"* (Bátora & Hynek, 2014, p. 155). As a new actor within the diplomatic system, the EEAS also is affected by isomorphic pressures of the field, but due to its interstitial character and ambiguity it brings heterogeneity to the organizational field and promotes processes of change (Bátora, 2013).

The next chapter will illustrate how and in which areas, not only the EEAS, but also the European Union affects bilateral relations of member states.

The Impact of European Integration on Bilateral Diplomacy

When addressing the issue of how European integration influences bilateral diplomacy of member states, the concept of Europeanization needs to be taken into account. The progress of European integration inspired scholars to investigate effects on member states under the label of Europeanization. However, there is no clear definition behind this term. Bulmer and Radaelli (2004, p. 4) for example found a comprehensive definition for Europeanization:

> *"Europeanisation consists of processes of a) construction, b) diffusion and c) institutionalisation of formal and informal rules, procedures, policy paradigms, styles, 'ways of doing things' and shared beliefs and norms which are first defined and consolidated in the EU policy process and then incorporated in the logic of domestic (national and subnational) discourse, political structures and public policies."*

Olsen (2002, pp. 923-924) instead argues that the term Europeanization consists of five different phenomena, which must each be considered in order to understand its character. The first phenomenon mentioned by Olsen are changes in the EU's external borders, because on the one hand, Europe becomes a single political sphere internally, while on the other hand, the EU further expands its territory. Secondly, he brings in the development of institutions at the European level, which leads to a certain kind of centralization with *"collective action capacity"*. These institutions and *"a normative order based on overarching constitutive principles, structures and practices both facilitate and constrain the ability to make and enforce binding decisions and to sanction non-compliance."* Thirdly, Olsen speaks of *"central penetration of national systems of governance"*. He refers to the EU's multilevel-governance framework, where supranational, national and regional forms of governance exist side by side and mutually influence each other. Europeanization in this context implies the adaptation of national and regional systems of governance to EU-wide norms. Fourthly, Olsen mentions the exporting of these norms of organization beyond the borders of the EU, such as when, for example, non-European actors are influenced by European forms of organization in the course of interaction with EU institutions. Olsen's fifth point is related to the intensity of European integration, which depends on all four dimensions of Europeanization mentioned above. However, Olsen does not necessarily perceive a positive correlation between each of these dimensions and a politically stronger Europe.

In the context of this work, the second and the third dimension of Europeanization are of particular importance. Participating in CFSP brings an EU-oriented approach to the member states' foreign policy making and diplomacy. With the EEAS, an intensified form of foreign policy coordination and coordination of diplomacy emerged, which supports collective action of the EU and its member states. Common objectives are determined in the Lisbon Treaty, based on a set of core values defining the EU's foreign policy spirit. Taking part in this new evolving system of foreign policy making and diplomacy creates the need for member states to adapt their individual forms of foreign policy making and diplomacy to this system.

In this context, it is interesting to consider the two key dimensions of Europeanization of foreign policy, depicted by Alecu de Flers and Müller (2012). The first dimension describes the process of uploading national foreign policy preferences to the EU-level, while the second dimension depicts the process of downloading CFSP policy elements to the national level. Relating this to the investigation of bilateral diplomacy implies considering processes of development and adaptation from two sides: from the perspective of adjusting the national diplomatic system to the needs of common European foreign policy making and from the perspective of adjusting it to the needs created by the aspiration to actively participate in EU decision making processes. These two perspectives represent the two sides of bilateral diplomacy investigated in this work, bilateral relations to third states and inner-EU bilateral diplomacy.

The following sections illustrate how these two sides of bilateral diplomacy are influenced by European integration and how the role of MFAs as well as the professional role and identity of national diplomats are affected.

Bilateral Diplomatic Relations within the EU

It seems that the process of European integration influences inner-EU bilateral diplomatic relations to a more minor extent than relations to third states, at least since the EEAS had been established. Hocking (2005a) is of the opinion that the structures of inner-EU bilateral diplomatic relations endure so far, and Bátora (2005a, p. 53) supports this statement with the example of Berlin. Berlin became the German capital city again after the country's reunification and the government moved there from Bonn in the year 1999.

The continued importance of inner-EU bilateral relations is shown by the fact that architectural sophisticated embassies were opened in Berlin at a time when European integration had already reached an advanced stage. The maintenance of established structures suggests that the process of European integration does not create a situation of radical change for diplomacy. It rather indicates a path-dependent adaptation of the institution to changes in its environment, where the role of bilateral embassies remains stable. However, it cannot be disregarded that one of the primary motivations of diplomacy, ensuring national security by threats from other states, becomes less important within the EU (Bátora, 2005a, p. 53). On the multilateral level the importance of interaction and cooperation in the form of diplomacy remains undisputed. When comparing bilateral and multilateral diplomacy, there is another difference beside the obvious fact of bilateralism containing relations between two actors, while multilateralism contains relations between three or more. The crucial difference between bilateralism and multilateralism is a qualitative one. In multilateral relations three or more parties must agree on a set of basic principles connected to certain expectations, even the strongest party has to do so. In contrast, bilateralism "*reflects the distribution of power between the parties*" (Wright, 2013, p. 180). In the EU these interstate power relations are out of their order, because the EU creates a rule-based legal environment within the state system, which had formerly been an anarchically structured setting (Bátora, 2005a, pp. 53-54). In Bátora's (2005a, p. 53) view, this circumstance could cause a metamorphosis of inner-EU bilateral diplomatic relations. Keukeleire (2003, p. 34) assumes that pre-EU bilateral diplomacy between states will either be structured within a new framework or even be absorbed by multilateralism.

Initial signs for a transformation have already been shown in the report by Paschke (2001), who investigated the work of 14 German inner-EU embassies in the year 2000 and perceived the development of a new type of *"European Diplomacy"*. This investigation illustrated that the role of German ambassadors is changing as they are no longer primarily negotiators and interpreters of German foreign policy interest, but communicators and mediators of German EU positions. Hence, bilateral relations keep their significance, but the core tasks of diplomatic missions are about to change. In the German example, trade promotion became the task of other institutions, analytical reporting and public diplomacy gained importance and certain traditional functions, like consular service, fostering cultural contacts and promoting German language, remained significant (Paschke, 2001, pp. 9-11, 17). In 2007, Bratberg conducted an analysis on changes in numbers of diplomatic staff in embassies in various European capitals. His objects of investigation were embassies of four EU member states (Britain, France, Denmark and Sweden) and one European Economic Area member state (Norway). He determined that the number of personnel remained relatively stable in the EU-15, while it even rose in the EU-27 (Bratberg, 2007). Bátora and Hocking (2009) explored the change dynamics in inner-EU bilateral diplomacy in member states' embassies in London and Vienna. They determined that the importance of consular service increases, because inner-European mobility increased and they as well perceived a trend towards *"European Diplomacy"*. The British Embassy in Vienna, for example, does not see a need for further developing the excellent relationship between Great Britain and Austria, but it does promote British EU positions, as they often differ from Austrian EU positions. Britain of course became a particularly noteworthy example after the BREXIT vote. Britain leaving the EU brings a new disintegrating dynamic to the diplomatic system, which will be an interesting object of investigation in the upcoming years. The results of the study of Bátora and Hocking (2009) furthermore show that analytical reporting gains significance, as reports from embassies often provide a basis for EU negotiations. Therefore, inner-EU bilateral embassies mediate between the traditional and the new EU-oriented form of bilateralism (Bátora & Hocking, 2009, pp. 173-179). Based on these results, Uilenreef (2013) investigated the task of diplomatic reporting in Dutch bilateral embassies in the EU, contrary to Dutch bilateral embassies in third states and discovered significant differences. Dutch bilateral embassies in the EU are also closely connected to other ministries at home than the MFA and their reports also deal with sectoral policies and to a large degree do follow topics on the EU agenda.

According to Bátora (2005a, p. 53), the reason for change of the standards of diplomatic appropriateness in bilateral diplomatic relations within the EU, contrary to bilateral diplomatic relations with third states, is obvious. Westphalian diplomacy enables states to survive in an anarchical environment by providing rules and norms, but inner-EU diplomacy is an arising set of norms and rules that regulates the interaction of states in a rule-based legal environment. In a setting of continuous interaction in supranational and intergovernmental ways, borders between multilateral and bilateral diplomacy become blurred. It appears that the traditional form of bilateral diplomacy, as it developed within the Westphalian state system, becomes less important or even redundant, in a post-Westphalian state order.

According to literature on globalized diplomacy, not only MFAs in the EU, but most MFAs and embassies around the world, are challenged by the demands of a changing society. Scientists and practitioners are proposing new concepts in order to meet the requirements of changes in the environment of diplomacy. Former British diplomat Riordan (2004), for example, suggests replacing expensive diplomatic representations and ambassadors, because their traditional representational role is out-dated. In contrast, former Indian ambassador Rana (2011, p. 135) perceives embassies and ambassadors as a "*country's diplomatic 'brand*". According to him, strategic objectives, diplomacy management, techniques, performance standards, human resource management, staff distribution and technology have to be the focus of reform (Rana, 2011, pp. 122-124). Rana (2011, p. 134) believes that multilateral diplomacy will not overtake bilateral diplomacy. He hints at the fact of cross-linkage between multilateral and bilateral diplomacy, especially in the case of regional cooperation: "*The bilateral and the multilateral are two legs of diplomacy*". The question is which role MFAs and bilateral diplomatic missions are going to play in the new emerging set-up of inner-EU bilateral diplomacy.

With accession to the EU, the nature of a state's relation to other EU member states changes. Major parts of national policies, including foreign policy, form a sort of European policy area within the EU, labelled by Höll (2002, p. 370) as *"Europäische Innenpolitik"* (European domestic policy) - a term that has also been used by Angela Merkel, in order to describe policy making in the EU. *"Europäische Innenpolitik"* represents a slim form of multilateral cooperation within the EU, where etiquette and diplomatic protocol are reduced to minimum (Krupa, 2013). Uilenreef (2013, p. 137) already detected consequences of this development in the work of Dutch bilateral embassies in the EU. According to him, diplomacy in the EU is conducted in a more technical manner than in non-EU countries.

The developments outlined above, namely the emergence of new tasks at embassies in the EU related to EU-coordination and the emergence of a slim sort of multilateral cooperation with reduced diplomatic forms of interaction, add a third dimension to the nationally and transnationally informed work of MFAs in the EU (Bátora, 2005a, p. 55). A transformation like this encourages the development of an additional repertoire of roles and identities in MFAs and therefore also encourages changes in training and socialization procedures (Bátora, 2005a, p. 54). How this third dimension will affect the assignment and the role of MFAs and diplomatic missions, as well as the role and the professional identity of diplomats working in bilateral diplomacy in the EU, must be observed.

Bilateral Diplomatic Relations to Third States

Previous chapters outlined how the EU stretches and re-interprets the rules of the institution of diplomacy in order to fit in, whereby it promotes mechanisms of change within the institution (Bátora & Hynek, 2014). Especially the EEAS represents a heterogeneous element within the diplomatic system, due to its interstitial character and ambiguity (Bátora, 2013). The EEAS could cause a change in diplomatic appropriateness in relations to third countries, as it challenges the role of states as so far only legitimate participants in bilateral diplomatic relations. Now the EU provides its own diplomatic service alongside those of the member states and imitates transnationally shared standards for organizing diplomacy (Bátora, 2005a, p. 62).

Representations of the EU already existed long before the implementation of the Lisbon Treaty, even already in the EC, but they only represented the EU Commission and not the EU in its entirety. The assignment of EU delegations primarily covered trade and aid policies. Implementing technical and financial cooperation programmes were the main duties of delegations before the Lisbon Treaty came into force. Therefore, political officials were rare in EU delegations, as political and security issues were handled by the embassies of the member state holding the EU presidency (Comelli & Matarazzo, 2011, p. 3). Today EU delegations also deal with foreign and security policy and represent the EU in its entirety in third countries as well as at international organizations.

Comelli and Matarazzo (2011, p. 3) draw attention to the fact that the CFSP remains essentially intergovernmental and the Lisbon Treaty does not provide a transfer of foreign policy competences from member states to the European Union. EU delegations do not overtake the assignment of member states' embassies. Hence, the EEAS represents a new actor within the diplomatic system and does not only challenge the role of national embassies in third states, but also the organization, procedures and processes in member states' MFAs (Bátora, 2011a, p. 10). The question arises as to how MFAs in the EU and national diplomatic services deal with this new actor in the diplomatic system.

According to Comelli and Matarazzo (2011, p. 5), many member states are very diffident concerning the EU's new role in foreign policy. Smaller states with fewer resources are more willing to transfer competences to the EEAS than is the case in well-equipped big member states. By 2013, Balfour and Raik, together with several authors, issued a paper on the EEAS and national diplomacies, comprising brief insights on 14 EU member states and their form of cooperation with the EEAS. The study is based on interviews with national representatives at the respective MFA and EU representatives. The investigation focused on the interaction between national foreign policy priorities and EU foreign policy, changes in the structure and resources of MFAs, national views on the function of the EEAS and EU delegations, working relations and information share between the EEAS and MFAs, recruitment of national diplomats to the EEAS, the prospects of a European diplomatic culture as well as European foreign policy leadership and the role of MFAs in it. Member states considered in this study have been chosen according to criteria of diversity. They differ in size, geographical position, attitudes towards European integration, duration of EU membership as well as foreign policy tradition (Balfour & Raik, 2013, p. 5).

The investigation of the German foreign service to some extent contradicts Comelli and Matarazzo's (2011, p. 5) assumption of bigger member states being less willing to transfer diplomacy competences to the EEAS. According to this paper, Germany would like to move forward in the discussion about joint representation at international organizations and also be willing to frequently share the information output of its diplomatic missions, reports and analysis, with the EEAS. Nevertheless, Germany has thus far not wanted to transfer consular duties to the EEAS, but would concur if smaller member states wanted to do so on a voluntary basis. Germany is the only one of the big three member states that is in favour of joint representation at international organizations (Adebahr, 2013, p. 16).

Contrary to Germany, which considers itself as one of the strongest supporters of the EEAS (Adebahr, 2013, p. 13), French diplomats do not perceive the EEAS as an instrument to develop European foreign policy, but rather as an instrument to implement French foreign policy to the EU. In the opinion of the French foreign service, the EEAS shall complement the work of MFAs and not replace them. France accepts the leading and coordinating role of EU delegations in third countries, but emphasizes a strong position for big member states, as they can bring added value, for example to EU *démarches* (Terpan, 2013, pp. 129-133).

Great Britain also ascribes a complementary function to the EEAS, which should only act in the field of EU competences, especially concerning the promotion of human rights and democracy (Carta & Whitman, 2013, p. 141). The French foreign service even perceives advantages in leaving sensitive issues, like human rights, up to the EEAS, because promoting such matters might hamper negotiations in other areas of interest, for instance in the field of economy (Terpan, 2013, p. 133).

Poland, as a new big member state in the EU, assesses the work of EU delegations in so-called *forgotten countries* – receiving states, where hardly any diplomatic services are represented – as quite positive. The Polish MFA uses the information provided by the EEAS on these countries. According to the paper, Polish diplomats however are of the opinion that EU delegations are not taken seriously by representatives of embassies of EU member states in important third countries. Poland also accepts the coordinating role of EU delegations in third states, but only concerning EU competences, not in bilateral issues (Gromadzki, 2013, pp. 68-70).

Estonia is an example of a small member state with limited resources in the study. The country has a strong interest in developing consular services at EU delegations, perceives diplomatic reporting of EU delegations as of huge benefit to its small diplomatic service and strongly supports the strengthening of political sections at EU delegations (Raik, 2013, pp. 79-80).

The Netherlands furthermore strongly supports the implementation of consular services at EU delegations and wants to give more visibility to the EU delegation in third states. The Netherlands emphasized that statements of the EU in third countries should always be made by the EU delegation and the member states. The big ones should show restraint (van Schaik, 2013, pp. 100-101).

Contrary to Estonia and the Netherlands, the Czech foreign service is generally sceptical about the ability of the EU to become a global player and therefore CFSP should remain intergovernmental. Accordingly, expectations concerning the EEAS are rather low. Czech diplomats do not classify the EEAS as diplomatic service and do not support the idea of leaving consular duties to the EEAS. Even still, diplomatic reporting from EU delegations is perceived as a benefit for the Czech foreign service (Beneš, 2013, p. 153).

Opinions and views on the EEAS and its future role differ among the member states. Generally, all country studies in the paper show that national foreign services perceive the EEAS and its delegations as a supplement to the existing national diplomatic services and do not expect the EEAS to take on their role. However, in a following paper Balfour and Raik (2015) describe first signs of adaptation in national diplomatic services in organizational structures and in the field of human resources management. The future development of the EEAS is strongly dependent on the scope of action the member states are willing to concede. Their individual approaches to CFSP will influence the EEAS' evolvement and strength in the diplomatic system and therefore also how the institution of diplomacy is about to develop.

The next chapter discusses how MFAs in the EU are affected by European integration and which direction their development and the process of adjustment might take.

The Future of Foreign Ministries in the European Union

Spence (2005, p. 18) raises the question if MFAs in the EU are in decline per se, or if they are involved in a subtle process of change and adaptation, as the diplomatic order changes. Although MFAs around the world are about to transform due to the process of globalization or the information revolution, Spence (2005, p. 18) observes aspects of uniqueness in the European experience because the EU clearly influences national administrative arrangements. MFAs play a monitoring and coordinating role, in order to guarantee the efficient production and representation of national policy. The idea of MFAs and associated diplomatic networks functioning as a filter between domestic and international environments, however, becomes questionable against the backdrop of policy processes linked to globalization and regionalization.

Hocking (2005b) describes two images of diplomatic systems with different roles for MFAs and diplomats. In the gatekeeper model, the territorial state as well as the control of boundaries and communication flows is central. In this concept the MFA takes the role of a dominant central agency. Thereby, coordination is structured as a hierarchical top-down process, influenced by the assertion of exclusivity in the management of international policy (Peters, 1998; Hocking, 2005b, p. 10). Obviously developments within the EU do call this model into question. Therefore, Hocking (2005b, p. 10) introduces another image, which is based on Ansell and Weber's (1999) discovery of the fact that actors possess the capacity to straddle or span boundaries. According to their concept, boundaries are uncertain, as they reconstitute themselves, responding to shifting patterns of interaction. Boundaries are enacted and re-enacted and so are able to maintain their relevance. Actors, so-called boundary spanners, are able to take the role of mediators or brokers, as they modulate, regulate or even control, which resources, signals and information pass the boundaries of the organization. Thereby, they operate both within and outside the organization (Ansell & Weber, 1999; Hocking, 2005b, pp. 10-11). While the key objective in the gatekeeper image is to control national boundaries and to isolate the state from its environment, the key objective in the boundary spanner image is to mediate within and across spaces, between the state and its environment through points of interface. This point of view strengthens the significance of bureaucratic actors outside the diplomatic service in international relations and weakens the identity of foreign policy as a category in its own right (Hocking, 2005b, pp. 12-13). Hocking (2005a, p. 285) assumes that an eventual transition from national to Europeanized diplomatic processes could occur. In such a case, national diplomatic systems would be rendered redundant. This speaks for Bátora's (2005a) assumption of change of diplomatic appropriateness. MFAs do play a significant role in a hybrid diplomatic EU arena, but this role does not meet with traditional expectations and clichés (Hocking, 2005a, p. 285).

In order to specify the dimension of change these developments may cause, Bátora (2005a) defined an analytical status quo for the constitution of modern diplomacy, which serves as point of orientation. This status quo contains features of the institution of diplomacy as well as features of the organizational culture of MFAs. Beyond that, the historical background of a certain MFA has to be taken into account, as in some states the management of international policy was traditionally conducted by several ministries (foreign, finance, trade) (Hocking, 2005b, pp. 9-10). Hence, historical developments as well as the organizational structure of MFAs must be considered in order to detect changes, caused by the process of European integration.

As pointed out above, bilateral diplomacy conducted by member states' MFAs is challenged on two levels, the level of bilateral diplomacy within the EU and the level of bilateral relations to third states. On the level of inner-EU bilateral diplomacy, former studies detected the development of a new form of *"European Diplomacy"* (Paschke, 2001; Bátora & Hocking, 2009), where processes and tasks are about to change. The question arises concerning the role MFAs and embassies will take in this new emerging system, where multilateral and bilateral elements intermingle. Against the background of former studies on changes in inner-EU bilateral diplomacy, two possible development trends are likely. The MFA as provider of structures and services for other institutions and ministries, which handle foreign and EU policy, and the MFA as a promoter of member states' EU policy issues, in order to build a basis for cooperation on the multilateral level. These development trends are explained in more detail in the chapter on the case of the Austrian MFA. Both developments would rather reflect a boundary spanner than a gatekeeper model of MFAs.

In relations to third states, the form of interaction and cooperation between member states' MFAs and the EEAS is central. Bátora (2011a, 2011b) therefore outlines three possible development patterns that reflect different forms of cooperation. These development patterns as well are explained in more detail in the chapter on the case of the Austrian MFA. Bátora (2011b, pp. 6-7) argues for the investigation of formal and informal structural connections between member states and the EEAS, as well as for the investigation of external representations and possible co-locations with the EEAS. Thus, investigating the changing role of MFAs in the context of European integration requires an evaluation with regard to structural and processual elements. In the paper issued by Balfour and Raik (2013, p. 6), which briefly evaluates the cooperation of 14 national diplomatic services with the EEAS, they conclude that structure and resources of MFAs did change, but not due to the EEAS.

Balfour and Raik (2013, p. 7) however identify one field in which MFAs had to adapt to changing circumstances caused by the EEAS. For all of the member states investigated, it was of high priority to bring national diplomats to senior positions in the EEAS. Thus, human resources management divisions had to develop strategies to do so. In the context of human resources, Bátora (2011b, pp. 7-8) argues for detecting possible EU-orientations in socialization and training procedures in MFAs. He further argues for taking the organizational demography of MFAs into account, because the educational background, age, sex and length of service of agents within an organization affect this organization and its decisions and behaviour (Egeberg, 2004, pp. 203-204; Bátora, 2011b, p. 7).

By reverting to Bátora and Hynek's (2014) definition of institutions as intermeshing of environments, structures and actors, the focus now shifts from the meso level to the micro level, from organizations to individuals and individual identities within organizations. Thus, not only the structural and processual level of the MFA is of relevance when investigating changes in the organizational field of the institution of diplomacy, but professional identities and mind-sets of diplomats working in MFAs are also able to provide significant information on how the organizational field develops.

Professional Identity in the Organizational Field of Diplomacy

Bátora (2005a) refers to March and Olsen (1989) as well as DiMaggio and Powell (1991a) in his conceptualization of diplomacy. DiMaggio and Powell (1991a) offer a primarily structural approach to institutions, where rules and practices are enclosed in structures of meaning and schemes of interpretation. Consequently, these structures and schemes legitimize certain identities as well as rules and practices related to these identities. In the concept of March and Olsen (1989), identity shapes action in the sense of a logic of appropriateness and because action is rule-based, certain identities therefore relate certain actions to certain situations. Within this context, the process of socialization is central, as it imparts rules and creates identities.

In the field of diplomacy, socialization plays a significant role. The profession of diplomacy is of a *"Janus-faced character"* (Bátora, 2005a, p. 45). In principle, diplomats guard and promote national interests. Beyond that, they are also part of diplomacy as an organizational framework, which enables communication and negotiation. Therefore, diplomats work within a professional group that acts in a transnational environment and shares a *"corporate culture, professional language, behavioural codes, entry procedures, socialization patterns, norms and standards"* (Bátora, 2005a, p. 45). Neumann (2005, p. 72) describes this as *"'third culture' in the sense that it is a locus for mediation between political entities with diverse cultures"*. The duality of representing a sovereign nation state within an anarchic international environment and being part of a transnational professional group creates an *"elementary tension within the institution of diplomacy"* (Bátora, 2005a, p. 45). According to Bátora (2005a, p. 45), this tension has been accommodated by professionalizing diplomats and socializing them into their dual role. This socialization process is carried out by MFAs in their own way, according to the respective organizational culture and national identity. Thus, when organizational cultures of MFA's are changing in the context of European integration, this process will also affect the professional identity and self-conception of national diplomats. Diplomats, who are socialized into their dual role, focused on handling national interests in a transnational environment, are now confronted with a third aspect in their professional life, the European Union and its possible socializing and identity-building influence.

Adler-Nissen (2009) illustrated that a high degree of socialization in EU institutions gives rise to a merging of national interests and EU-interests among national representatives in multilateral diplomacy. But it cannot be assumed that national diplomats will spontaneously carry a European identity as soon as they face some kind of EU socialization. Checkel's (2005) approach shows that socialization does not necessarily lead to the internalization of norms and values or to the adoption of a certain role and identity. Checkel (2005, pp. 808-813) offers a model of three mechanisms of socialization - strategic calculation, role playing and normative suasion - connected to two types of internalization, which represent two different ways of following a logic of appropriateness. Type I internalization represents role-playing in order to act according to expectations, regardless of whether role-players agree with the norms and values of their role. Type II internalization goes beyond role-playing and implies the acceptance of norms and rules among agents of a community or organization. Therefore, interests and even the identity of the respective community or organization can be adopted (Checkel, 2005, p. 804). Hence, acting in accordance with certain expectations does not imply that the actor identifies with a community or organization, or carries the identity of this community or organization. Therefore, it not only is of importance to examine adaptations in socialization and training procedures in MFAs in order to detect possible Europeanization trends, but it is of similar importance to consider the behaviour, attitude and mind-sets of individuals working in an organization. Consequently, a broad methodological approach is needed in order to examine how a national MFA, its bilateral diplomatic missions and the diplomatic staff working within the MFA and the diplomatic missions are affected by European integration on the levels outlined above. The following chapter displays a research design created for the investigation of the Austrian MFA.

The Case of the Austrian Ministry of Foreign Affairs

Methodology and Development Patterns

This book is concerned with the question of how bilateral diplomacy changes in the context of European integration, illustrated by the example of the Austrian MFA. Thereby, two levels of investigation are treated separately, because they are influenced by different developments and consequences of European integration: the level of inner-EU bilateral diplomacy as well as the level of bilateral relations to third states.

In the Westphalian system of states, MFAs represent the common organizational framework to support the conduct of diplomacy. Investigating their structures, practices and organizational identity allows the drawing of conclusions surrounding the interconnectedness between the core function of diplomacy and its current organizational framework. Such an investigation also gives rises to an explanation of possible changes in the institution of diplomacy (Sonnleitner, 2015, p. 7). MFAs are organizations within this institution (Jönsson & Hall, 2005, pp. 25-26). Modern diplomacy is inseparably linked to this organizational framework, even though other organizations are becoming important actors in the field of diplomacy (Hocking, 2013). Empirical access to the institution of diplomacy is possible via the organizational framework of the MFA. Conducting an in-depth investigation of a single MFA concerning changing processes in bilateral relations in the context of European integration not only promises to give insights into the transformation of the organizational framework, but also promises to give insights into how MFAs develop within the institution of diplomacy.

A methodological approach had to be found that enables an investigation of the effects of European integration on the Austrian MFA and Austrian bilateral diplomacy. Thornton, Ocasio and Lounsbury (2012) offer a metatheoretical perspective on the constitution of institutions and argue that institutions consist of material as well as symbolic elements. Structure and practices of an institution are classified as material elements, while ideation and meaning are categorized as symbolic elements (Thornton et al., 2012, p. 10). These elements are not only to be found in the institution itself, but also in the organization within the institution. The investigation of material elements can be easily transferred to the organizational framework of a

MFA. On the material level, structures are represented by the legal framework, the infrastructure, personnel as well as the organizational set-up of a MFA. Practices are established tasks and working procedures within the MFA's organizational culture. Symbolic elements are rather difficult to transfer to the organizational framework. They are, however, especially important for the investigation because changes on the level of symbolic elements are of a more sustainable nature than changes on the level of material elements (Dobbin, 1994; Thornton et al., 2012). Symbolic elements of the institution of diplomacy are represented by aspects of the occupational image as well as the professional identity of diplomats (Sonnleitner, 2015, pp. 7-8).

There are intersections between Thornton, Ocasio and Lounsbury's (2012) approach on institutions consisting of material and symbolic elements and Bátora and Hynek's (2014) conceptualization of the institution of diplomacy as the intermeshing of environments, actors and structures. Structures in the concept of Bátora and Hynek can clearly be integrated to Thornton, Ocasio and Lounsbury's material elements. Actors as components of institutions can be categorized as material as well as symbolic elements. Practices and tasks conducted by diplomats represent material elements within the institution. The professional identity that diplomats carry along with their occupational image, leads rather to a classification as symbolic elements. Thornton et al. do not explicitly mention the environment, but it also consists of both material and symbolic elements, because the environment itself is constituted by institutions (Bátora & Hynek, 2014, p. 48). The investigation of the organizational level of the institution of diplomacy requires to regard this complex composition and also requires to consider material and symbolic elements on several levels of the organization (Sonnleitner, 2015, p. 8). Concentrating on a single case therefore enables an intensive investigation of these levels and also provides reference material for similar studies in the future concerning changing processes in the organization of MFAs.

The case chosen for this investigation is the Austrian Federal Ministry for Europe, Integration and Foreign Affairs. Austria is a small and neutral member state, which accessed the EU in 1995, together with the two other neutral states Finland and Sweden. The investigation focuses on Austria's first 20 years of membership and is to be guided by the question of how Europeanization processes change Austrian bilateral diplomacy, conducted by the Austrian MFA.

The impact of EU accession on the Austrian MFA had already been an object of research in an investigation conducted by Neuhold in the year

2002. In his conclusion on this investigation, re-printed in 2005, he argues that the traditional function of the Austrian MFA as a gatekeeper (Hocking, 2005b) diminished, but the MFA was able to increase its political importance in the context of multilateral diplomacy because it coordinates Austria's EU policies (Neuhold, 2005, p. 52). Fundamental organizational reforms did not occur at the time of Neuhold's investigation. Concerning bilateral diplomacy, he did not find any evidence for the redundancy of embassies and consulates abroad in 2002, although he notes that their activities change. Like Paschke (2001), Neuhold (2005, p. 50) perceived growing significance of the field of public relations and points out that the curricula of diplomatic academies should take this into account. By 2002, maintaining bilateral relations in the EU was particularly important for the new member state Austria, in order to tighten relationships with other member states. Today Austria is no longer among the new members and gained experience in EU relations, multilateral EU diplomacy and CFSP issues. Investigating the role of the MFA after 20 years of membership therefore promises to bring new insights. Investigations for this book were conducted in the years 2014 and 2015. A working paper as well as a doctoral thesis stemming from the results were published in 2015. By 2016, Maurer (2016) published an article on Austrian diplomacy, which partly also regards effects of European integration, that confirms these results.

This work is based on Yin's (2009) approach on case study analysis, which serves as methodological guideline. In this case, a so-called embedded case study is conducted, in which two or more units of analysis are of relevance. One distinction has to be made between inner-EU bilateral relations and relations to third states, because the preconditions for bilateral diplomacy are different inside and outside the EU. Therefore, the first unit of analysis is addressed to inner-EU bilateral diplomacy, while the second unit is addressed to bilateral relations to third states. Investigating these two units means to predominantly concentrate on changes in material elements, namely structures, practices and tasks. A third unit of investigation concentrates on symbolic elements, ideation and meaning, by focusing on changes in the occupational image and professional identity of Austrian diplomats.

Compared to other qualitative research methods, theory plays a major role in Yin's (2009, pp. 35-36) concept of case study research. Not in the sense of a grand theory, but as a guiding blueprint for the study. Regarding different dimensions within the case implicates the consideration of several levels of theory (Flick, 2012, pp. 75-76). Organizational analysis, sociological new-institutionalism and the definition of diplomacy within this setting serve as theoretical framework. Studies and theoretical assumptions on

Austrian foreign policy and diplomacy serve as content-related theoretical background. Beyond that, context-theories on relevant topics such as Europeanization, European integration, IR as well as research on identity-building provide orientation on several levels of the analysis. These context-theories are the foundation for propositions, to which collected data may be linked.

Yin (2009, pp. 136-141) provides several analytic techniques in his concept of case study research. In this book, *"pattern matching"*, a technique that attempts to compare empirical data with predicted patterns, will be used. These patterns are constructed as ideal-types according to Max Weber, which allow access to a complex empirical reality (Bátora, 2011a, p. 7). These patterns do not only result from preliminary observations, but are also informed by previous studies and theoretical assumptions. Hence, they are used as a kind of informed hypothesis. These patterns are not mutually exclusive, but should enable to indicate the overall direction of the development.

While considering the Austrian position as a small and neutral member state, two development patterns are likely on the level of inner-EU bilateral diplomacy. One possible option for the Austrian MFA would be to act as a provider. Due to the fact of growing interconnectedness between member states on the Brussels-level as well as between political resorts of member states, MFAs lose traditional competences within the EU. The inner-European policy area became the domain of others. Hocking (2013) found an appropriate label for this development. He describes the MFA not as national diplomatic system, but as a subsystem of the national diplomatic system. MFAs could act as providers within this framework in two respects. If bilateral diplomacy in the EU decreases, due to less bureaucratic interaction possibilities between member states on the multilateral level, MFAs could focus on providing support for these interaction processes in organizational terms and provide their outcome of political reporting to other institutions.

If high diplomacy remains of high importance in the structure of the Austrian MFA, it could also take a more active role in inner-EU bilateral diplomacy. Small member states operate under particularly unfavourable conditions, if they try to upload their policies to the EU-level. They do not only have fewer votes, but also fewer financial and personnel resources. According to Panke (2010, p. 802), small member states have the possibility to strengthen their bargaining power through regional cooperation or alliance with bigger states. In order to promote such forms of cooperation on a multilateral level, well-functioning bilateral relations are necessary. From this point of view, inner-EU bilateral diplomacy achieves new significance.

MFAs would be in a key position between multilateral and bilateral cooperation, while EU issues would be the essential element of bilateral diplomacy. Diplomatic missions would be promoters of the country's respective EU position, not only in interaction with the government of the receiving state, but also in interaction with interest groups and representatives of business as well as the public. Public diplomacy would be central. In this case, MFAs could take the position of promoters in the EU and would develop a certain diplomatic brand.

On the level of bilateral relations to third states, the investigation is oriented towards three development patterns, created to investigate the form of interaction between MFAs in the EU and the EEAS. Bátora (2011a) offers three different directions, the development of the EU foreign policy making system, in which the EEAS and MFAs interact, could take. These patterns are of a two-dimensional kind, because they take MFAs and the EEAS into account. One dimension, respectively the view on the role of MFAs within the EU foreign policy making system, is used for the second unit of analysis in this investigation. In using organization theory and new-institutionalist approaches, Bátora (2011a, p. 3) describes foreign policy developments within the models of a foreign policy market, a foreign policy hierarchy and a foreign policy network.

Features of a market system are low integrative effects on actors, opportunism and cost-orientation. Prices are the main factor for regulating relations between actors and the maintenance of these relations. Therefore, relations are flexible and non-coercive, trust is low and communication in a market system is fast and simple. Profit maximization is a central category in this system (Bátora, 2011a, p. 6). Applied to the relation between the EEAS and the Austrian MFA, a foreign policy market would imply that the main objective of the MFA is cost efficiency and cost reduction. The MFA would only use EEAS facilities in order to reduce transaction costs, and loyalty would not go beyond individual external actions. Member states would be in competition in offering foreign affairs expertise to the EEAS. For small member states in a foreign policy market, special regional or cultural competence would be an asset. Offering a certain foreign policy expertise could support Austria in enforcing its own interests in the foreign policy making system (Bátora, 2011a, p. 6).

Hierarchically structured systems have clear boundaries. Transactions within these boundaries are structured by clear lines of authority which define roles of actors and relations between actors. Applied to EU foreign policy, a hierarchy system would provide similar conditions as usual in federal states. Austria would maintain its external relations, while the EEAS would be in charge of the EU's external relations and in charge of balancing member states' foreign policies. Stable roles and competences would develop and member states would be in the position to report to and support the EEAS. Thereby, hierarchical structures reduce opportunistic tendencies of member states, and their foreign policy action would be influenced by their level of identification with the EU (Bátora, 2011a, p. 7).

Network forms of organization emerge in the context of recurring and long-term interaction between actors. The items exchanged are not easy to measure in this case. Mutual obligation is the linking element between actors, rather than legal frameworks. Therefore, sanctions are mostly of a normative nature. Dependence of one actor upon another, advantages from pooling resources and continuity are elementary in this concept (Bátora, 2011a, p. 6). In this model, the EEAS represents the central hub of the EU foreign policy making system, while interaction processes between the EEAS and the Austrian MFA would be based on a *"sense of mutual obligation"* and would be oriented towards the achievement of EU foreign policy goals (Bátora, 2011a, p. 7). In a foreign policy network, Austria would reduce its individual foreign policy activity in order to co-organize and participate in EU foreign policy activities. The concept of mutual obligation therefore makes it considerably easier to upload one's own foreign policy preferences to the EU-level if Austria is eager to support the EEAS' foreign policy focus in general.

Data Collection and Evaluation

Investigating the Austrian MFA as an organizational representation of the institution of diplomacy requires a consideration of a complex composition of environments, actors and structures (Bátora & Hynek, 2014) as well as symbolic and material elements (Thornton et al., 2012) on several levels. Structure is a central material element and is represented by the historical development and the legal framework as well as the organizational set-up, infrastructure and staff development of the Austrian MFA. In the field of practices, tasks and working procedures, developments in significant divisions of the MFA as well as in selected missions inside and outside the EU are considered. Divisions of the MFA were regarded as significant if their assignment is directly linked to bilateral diplomacy and/or EU-coordination. In order to analyse the multilevel influence of the developing EU foreign policy system on Austrian bilateral diplomacy, Austria's Permanent

Representation to the EU is considered as well. Selected examples of Austrian embassies in third states are also part of the investigation, whereby special attention was paid to their cooperation with EU delegations. Similarly, examples of Austrian embassies in the EU were investigated, concerning tasks and working procedures in order to draw conclusions on their role within the inner-EU diplomatic system. Embassies had been selected according to several criteria regarding the receiving state, like political, historical and cultural relations to Austria. In third states, political conditions in the respective state, the state's relation to the EU and the geographical location were decisive factors for the selection of investigated embassies. Within the EU, the time of EU accession of the respective state also had to be considered.

On this level, documentation and qualitative interviews were used complementarily. The material contained historical and contemporary documents on the Austrian MFA, studies on Austrian foreign policy and interviews with representatives of the areas mentioned.

On the symbolic level, which focuses on ideation and meaning (Thornton et al., 2012, p. 10), change in the dual role of diplomats, comprising a national and a transnational side, has been considered in the context of EU socialization and European identity. Here, the investigation was based on interviews focusing on attitudes towards the occupational image as well as norms and values related to the occupational image. Beyond that, attitudes towards Austria and the EU as well as the importance of bilateral diplomacy in this context, plus training and socialization procedures in the Austrian MFA, were part of the interview guide. This approach allows a determination of whether diplomatic socialization and education in the Austrian MFA and consequently norms, rules and identities within the Austrian diplomatic corps are influenced by European integration.

For this part of the analysis, three target groups were specified, in order to assess if identity-constructions among Austrian diplomats are about to change in the course of European integration. Interview partners were selected from three generations of diplomats. Target group I consists of diplomats, who spent a substantial part of their professional career in the Austrian MFA before EU accession. Target group II consists of diplomats currently in office with several years of professional experience. Target group III consists of diplomats at the beginning of their career or in training at the Austrian MFA. This approach offers a multi-dimensional perspective on changing processes of the professional identity and occupational image of diplomats, as members of target group III referred to contemporary experiences, while members of target group I and II had the possibility to compare contemporary and past images and identity-constructions.

The multi-layered character of this case study required the preparation of several versions of interview guides, especially on the level of material elements. Different units of the organizational framework of the Austrian MFA were investigated on this level. A basic interview guide with additional questions for different organizational units, like embassies inside and outside the EU as well as divisions in the MFA, supported the determination of a possible overall development trend. On the level of symbolic elements, as well a basic interview guide was adapted with additional questions regarding the specific situation of each target group.

Interviews were conducted in three research cycles. First, examples of Austrian representations inside and outside the EU were investigated. Based upon this data, a final specification of significant divisions and interview partners in the Austrian MFA was set, in order to implement the second research cycle. Research cycle three covers the three generations of Austrian diplomats. The three target groups were interviewed side by side.

Interviewees were all members of the MFA's diplomatic service. At Austrian missions, interviews were conducted with the respective ambassadors or counsellors, and in the MFA with persons in a leading position in the respective division. Among the three generations of diplomats, special attention was paid to diversity within the target groups concerning educational backgrounds and career paths of interviewees. It should be mentioned that due to the rotating system in the diplomatic service, most diplomats interviewed had already a variety of work experiences at different posts and did not only refer to their current working situation, but also compared different experiences from different posts, what multiplied the outcome of these interviews and further enriched the investigation.

In total, 29 interviews were conducted, 6 at selected embassies inside the EU, 6 at selected embassies in third states, 2 at Austria's Permanent Representation at the EU, 3 in selected MFA divisions and 12 with representatives of different generations of diplomats. A detailed listing can be found at the end of this work. Most of the interviews were conducted on a face-to-face basis. In exceptional cases, interviews were conducted by phone or the interviewee sent written statements. The interviews were recorded and transcribed. In a few cases, notes were taken because interviewees requested not to be recorded. Interviewees were granted anonymity.

All interviews were evaluated according to the guideline of Froschauer and Lueger (2003). They offer three types of interpretation strategies for different research projects. In this case study, the interviews placed focus on the knowledge of interviewees, concerning the social system in which they interact. This perspective is labelled as internal reflection expertise and in such cases Froschauer and Lueger (2003, p. 92) recommend conducting a system-analysis or a micro-structure-analysis. The system-analysis is most suitable for this investigation as it is designed to analyse process dynamics in complex social systems. It is also suitable to evaluate a greater amount of text. The system-analysis is grounded on the idea that the specific dynamic of a social system can be understood by the interpretation of specific constellations of collectivities and actors. This concept follows the assumption that activities of actors are shaped by the structural conditions of the investigated system. Simultaneously, activities of actors reshape the structural conditions of the system (Froschauer & Lueger, 2003, pp. 108-109). This analytical method concentrates on the extensive interpretation of the issues addressed and their related contexts (Froschauer & Lueger, 2003, p. 142).

Considering these contexts, it has to be taken into account that not only the organizational set-up and culture of a MFA, consisting of material and symbolic elements, defines its essence, but also the foreign policy background of the respective country. The national identity of the state represented in the diplomatic system is a core element of the profession of diplomacy and also shapes the country's foreign policy. Therefore, the following chapters concentrate on identity-building elements related to Austrian foreign policy and diplomacy. Austria's nation-building process, its status within the international system, influencing aspects of Austrian domestic policy as well as identity-building elements in its foreign policy history shall illustrate Austria's foreign policy disposition and provide a policy-oriented basis for the research on developments in the Austrian MFA.

It should be noted that the terms foreign policy and diplomacy cannot be equated, although in some cases they are used synonymously. Watson (1984, p. xvi) defines foreign policy as *"the substance of a state's relations with other powers and agencies and the purposes it hopes to achieve by these relations"* and diplomacy as *"the process of dialogue and negotiation by which states in a system conduct their relations and pursue their purposes by means short of war"*. Although Watson's definition of diplomacy is a rather narrow one, his differentiation between substance and process is significant (Bátora, 2005a, pp. 45-46). In order to analyse the process, knowledge of the substance is essential. Thereby, the substance consists of several distinctive features. According to Pelinka and Rosenberger (2003, p. 237), Austria's geopolitical situation, its role as a small state and its economic interests define its foreign policy focus. Despite Austria's millenary history, the steps taken in its re-orientation after the Second World War created a particular national identity that certainly is path-dependent, but also significantly shaped by certain incidents in the course of the nation-building process. Elements of this new emerging national identity became guiding principles in Austria's foreign policy (Röhrlich, 2009, p. 31).

Nation-building in the Second Republic of Austria

The nation-building process of the Second Austrian Republic is primarily the outcome of incidents during the first half of the 20th century (Doktor, 2007, p. 61). Its development after the Second World War is structurally connected to the *"Ständestaat" ("corporate state")* of the interwar period. Austria is a parliamentary republic with presidential elements and is considered to be a centralized state, as the Austrian federalism is less powerful compared to others (Pelinka & Rosenberger, 2003, p. 25). The Second Republic of Austria gained sovereignty in 1955 and proclaimed permanent neutrality, based on the Swiss model. It is hence positioned as small and neutral state in the international state system.

According to Doktor (2007, pp. 64, 68), the State Treaty, neutrality and the self-conception as first victim of Nazi Germany's policy of conquest, mainly defined the Second Republic's identity until the end of the 1980s. The importance of the State Treaty results from the fact that it brought a ten-year period of occupation to an end. Although the Second Republic was founded after the Second World War in 1945, the State Treaty, signed in 1955, and the recovery of sovereignty both still mark the beginning of the republic to many Austrians.

Permanent Neutrality as Foundation for Austrian Foreign Policy

In the process of nation-building of the Second Austrian Republic, the concept of neutrality played a major role. It did and still does strongly influence Austria's national identity and therefore to a certain extent still affects Austria's foreign policy and diplomacy. The prevailing opinion is that Austria's confession to neutrality is anchored in the State Treaty and was a precondition for the troop withdrawal of the occupying powers and a precondition to gain sovereignty. Former Foreign Minister Willibald Pahr (2002, p. 4), however, stated that declaring permanent neutrality had already been discussed among leading Austrian politicians years before the State Treaty negotiations started. Both leading parties tried to keep Austria away from the burgeoning Cold War and thought about the confession of neutrality in order to free the state from the occupying powers (Luif, 2003a, p. 96). The declaration of permanent neutrality was part of the negotiation process on the State Treaty, but is not mentioned within it. Luif (2003a, p. 96) counts this as one of two important concessions that the Austrian government was able to achieve in the negotiation process. Only after the withdrawal of the occupying troops did the Austrian National Assembly pass a federal constitutional law on permanent neutrality. Firstly, Austria was in the position to present its status as a neutral country as not imposed by the occupying powers, but as a self-defined element of the new state, and secondly, the country had the chance to establish its own implementation of neutrality (Doktor, 2007, pp. 69-70). Austria adopted Switzerland's concept as a role model concerning its approach to armed neutrality, instead of adopting a more unassertive model of neutrality as practiced in Yugoslavia or India at that time (Luif, 2003a, p. 96). Like in the Swiss model, Austria's concept of neutrality is legally binding under international law because the government asked all states it maintained diplomatic relations with to notify the declaration of neutrality. Most states fulfilled this request which created a quasi-contractual status at the level of international law. So from a legal point of view, Austria is not able to modify or discard its status of neutrality; it is legally bound to the fulfilment of its duty of neutrality towards the recognizing states (Neuhold, 1992, p. 88). The law of neutrality thereby must not only be observed during wartimes, but also during times of peace, a neutral state has to maintain its ability to fulfil its duty of neutrality in a possible upcoming war. This includes not supporting warring parties and not tolerating acts of war on the state's territory, including the airspace. The status of permanent neutrality prohibits the participation in military alliances as well as the membership in primarily economical supranational international organizations, if this membership contains the obligation to act against the law of neutrality, for example in the case of an unilateral embargo on the export of war materials. This is because the status of permanent neutrality requires an application of restrictions on the private trade of war material in equal parts on all war parties (Neuhold, 1992, pp. 88-89). The law of neutrality was codified in the Hague Convention of 1907 and was primarily advanced through international customary law (Neuhold, 1992, p. 88). In Austria's federal constitutional law on permanent neutrality from 1955, only the prohibition of entering a military alliance and the prohibition of foreign military bases on its territory are mentioned.

Neutral states pursue their individual neutrality policy, in order to position themselves in the international state system. Austria's neutrality policy was defined as an active one from the beginning. Austrian Foreign Minister Leopold Figl stated shortly after the signing of the State Treaty in 1955 that Austria would make a contribution to international understanding and peace through an active participation in global treaty organizations (Pahr, 2002, p. 4). Although this is the case, Pahr (2002, p. 4) does not interpret Austria's confession to neutrality as value-based, but as Realpolitik-oriented. The declaration speaks of the implementation of neutrality for the purpose of securing external sovereignty and the protection of the state territory. In contrast to the role model Switzerland, Austria's interpretation of active neutrality policy led to UN membership in 1955 and Council of Europe membership in 1956. Hence, Austria's status of permanent neutrality did not induce a reluctant attitude in foreign policy, but was rather used to re-establish the small state in the international arena through active engagement in international organizations and peace policy (Doktor, 2007, p. 71).

The chancellorship of Bruno Kreisky from 1970 to 1983 particularly strengthened Austria's positive attitude towards neutrality. Höll (1994, p. 37) states that Kreisky was convinced of permanent neutrality being the only way to secure Austria's unity and to recover its independence, while also making a contribution to the balance of power during the Cold War. Austria played a major mediating role in the Middle East conflict that time and Kreisky used Austria's geographical and political position between East and West to support their rapprochement. Gehler and Bischof (2006, p. 7) point out that the two opposing theses related to Kreisky's foreign policy efforts, Austria's destiny as a *"bridge-builder"* between East and West and Austria as a *"secret ally of the West"*, had never been the object of an in-depth investigation by scholars and therefore both have not been deconstructed so far. Gehler and Bischof (2006, p. 7) further state that Kreisky's *"at times feverish foreign policy activism"* did not relate to Austria's real political or military power. Considering this against the background of Goetschel's (1998, p. 19) assumption on small states, whereupon the small state status is characterized by a deficit in influence and autonomy, Kreisky's activism could be interpreted as a form of compensation. Nevertheless, Kreisky's efforts and his concept of neutrality became *"one of the most important identity-promoting characteristics of the Second Republic"* (Wodak, De Cillia, Reisigl, & Liebhart, 2009, p. 63), an identity-constituting norm. After two lost World Wars, the concept of permanent neutrality was easily accepted by the Austrian population. Bruckmüller (1994, pp. 134-135) argues that neutrality in Austria over time gained a *"mythological quality"* and the identification with it is considered to be an evidence of the acceptance of the Second Austrian Republic.

After the era Kreisky, Austria's reputation as diplomatic agent in the international arena was heavily damaged when Austria's role in the Second World War became a controversial topic in the context of the Waldheim Affair. Developments of the late 1980s dramatically changed the basis for Austrian foreign policy making and diplomacy, especially regarding its concept of neutrality.

When Austria accessed the EU in 1995, the acquis communautaire, the body of EU law, was incorporated into Austrian law, including clauses concerning CFSP as well as the perspective of a common defence policy, formulated in the Treaty of Maastricht. Nonetheless, two thirds of the delegates of the Austrian parliament before voted in favour of joining the EU. The federal constitutional law on neutrality remained intact, but a special provision had been added to the constitution, which determines that Austria's participation in CFSP will not be impaired by its status of neutrality. Beyond that, a further clause was added after the ratification of the Treaty of Amsterdam, which enables Austria to fully participate in the so-called Petersburg tasks, which include military action in peace-making operations and crisis management (Krüger, 2003, pp. 9-10).

Although these developments reduced Austria's approach on neutrality to a minimum, in concrete terms to the permission of stationing foreign troops on its territory and the permission of joining a military alliance (Krüger, 2003, p. 10), the abolition of neutrality currently is no issue of debate. People's Parties' politicians, who brought up this issue by the end of the 1990s, changed their mind by the middle of the 2000s, because the majority of the Austrian population seemed to adhere to neutrality (Kramer, 2013, pp. 94-95). In a public opinion poll in 2013 on the abolition of Austria's compulsory military service, 59.7% of the votes cast were in favour of continuation of compulsory military service. An analysis of the results displayed that 58% of the pro-military service voters were motivated by the assumption that compulsory military service is an essential feature of neutrality (SORA/ISA, 2013). Many Austrian politicians are still convinced by the idea of permanent neutrality, or at least realize that it still is a central component of Austria's national identity. This was proven in December 2013 by social democratic President Heinz Fischer in the context of protests against the inauguration of the new government, triggered by the integration of the Ministry of Science and Research into the Ministry of Economy. In an interview a journalist of the Austrian Broadcasting Company (ORF) pointed out that the President of the Republic would be in the position to prevent the inauguration. President Fischer answered that he would do so, if a government would agree on the abolition of neutrality (Zirnig, 2013). Beside social democrats like Heinz Fischer, also parts of the People's Party and especially the right-wing populist Freedom Party promote the retention of neutrality.

Karsh (1988, p. 79) points out that neutrality is *"the most extreme manifestation of the aspiration to assure one's security through the avoidance of identification with or reliance on additional states"*. Although the status of neutrality was reduced to its essence with Austria's accession to the EU, the importance that the population still ascribes to this status is a potential source of conflict in future CFSP-related foreign policy decision making.

Permanent neutrality only is one perspective through which Austria's position in the international state system can be classified. Kramer (2006, p. 807) states that the foreign policy of the Second Republic can be seen from various viewpoints; permanent neutrality is therefore just one of them. Like Pelinka and Rosenberger (2003), he also moves Austria's economic situation to the centre. After the Second World War the new nation state started off from an unfavourable position but was able to develop as successful industrial country, supported by the European Recovery Program. Kramer (2006, p. 807) is of the opinion that flexibility and initiative in Austrian foreign policy promoted this development. Closely connected to the country's economic situation is Austria's status as a small state within the international state system, another aspect that has to be taken into account when regarding the Second Republic's foreign policy alignment.

Small State Status

In a scientific context, the term small state is a controversial one. Definitions range from purely quantitative descriptions, focusing on GDP and/or population, to qualitative ones, where a state's status within the international system is central. Qualitative approaches require the consideration of political, diplomatic and economic relations, as well as the consideration of a state's power in these terms within the international system and in relation to other states (Pospisil & Khittel, 2008, pp. 16-17). Irrespective of the approach - qualitative or quantitative - the size of a state is a social construction (Thorhallsson, 2006) and many scholars conclude that despite decades of research, there is no generally accepted definition of a small state.

In summarizing treatises on small states, Hey (2003, p. 2) identifies at least three different communities: microstates with a population of less than one million, small states in the developed world, which includes Austria, and small states in the so-called third world. Within the third category, many states are much larger than among the first two. Goetschel (1998, p. 19) is of the opinion that *"the term small state characterizes a state's position towards its environment. This position is characterized by a deficit in influence and autonomy."* A small state's foreign and security policy is an expression of this circumstance. Minimizing and compensating these power deficits thereby is central. This statement is of special interest when regarding small states in the EU. Small states often join the EU in order to compensate their smallness through being part of a large economic area and a political actor with growing influence. At the same time, they become part of another system of classification with its own rules. In an institutionalized system like the EU where interaction between member states follows its own legal framework, the differentiation between big and small states is based on different factors, mostly quantitative criteria. The influence of a member state on decision making processes as well as its influence on interaction processes between the member states determines its status in the EU (Pospisil & Khittel, 2008, p. 17). Panke (2010, pp. 800-801) uses the distribution of votes in the Council of Ministers in qualified majority voting in order to distinguish between big and small EU member states. Small member states are those with less than the average of votes in the Council, including Austria. However, fewer votes are not the only feature by which small member states in the EU are characterized. Smaller budgets and thus fewer resources classify states as small ones, due to the fact that they cannot participate in as many areas of EU policy making as big member states which are able to operate with a high number of specified staff members in Brussels (Panke, 2010, p. 801). This also affects the field of foreign policy because small member states are not in the position to cover a broad variety of foreign policy topics, but rather have to focus on specific areas. Concerning bilateral diplomacy, having fewer resources means to have fewer and less well-equipped representations abroad as well as fewer resources in the MFA to deal with certain issues. However, concerning the size of the network of diplomatic representations, Austria at the moment still holds a middle position in the EU (Balfour & Raik, 2013, p. 167). These aspects must be considered when concentrating on Austrian foreign policy and diplomacy.

Besides the basic factor of size and the identity-promoting factor of permanent neutrality, the Second Republic's foreign policy and diplomacy is also influenced to a high degree by Austria's domestic policy structure. The next chapter will outline significant features of this structure, which are of relevance for the investigation of Austria's action in an international environment.

Relevant Aspects of Austrian Domestic Policy

First and foremost, Austria operates under the system of federalism. Thus, the state's duties are shared between the Austrian government and the governments of the nine provinces, the so-called *Bundesländer*. This distribution encompasses the fields of legislation, execution of law as well as financial management. The state and the *Bundesländer* have their own bodies of legislation and execution as well as their own budgets. Compared to other states operating under federal systems, Austria is centralized to a rather high degree, resulting from historical events. Nevertheless, Austria has a vital federal system and the *Bundesländer* each have strong regional identities (Bußjäger, 2012, pp. 43, 52).

In the context of foreign policy, diplomacy and EU policy making, Austrian federalism matters, as the *Bundesländer* gain importance with the EU's initiative of an *Europe of the regions* and the principle of subsidiarity (Dialer & Mast, 2012, p. 74). According to this, regions are also classified as decision making actors beside nation states and the supranational institutions in the EU's multilevel-governance system. The *Bundesländer* also have offices in Brussels, which are mainly concerned with gathering information and forwarding this information to the government of the respective Austrian region. Besides that, lobbying is among the tasks of these offices. Advantages of the regions shall be promoted and networks shall be expanded. Although this is clearly part of multilateralism, it also includes a bilateral dimension. Seven of the nine Austrian *Bundesländer* have individual offices in Brussels, one has no office (Vorarlberg) and one of the *Bundesländer* participates in a bilateral cooperation between three neighbouring regions in two countries. The Austrian region Tyrol as well as the Italian regions South Tyrol and Trentino operate a shared office in Brussels since 1995, the year Austria accessed the EU. The aim of this office is to promote shared positions in several policy areas (Dialer & Mast, 2012, pp. 83-89). This association is influenced by the common past of these regions, what is outlined in the following chapter, and illustrates how other actors than the MFA conduct EU-related bilateralism.

A further relevant aspect of the Austrian domestic policy structure is social partnership. Austrian social partnership is a special form of corporatism that provided long-lasting stability and thus is of high importance in Austria's political system. Main components of this form of corporatism are a central role of the government and the government's administration on policy making, a specific form of representing interests in professional public associations as well as interaction between state bureaucracy and these associations (Tálos, 2008, pp. 7, 13). In Austria, four of these associations exist, whereby two are responsible for the interests of employees (Chamber of Labour and Austrian Trade Union Federation), one is responsible for the interests of employers (Federal Economic Chamber) and one represents the interests of farmers and foresters (Chamber of Agriculture). Based on Austria's federal system, all associations are divided into subsidiary organizations in the nine Austrian *Bundesländer* as well as further specialized subsidiary organizations. Like the *Bundesländer*, some of these associations are also represented in Brussels. Particularly interesting in this context is the foreign trade activity of the Federal Economic Chamber. Austria's system of social partnership creates a special situation in foreign trade policy that also affects Austrian bilateral diplomacy. The Federal Economic Chamber operates its own foreign trade service, which supports Austrian companies abroad and its Foreign Trade Centres exist alongside Austrian bilateral embassies in EU member states as well as in third countries. Thus, Austrian social partnership not only affects domestic policy making, but has significant impact on the structure of Austria's diplomatic service. Details on the duties of Foreign Trade Centres, the form of cooperation between Foreign Trade Centres and Austrian embassies as well as the influence of this cooperation on Austrian bilateral diplomacy are outlined in the chapter on the MFA's organizational set-up as well as the chapter on economy in Austrian bilateral diplomacy.

Austrian social partnership emerged from developments of the immediate post-war period. The Second Republic is based on an elitist consensus between the Social Democratic Party and the conservative People's Party. This consensus originated from the idea to overcome the differences that led to civil war in the First Republic, and this consensus predetermined the political and structural development of the Second Republic (Pelinka, 2002, pp. 73-74). Social partnership, with its four main associations, is deeply rooted into this tradition, as the Chamber of Labour and the Austrian Trade Union are related to the Social Democratic Party, while the Federal Economic Chamber and the Chamber of Agriculture are related to the People's Party. The initial situation after the Second World War created this specific form of Austrian corporatism and also defined the framework for political competition. During the first years of the post-war period, the grand coalition between the Social Democratic Party and the People's Party was perceived as the only possible form of government to stabilize the new republic. However, also after the country's situation had stabilized internally as well as externally, the grand coalition remained to be the most common form of government (Pelinka, 2002, pp. 74-81). According to Pelinka (2002, p. 81), this is not the expression of a specific political culture, but rather is caused by tradition and limited experience with other forms of coalition as well as the outsider role of the third political force in Austria, the right wing Freedom Party. So the grand coalition can be seen as another specific aspect of Austria's domestic policy. However, the stabilizing effect of grand coalitions in Austria made way for a political stalemate, where the two governing parties are captured in ongoing disputes over fundamental questions. This situation also affects Austria's foreign policy making. Höll (2002, pp. 373-374) argues that ongoing disputes over central foreign policy and security policy issues and a missing common strategy are noticed abroad and harm Austria's international reputation.

These three domestic policy elements - federalism, social partnership and the dominance of grand coalitions - are influential features for Austrian foreign policy making, besides its status of neutrality, as well as the classification of being a small state.

The introductory statement to this chapter defined foreign policy as the substance of a state's relations to others, while diplomacy is the process of dialogue and negotiation within these relations (Watson, 1984, p. xvi). Obviously, distinct knowledge of the substance is necessary, in order to analyse the process. Thereby, the necessity is not to identify immediate foreign policy interests. Knowledge of the substance rather is generated by unfolding the underlying framework of Austrian foreign policy making in order to gain access to an Austrian foreign policy identity. The following chapter shortly exposes the concept of foreign policy identity, before certain identity-building events and periods in the history of the Second Republic of Austria are illustrated.

Identity-building in Austria's Foreign Policy and Diplomacy

In the formation of identities, the construction of the *self* in relation to others is a central process. Tulmets (2014, p. 13) exposes two interrelated concepts in the context of investigating a country's foreign policy identity. The preceding chapter of this work outlined several aspects, which serve as foundations of Austria's foreign policy in legal terms, in political terms as well as in terms of geographical situatedness. These aspects can be classified under the concept of the *political self*, a kind of *"first order identity"* that is represented by a set of generally accepted norms and values. Tulmets (2014, p. 13) refers to Marcussen et al. (Marcussen, Risse, Engelmann-Martin, Knopf, & Roscher, 1999) who show that nation state identities either further develop or refuse to develop when different political orders meet. Through the examples of Germany, France and Great Britain, the authors illustrate how prevailing political orders influenced the countries' modes of evolving a European identity. According to Tulmets (2014, p. 15), the *political self* or the political identity of a state is characterized by its core foreign policy roles or ideologies. With regard to the preceding chapter, the status of neutrality, the precondition of being a small state as well as relevant characteristics of Austria's domestic policy structure shape Austria's *political self*. The *political self*, however, does not exist on its own, it *"has to accommodate with a historical past, the historical self, which refers to a set of historical events, which can be interpreted – and thus negated or accepted – in different ways"*. The *historical self* represents a *"second order identity"* that is based on commonly shared narratives. A country's foreign policy identity results from the coherence of these two elements, the *political self* as well as the *historical self* (Tulmets, 2014, p. 14). A country's diplomatic identity is also affected by characteristics of the institution of diplomacy. The professional conduct of diplomats is influenced by several sources of appropriateness: transnationally shared diplomatic rules and norms, like the legal basis of diplomacy, including immunity and extraterritoriality; a transnationally shared professional language as well as transnationally shared working methods; national identity and the organizational culture of the respective MFA (Bátora, 2005a, p. 49). The Austrian diplomatic identity, imparted by the MFA and carried by Austrian diplomats, is covered in following chapters. This chapter is dedicated to the second element in Austria's foreign policy identity, the *historical self.*

The discussion on identity-building aspects in the Second Republic's foreign policy past and its implications to diplomacy have to be based on research done in the field of foreign policy history. Here, one specific work offers comprehensive insights to the Second Republic's foreign policy making. Historian Michael Gehler (2005a) composed a detailed depiction of important developments in Austria's foreign policy within a comprehensive monograph. His approach is problem-based and places the role of the Austrian MFA and the Austrian diplomatic corps as well as activities of Austrian foreign ministers and governments at the centre. This actor-centred approach focuses on the question of priorities and targets of individuals, as Gehler accredits many foreign policy developments to outstanding diplomats, who operated against the background of different motivations. In order to achieve a holistic perspective, state interests and foreign policy goals of different governments complement Gehler's (2005a, p. 15) illustration of Austria's foreign policy in the Second Republic. He thereby deconstructs several myths which are deeply connected to the Second Republic's national identity concept and self-perception. Due to its in-depth focus and detailed depiction of certain events, Gehler's monograph serves as basis for identifying identity-building moments in Austria's foreign policy history.

Gehler (2005a) as well as Gehler and Bischof (2006) divide the Second Republic's foreign policy before the country's EU accession into four periods, while Kramer (2006) defines five, based on foreign policy objectives as well as thematic and geographical scopes, with regard to a variable international environment. Kramer's (2006) first period (1945-1955) describes the time between the end of the Second World War and the signing of the Austrian State Treaty. The first period of Gehler (2005a, 2005b) as well as Gehler and Bischof (2006) is labelled as *"the long fifties"*, ending by 1961, a time span of growing independence and emancipation. Kramer (2006) instead stresses the period between 1955 and 1968/70 as a term of emancipation, whereby neutral foreign policy was a tool for integration. Gehler (2005a, 2005b), Gehler and Bischof (2006) focus in their second period *"the short sixties"* (1961-1969) on the emerging Western orientation of the Second Republic and its Eastern policy. Kramer's (2006) third period (1968/70-1983/84) concentrates on the globalization of Austria's foreign policy and neutrality, while Gehler (2005a, 2005b), Gehler and Bischof (2006) describe a new kind of neutrality in *"the long seventies"* (1970-1986). Between 1983/84 and 1989, Kramer (2006) detects a re-orientation of Austria's foreign policy towards Europe. Gehler (2005a, 2005b), Gehler and Bischof (2006) instead focus on Austria's isolation and its liberation from the past in *"the short eighties"* between 1986 and 1992. Kramer (2006) finishes by outlining the road to the European Union between 1989 and 1994/95.

For illustrating identity-building aspects in the foreign policy history of the Second Austrian Republic, foreign policy developments shall not be outlined alongside decades and time periods in this work, but on the basis of significant events, alignments, orientations and leading ideas policy makers have implemented to the foreign and diplomatic service before Austria accessed the EU.

There is no claim to completeness, this exposition is an attempt to characterize identity-building elements in the period between 1945 and the early 1990s, when Austria's EU accession was prepared. Therefore, Gehler's (2005a, 2005b) comprehensive monograph on Austrian foreign policy serves as the basis, complemented by literature dealing with specific issues of Austrian foreign policy. Thereby, several topics were identified to illustrate key questions, turning points as well as foundations of Austrian foreign policy making before the country's accession to the EU.

Period of Occupation and the Issue of South Tyrol

Despite different approaches in classifying and labelling significant time periods in the Second Republic's foreign policy, the influence of the four occupying powers, Great Britain, France, the Soviet Union and the United States is uncontested. Heer (1981, p. 17) stated that no other historical and political entity in Europe had been affected more dramatically by external influences than Austria. Especially in the field of foreign policy, the Second Republic had been exposed to *"an unusual amount of interference"* (Gehler & Bischof, 2006, p. 1) from the international arena. Before 1955, Austrian foreign policy was highly dependent on the interests and decisions of the occupying powers. The primary goal of Austrian foreign policy after 1945 was to achieve independence and the withdrawal of the occupying troops. During the years of occupation, the Second Republic's first Foreign Minister Karl Gruber was confronted with a special situation, as he not only had to regenerate Austria's foreign policy and diplomacy, but he also had to deal with four occupying powers in the country. Gehler (2005a, p. 63) characterized this assignment as *"domestic"* foreign policy. So Gruber's scope of action to a large extent was defined by the interests of the Allied powers and their relation to each other, especially concerning the East-West-conflict. Gruber inclined to orient towards the position of the US, especially after they had shown their reliability with the European Recovery Program (ERP) or Marshall Plan.

Beyond that, another topic gained importance in the nation-building process of the Second Republic and remained to be a key foreign policy question for several decades. The region of South Tyrol had been part of the Austrian province Tyrol until the end of the First World War. Afterwards the region became part of Italy in the course of the ceasefire agreement between the Austrian-Hungarian monarchy and Italy, as well as in the course of the Treaty of St. Germain. The majority of the population of South Tyrol was German-speaking and there was hope for reunification with Tyrol among many South Tyroleans after the end of the Second World War. Supporting these efforts was one of the major concerns of the Second Republic during the first years of its existence (Gehler, 2005a, pp. 27-28). Foreign Minister Gruber had been governor of Tyrol in the past and placed the issue of South Tyrol at the centre of his agenda. To this end, Gruber banked on the support of the Western powers. However, according to Gehler (1996, pp. 38-51; 2005a, pp. 237-241), Gruber evaluated the situation incorrectly, because of his inexperience in the international arena and his disregard of advice by experts of South Tyrol policy as well as experts of international law. Thus, he and Chancellor Figl misinterpreted the situation at the first stage as a case of retrieving South Tyrol, although the subject of negotiation was the right to self-determination of the population of South Tyrol. Although Gruber maintained a close relationship with British and US representatives, his transfer of information concerning South Tyrol to the US and sharing his thoughts had not always been advantageous for the Austrian position. Furthermore, he missed the promising period for negotiation in 1945/46 when Italy still was in a weak position. Gehler (2005a, p. 243) refers to Stadlmayer (2002), an expert on South Tyrol, when he states that Gruber took a rather passive position in the Paris Peace Conference in 1946. At that time, the negotiations on the State Treaty had already been of higher priority than the issue of South Tyrol (Stadlmayer, 2002). In the course of this conference, Gruber and the Italian Prime Minister Alcide de Gasperi signed the Gruber-De-Gasperi Agreement which ensured equality of rights between the German-speaking and the Italian-speaking population of South Tyrol, and moved Austria to the position of a protecting power for this minority. This agreement was, however, not a full success for either side. Gruber and Figl had to give up their idea of returning South Tyrol to Austria and Italy lost some of its sovereignty over a part of its territory. From today's perspective, this step did however enable the development of solid bilateral relations between Austria and Italy, as Austria's waiver of territorial claims was a contribution to Italy's stability (Gehler, 2005a, p. 244).

Whether Austria was able to accomplish its task as protecting power for the German-speaking minority in South Tyrol is a controversial issue. On the one hand, the Italian government deferred the implementation of the Gruber-De-Gasperi Agreement. On the other hand, the Austrian interest in South Tyrol decreased due to the rise of new conflicts (Gehler, 2005a, pp. 250-252). During the Cold War, the issue of South Tyrol received lower priority in Austrian foreign policy. Nevertheless, Foreign Minister Bruno Kreisky claimed that the topic was put to the agenda of the UN General Assembly in 1960 and the following UN resolution declared that the implementation of the Gruber De Gasperi Agreement is binding for the Italian government. In 1972 the so-called Second South Tyrolean Autonomy Statute was signed, but only after the end of the Cold War a comprehensive solution was found.

State Treaty and Western Orientation

Although Austria became part of Nazi-Germany in 1938 without an act of war, the country has mainly been treated as liberated and not as defeated by the Allied powers (Stourzh, 2005, p. 35). Austria had been occupied for a period of 10 years, between the end of the Second World War in 1945 and the signing of the State Treaty in 1955. This might be one reason explaining why the Allied powers are still perceived as occupying and not as liberating powers in Austria's public discourse. According to Gehler (2005a, pp. 42-43), Austria's foreign policy had been determined by three significant topics in this period, which had been central for creating a reliable foundation for the Second Austrian Republic.

First of all, negotiating the State Treaty and liberating the country from the occupying troops was a significant element in the government's policy efforts. Between 1945 and 1946, basic domestic policy issues had to be addressed first and South Tyrol was of prime importance on the agenda of Foreign Minister Gruber. This was followed by a time of intense negotiation between 1947 and 1949, when the Soviets showed a tendency of willingness to make concessions. Gehler (2005a, pp. 42-43) labelled this period as *"crunch mode"*, while he choose the term *"state mate"* for the period between 1950 and 1953, when negotiations stagnated and even stand still due to delaying tactics of the Western powers and Soviet obstructionism. This was followed by a period of re-orientation towards non-alignment and neutrality between 1953 and 1955, what supported a positive conclusion of the negotiations.

The second important aspect of Austria's foreign policy orientation identified by Gehler (2005a, pp. 42-43) in the period between 1945 and 1955 is foreign trade policy. In 1945 and 1946 compensation contracts for bilateral trade were negotiated. In 1946 and 1947 a customs union project was discussed, but not realized. With the ERP and the membership in the Organization for European Economic Cooperation (OEEC) from 1947/48 on, Austria participated in trade liberalization and from 1950/1951 on, it also participated in multilateral clearing as associated member of the European Payment Union (EPU). With the end of the ERP, trade was further liberalized and Austria intensified its trade relations with the Federal Republic of Germany (FRG).

Security policy is the third field identified by Gehler (2005a, pp. 42-43) in Austria's foreign policy efforts in the period between 1945 and 1955. In 1946 and 1947 Austria was demilitarized, based on decisions by the Allied powers, but the Austrian government promoted the country's rearmament. In 1947 the Foreign Ministerial Conference in Moscow brought the decision to legalize controlled and limited armament. After 1948/49, the Cold War encouraged Austrian rearmament and Austria's security concepts were linked to Western defence concepts and the US Mutual Assistance Program. With the foundation of the NATO, this form of cooperation was intensified from 1951/52 on.

Austria's definite Western orientation was marked by an event in 1947, referred to as "*Figl-Fischerei*". Chancellor Leopold Figl organised private talks between himself and Communist Party official Ernst Fischer, who encouraged staff changes in the government, as the Soviet Union would otherwise not agree to sign a treaty. Foreign Minister Gruber, well-known for his pro-Western orientation, was informed by Figl and passed this information on to the US occupation authorities as well as the media without authorization (Gehler, 2007b, p. 350). The release of this information entailed resentments on the domestic policy level and introduced preconditions for a definite waiver of an East-orientation of Austria (Gehler, 2007b, p. 381). According to Gehler (2005a, p. 52), the Figl-Fischer affair did not mark a severe turning point in Austria's alignment policy, but it strengthened its Western orientation. The Social Democratic Party as well as the People's Party gave their consent for participating in the ERP, which started in its first round in 1948 and ended in 1953. Karl Gruber stepped back from the position of foreign minister after he published a controversial book on his time in the MFA. Leopold Figl became his successor. He was replaced as chancellor after being criticized for his compromising attitude towards the social democrats. Figl became one of the most famous foreign ministers of the Second Republic as he negotiated the State Treaty. However, before all of this, the future development of Austria had to be separated from the discussion on Germany's future. Between 1947 and 1954 Austria's concern for independence was upstaged by the much more complex conflict around Germany. The Second Republic's first Foreign Minister Gruber always argued for separating Austria from Germany's future, as the maintenance of Austria's unity was his main concern in this context (Gehler, 2005a, pp. 75-76). For the first time in 1955, the Soviet Union's Foreign Minister Wjatscheslaw Molotow noted that the case of Austria could be treated detached from Germany. Austria's diplomatic representative in Moscow, Norbert Bischoff started exploratory talks, in order to determine the extent of willingness of the Soviet regime to support an Austrian State Treaty. Based on Bischoff's assessment, the Austrian government sent a delegation for preliminary negotiations to Moscow, followed by a government delegation (Gehler, 2005a, pp. 102-103). These talks resulted in the Moscow Memorandum, which had shortly been followed by the signing of the State Treaty and Austria's declaration of permanent neutrality.

Hungarian Uprising as Touchstone of Neutrality

As soon as the year after the Austrian State Treaty was signed and Austria declared its status of permanent neutrality, these foundations were challenged by a major event in Austria's neighbourhood, the Hungarian Uprising in 1956 and its suppression by the Soviet army. Gehler (2005a, p. 161) indicates an indisputable connection between the Austrian State Treaty, the country's establishment as a neutral state in 1955 and the Hungarian Uprising in 1956. He cites French ambassador Francois Seydoux, who argued that Austria as a neutral state was not a role-model of the West for the development of Germany, but a Trojan horse for Middle and Eastern Europe (Gehler, 1995, p. 272; 2005a, p. 161).

The Hungarian Uprising was a challenging situation for the Austrian government because Austria had to position itself as a neutral state between East and West for the first time. Chancellor Raab formulated a clear statement in which he called the Soviet Union to participate in stopping the military operations and he pleaded for the restoration of peace and human rights. Within this crisis, the Second Austrian Republic had the first opportunity to define its foreign policy profile in displaying behavioural patterns which are connected to neutrality in international law, such as humanitarian aid, political mediation as well as military self-protection. Austria unambiguously demonstrated its Western and pro-democratic orientation. The government issued several measures in order to display Austria's neutrality. It established a restricted zone and allowed the inspection of these zone by ministers of defence and military attachés of the superpowers, it enacted a visa-ban on foreign passports, reinforced controls on the Western border, banned political activities by refugees and expatriates, and disarmed and interned armed subjects (Gehler, 2005a, p. 162). Beyond that, Austria supported Hungary with aid consignment and medication supplies and suggested the surveillance of aid programs for Hungary by an UN coordination committee.

Thus, Austria already at an early stage positioned itself as a self-confident neutral power. According to Gehler (2005a, pp. 163-164), the Soviets at that time could not have an interest in discrediting this concept, which had been invented with the help of the Soviet Union. Therefore, Austria's reaction to the Hungarian Uprising represents the first test for the feasibility of its neutrality concept. The successful overcome of this crisis had a major impact on the future development of the foreign policy strategy of the Second Republic (Schlesinger, 1972, pp. 51-52; Rauchensteiner, 1981, p. 107; Gehler, 2005a, pp. 180-181). Gehler (2005a, pp. 171-172) even detects a first movement towards peace keeping when the Austrian government expressed that it is the duty of non-aligned states to support Hungary in stabilizing the situation.

Austria's action in the Hungarian Uprising was a boost for the development of the country's foreign policy identity. The event itself hindered Austria to take further steps towards the West. The Austrian government had applied for accession to the European Coal and Steel Community (ESCS), although all of the founding states were NATO members and were about to plan an economic community, including common external trade policy. However, the developments in Hungary in autumn 1956 motivated the Austrian government to withdraw the application for admission (Angerer, 2014, pp. 201-202). For Gehler (2005a, p. 169), this represents an example of the immaturity of the idea of neutrality in the Second Republic before the Hungarian Uprising sharpened Austria's profile as neutral state. Beyond that, the insufficient equipage of the Austrian armed forces built a basis for neutrality as security policy concept in the Second Republic because with the status of neutrality, Austria was protected without the need for presenting major military power (Gehler, 2005a, p. 169).

One particular Austrian policy actor intensively influenced and promoted Austria's development during the Cold War period and the country's further positioning as neutral state in the international state system, as well as the country's specific concept of neutrality. The next section illustrates how Bruno Kreisky's concept of *positive neutrality* shaped Austria's foreign policy profile and also how his personal background and his personal preferences became influential factors for Austrian foreign policy making.

The Kreisky Era

Bruno Kreisky was one of the most influencing characters of the Second Republic of Austria, especially in terms of foreign policy. According to Luif (1982, p. 216; 2007, p. 77), Kreisky *"globalized"* Austria's foreign policy. He was foreign minister from 1959 to 1966 and long-term chancellor from 1970 to 1983. According to Gehler (2005a, p. 291), foreign policy played an essential role for Kreisky and was potentially even his first priority in policy making. Maintaining and strengthening Austria's independence was probably his most important goal and he adopted an active foreign policy approach in order to achieve it. He was eager to normalize the relations with the Eastern neighbours and Kreisky used Austria's geographical position between East and West, as well as its legal status as neutral state to mediate between the blocks. Despite this attempts of mediation and his social democratic background, Gehler (2005a, p. 292) describes Kreisky's ideological orientation as Western-democratic and anti-communist. Kreisky was a proponent of the containment policy of the US against communism and the Soviet Union (Höll, 1994, p. 39; Rathkolb, 1998, p. 99). The status of neutrality, however, hindered Austria in actively participating in it or in the following rollback policy of the Eisenhower-Dulles administration (Gehler, 2005a, p. 294). According to Gehler (2005a, p. 294), Kreisky had a rather optimistic view on the development of the United States as bearer of the world's moral and political responsibility. He accepted the hegemonic position of the US and esteemed its democratic achievements (Höll, 1994, p. 40). Beyond that, to his understanding, non-alignment was an obligation to support the resolution of international conflicts.

Höll (1994, p. 35) distinguishes Kreisky's foreign policy work into three periods. The years between 1970 and 1975 were still characterized by the reconstruction of Austria's foreign policy and only showed first attempts and preparations towards a global orientation. Relations to the European neighbourhood and the developing South were at the fore during this period. Furthermore, Austria was part of the UN Security Council in 1973/74. In the second period from 1975 to 1981, Austria's foreign policy scope became broader and Kreisky took the role of a mediator in the Middle East conflict and started to advocate for the provision of development aid for developing countries. The last years of his political career between 1981 and 1983 were characterized by a declining foreign policy activity according to Höll (1994, p. 35), caused by changing circumstances in the international environment and increasing criticism from the opposition.

Due to his social democratic and pacifist orientation and as a member of the youth association of the social democrats in the 1930s, Kreisky was in favour of the idea of the liberation of oppressed nations outside Europe. He was eager to establish relations to nations which were able to emancipate from colonialism. In his term of office, several Austrian bilateral missions were opened in Africa, Asia and Latin America. Kreisky had the vision of adopting the concept of the European Recovery Program for developing countries and argued for their industrialization and against the assumption that this would harm the already industrialized part of the world. However, the resistance against comprehensive development aid programs was rather strong in Austria, because capital requirements were high and the Austrian economy was only about to recover after the Second World War. Beyond that, the responsibility for development aid was not clearly defined in the Austrian government and between the two governing parties. Furthermore, the prevailing opinion in Austria was that the colonial powers rather than Austria would have to take this responsibility (Gehler, 2005a, pp. 308-309).

Kreisky had the idea of prominently positioning Austria in the international sphere, especially concerning its importance for the neighbouring countries. In the role of the successor state of the Danube Monarchy, to Kreisky, Austria had a foreign policy responsibility for this area and should be present in ideological and political terms. Kreisky had a realistic view on Austria's possibilities for transition in this area under the conditions in the Cold War, but still he was eager to establish good relations, especially through visiting diplomacy. One of his first visits as foreign minister led him to Warsaw. Poland was one of the most nationalistic-oriented countries among those in Central and Eastern Europe and the first in which a process of liberalization started. Between Austria and Yugoslavia, bilateral relations were occasionally stressed, due to the insufficient implementation of minority rights for the Slovenian minority in Carinthia. Here as well, Kreisky's approach was to strengthen the relation through diplomatic interaction. The relations to Rumania and Bulgaria were improved when a regulation for compensation of the expropriation of Austrian citizens was found. Bilateral relations to Hungary were more difficult to improve as the Hungarian crisis continued to have an effect and also delayed the compensation for Austrian property. In 1964, Hungary agreed to pay a lump sum and in the same year Kreisky was the first foreign minister from the West to visit the country (Gehler, 2005a, pp. 294-296). According to Bielka (1983, p. 224), Czechoslovakia was the most difficult Eastern neighbour of Austria at that time. Disputes in the Habsburg Monarchy which date back to the sixteenth century still affected the relation. The suppression of the communist reformist movement, called the *Prague Spring*, by Soviet troops in 1968 put the bilateral relation between Vienna and Prague on ice (Höll, 1994, p. 41). Relations only became better in 1974, when a regulation for the compensation of Austrian property was found (Gehler, 2005a, p. 296).

Kreisky's open and consensus-oriented East policy had not been appreciated all over the West. Kofler (2003, p. 38) cites British ambassador James Bowker, who was of the opinion that Austria often avoids to anger the Soviet Union with the disadvantage of irritating the Western friends. In the 1960s, Kreisky's reaction to hostilities like this were modest. He explained that Austria's foreign policy does not have the leverage to allow a bridging function between East and West, but unofficially he persisted with his policy of détente. In Kreisky's view, his approach should not annoy the West, but rather further strengthen the West's confidence in Austria and Austrian foreign policy (Kofler, 2003, p. 38). Kreisky however had one major concern, which necessitated a certain degree of Western integration. He strived to lead Austria's economy to the European market because a vital economy to him was a precondition for an independent state, and permanent self-exclusion from the European Economic Community (EEC) would have harmed the economic development of the Second Republic. Conducting European economic integration policy without becoming part of supranational attempts was a challenging task. Moreover, permanent neutrality could have become a controversial topic among the Austrian population if a consequence would have been economic disadvantages. Kreisky was well aware of this risk (Gehler, 2005a, p. 300). Austria had chosen its status of permanent neutrality independently and therefore was able to interpret this status in its own way. This circumstance opened possibilities to approach to systems of integrated policies through concepts like *association* or *arrangement*. The Soviet Union was not in favour of Western European integration of Austria and insisted on strict compliance with the State Treaty. In the 1960s, however, the Soviet Union was not in the position anymore to offer economic incentives, and the Austrian State Treaty does not contain a concrete clause which contradicts an economic orientation towards the EEC. Hence, slow and cautious steps by Austria towards the EEC were possible (Gehler, 2005a, pp. 301-304). Kreisky developed a three-step-model for the integration process. At the first level, an economic agreement with the EEC was planned. At the second level, Austria should achieve the same advantages as members of the European Free Trade Association (EFTA) and at the third level, Austria should become an associated member. After a loss in the elections in 1962 the matter of integration was moved from the Social Democratic Party to the People's Party and therefore from the Ministry of Foreign Affairs to the Ministry of Trade and Reconstruction. Conservative Minister Fritz Bock followed a different strategy than Kreisky and tried to achieve EEC-association within a single step, but failed (Gehler, 2005a, p. 305).

Concerning the predominant topic of South Tyrol in Austria's foreign policy, Kreisky's active approach, including placing this issue on the agenda of the UN General Assembly, might be surprising in the context of his social democratic background because this topic rather was popular among conservative movements. Gehler (2005a, p. 311) ascribes Kreisky's effort in the case of South Tyrol to a bolstering of his public relations. Kreisky wanted to avoid being condemned for not caring enough about South Tyrol because of his social democratic and cosmopolitan view. Through concerning himself with the issue of South Tyrol, he created his image of an Austrian patriot. This seemed to be necessary because criticism from conservative parts of the Austrian population was not only limited to his social democratic and cosmopolitan attitude. His Jewish origin was also a source of suspicion as the anti-Semitic propaganda of the Third Reich continued to have an effect in Austria. In the election campaign of 1970, the People's Party tried to take an advantage of Kreisky's non-Catholic origin and used the slogan *"Ein echter Österreicher (A real Austrian)"* to promote their candidate Josef Klaus (Gehler, 2005a, p. 393).

Höll (1994, p. 33) states that Kreisky's political orientation was heavily influenced by his bourgeois home where he was raised in a liberal-Jewish intellectual tradition. However, his relation to his Jewish origin was ambivalent. Gehler (2005a, p. 394) indicates that Kreisky had no anti-Semitic or Israel-hostile attitude, but he was not a Zionist and his approach on neutrality also concentrated on equation and the establishment of peace in the Middle East, what required the inclusion of the Arabic world. Therewith, he overcame the US-friendly und Eurocentric positioning of his predecessors. At least once, in 1975, Kreisky openly attacked the Jewish population in stating that "*the Jews are no people, and if they are, they are lousy people*" (Böhler, 2007). This statement was the result of an intense political and personal dispute between Kreisky and Simon Wiesenthal, a well-known Holocaust survivor and hunter of war criminals. Wiesenthal criticised Kreisky's collaboration with Freedom Party leader Peter Friedrich, who had withheld details of his SS-past. Despite Wiesenthal's accusations against Peter, Kreisky fully supported him and heavily attacked Wiesenthal. Böhler (2007, pp. 526-531) states that several aspects explain Kreisky's behaviour. First of all, the domestic policy situation, which seemed to make Kreisky dependent upon Peter. Beyond that also his biography, his antipathy against the People's Party and his temper had an influence on the intensity of this dispute. Scholars also discussed Kreisky's Jewish identity and its psychological impact in this context. Whether Kreisky tried to compensate his Jewish origin in mainly Catholic environs and therefore separated himself from his Jewishness (Wistrich, 1992), or if the dispute was an inner-Jewish conflict between the assimilated and antireligious Jew Kreisky and Wiesenthal, who remained attached to the Jewish tradition, is unclear (Embacher & Reiter, 1998, p. 184; Böhler, 2007, pp. 529-531). For Austria's foreign policy identity, Kreisky's behaviour had a major impact and supported the country's self-conception as first victim of the Third Reich, which enabled a self-assured positioning in the international arena.

Already in the 1960s, Austria successfully positioned itself in the international state system with its concept of *positive neutrality*. This circumstance and Austria's geopolitical position between East and West made it an interesting location for international institutions and organizations as well as for holding international conferences (Knitel, 1986; Gehler, 2005a, p. 458). Austria had actively used its UN- and Council of Europe-memberships to support the development and compliance of human rights. Austria was a regular participant in the UN Human Rights Commission, starting in the 1950s, and Vienna became one of the most important sites for developing the legal foundation for the conduction of diplomacy. The Vienna Convention on Diplomatic Relations, the Vienna Convention on Consular Relations and the Vienna Convention on the Law of Treaties were all negotiated in the 1960s. Austria offered expertise in human, minority and international law. According to Gehler (2005a, p. 458), these developments were closely connected to the foreign policy intention of Foreign Minister and Chancellor Kreisky. Gerald Hinteregger (2008, p. 150), who was chief of cabinet in the MFA during Kreisky's chancellorship and had been part of Kreisky's cabinet during his term as foreign minister, states in his memoirs that the concept of *positive neutrality* mainly was built on the following pillars: maintaining good relationships with the four State Treaty powers, active neighbourhood policy, intensifying relations to developing countries, active participation in international organizations and establishing Vienna as site for international exchange and cooperation. The Vienna International Centre (VIC) was opened in 1979 and contrary to Switzerland, which only offered the building ground in Geneva to the UN, Austria took over all construction costs and rented the buildings to the UN for a symbolic rent of one Schilling per year. Vienna had already been an official seat of the International Atomic Energy Agency (IAEO) and the United Nations Industrial Development Organization (UNIDO) from the 1950s and 1960s on. The constant growth of these organizations required a comprehensive solution in terms of accommodation. The offer to the UN to host some of its organizations was not made by Kreisky, as the Social Democratic Party was in opposition in 1967, but by a People's Party government together with the social democratic-led city of Vienna. The final dimension of the project was set after 1970, when Kreisky came into power as chancellor with a minority government. Although the project was initiated by a People's Party government, it was a point of contention between government and opposition when the Social Democratic Party came into power again. Kreisky was faced with the accusation that the choice of the architect was guided by personal preferences and during the oil crisis the costly project was difficult to promote among the population. Besides that, Hinteregger (2008, p. 164) describes the negotiations with UNIDO and IAEO as complicated and the oil crisis also reduced the optimistic growth forecasts for international organizations. Empty UN office buildings in Vienna would have been rather unpleasant for the Kreisky government and so Austria offered to accommodate further units of the UN Secretariat in Vienna. This was controversially discussed within the UN because US delegates did not appreciate a devitalisation of New York as the major UN-site. The Soviet Union and China, however, as well as some developing countries were in favour of Vienna becoming a new host for the United Nations. It took several weeks of lobbying and negotiations until the course for the Vienna International Centre was set (Hinteregger, 2008, pp. 164-170). So although it was not the Kreisky government that offered the UN further accommodation facilities in Vienna, it was Kreisky's attempt to establish the city as a major site for international cooperation that strengthened Vienna's image as city of diplomacy.

According to Röhrlich (2009, p. 276), Kreisky's foreign policy followed a *"grand design"*, with the aim to create a distinct foreign policy profile for Austria that enables the country to serve as meeting point in world politics. Kreisky's *"at times feverish foreign policy activism"* (Gehler & Bischof,

2006, p. 7) had the effect that Austria's population to a high degree perceived Austria's foreign policy initiatives as Kreisky's foreign policy initiatives, even after his term as foreign minister had ended. Foreign policy was also a central issue during Kreisky's chancellorship (Wittmann, 1983, p. 138). Höll (1994, p. 36) mentions ironic anecdotes in which Kreisky had stated *"that he would not interfere in foreign policy matters, with the exception of the East-West affairs, the North-South relations and the Middle East conflict as well as development policy*". To Höll (1994, p. 36) it appears unlikely that Kreisky directly intervened into day-to-day foreign policy making during his chancellorship, but Kreisky was the major representative of Austria's foreign policy during that time and could rely on a broad network of international contacts as well as his excellent relations with domestic and international media, which supported or even created his prominent position in Austrian foreign policy.

Nevertheless, Höll (1994, p. 53) as early as 1994 came to the conclusion that there was nothing remaining from the era Kreisky in Austria's foreign policy, because several events dramatically changed its foundation: the Waldheim affair, the fall of the Iron Curtain and Austria's orientation towards the EU.

Waldheim Affair and Victim Thesis

Kurt Waldheim was an Austrian diplomat and non-party aligned politician, who had been foreign minister in a People's Party government from 1968 to 1970. From 1972 to 1981 Waldheim was UN secretary general and in 1986 he ran for the post of president of Austria for the People's Party. Due to his international experience and reputation, Waldheim was leading in the polls from the very beginning (Gehmacher, Birk, & Ogris, 1986, p. 92; Lehnguth, 2013). His social democratic opponent, Health Minister Kurt Steyrer, had the disadvantage of being perceived as part of the current social democratic and Freedom Party led government, which had to deal with economic and labour market problems as well as with several affairs (Trettler, 2007, pp. 592-594; Lehnguth, 2013, p. 92).

One such affair that the government had to deal with is described by Gehler (2005a, p. 539) as *"precursor"* of the Waldheim affair, the so-called Frischenschlager-Reder affair. In 1985, former SS-officer Walter Reder, who was detained in Italy after his conviction of war crimes, was released by the Italian government and returned to Austria. Friedhelm Frischenschlager, a liberal-oriented Freedom Party member, was minister of defence that time. According to Trettler (2007, p. 598), the requirements of the Italian authorities made the involvement of the Ministry of Defence reasonable and Frischenschlager appeared in person to overtake Reder from the Italian authorities. In Austrian historiography, this event and the following estimation also is labelled as *handshake affair*. It is not completely clear if Frischenschlager really shook hands with Reder at the airport (Trettler, 2007, p. 599), but the appearance of an Austrian minister at such an event evoked contradictory reactions among politicians, the press and the public. On the one hand, Frischenschlager was heavily criticised for welcoming a Nazi war criminal in Austria, especially because the right wing of the Freedom Party was regarded as a stronghold of former Nazis. On the other hand, some appreciated Frischenschlager's action and interpreted it as a welcome gesture to the last homecoming prisoner of the Second World War (Trettler, 2007, pp. 601-607). Frischenschlager apologized in Austria, apologized to the Jewish people and could remain in office (Trettler, 2007, pp. 608-610). Nevertheless, this event showed a first flaring up of Austria's NS past, which caught up with the country in the course of the Waldheim affair.

During Waldheim's earlier candidature for the office of Austrian president in 1970, which he lost, first rumours on his wartime past were in circulation (Gehler, 2007a, p. 617). Gehler (2007a, p. 618) assumes that the social democrats initiated the campaign against Waldheim by handing Waldheim's *Wehrstammkarte*, a document of the German Wehrmacht, to the media. In spring 1986, journalists of the Austrian investigative magazine *profil* and of the *New York Times* exposed details of Waldheim's past. His *Wehrstammkarte* stated that he was part of the *NS Sturmabteilung's Equestrian Corps* as well as a member of the *National Socialist German Students Union* between 1938 and 1945. Even more controversial was the revelation that Waldheim was part of an army group controlled by Alexander Löhr in 1942/43, which carried out brutal actions against partisans in Yugoslavia and executed mass deportations of Jews in Greece (Lehnguth, 2013, p. 93). In a TV-Interview in 1986 for the Austrian Broadcasting Company (ORF) Waldheim claimed that all assertions on his NS past are untrue and that he is the victim of a comprehensive defamatory campaign. The first reaction of Waldheim and the People's Party was therefore a campaign against the campaign (Gehler, 2007a, p. 622; Lehnguth, 2013, p. 94). Soon the topic attracted international attention and the World Jewish Congress (WJC) strongly supported the exposure of Waldheim's past and provided the media and the public over the course of one year with material and information collected by middlemen in Austria (Rosenbaum & Hoffer, 1993, pp. 7-8; Lehnguth, 2013, p. 93). Waldheim denied accusations, indicating that he just did his duty and only admitted certain circumstances of his biography, and only when they had already been proven by documents. This strategy of denial negatively affected his credibility (Lehnguth, 2013, p. 94) and the whole affair had a negative effect on the international reputation of Austria, as Austrians, national socialism, the holocaust and Kurt Waldheim were intermingled in an undifferentiated way (Gehler, 2007a, p. 626). The thesis of Austria as the first victim of Hitler-Germany now was challenged by the revelations of the WJC and Waldheim's refusal of guilt. Especially his reference to the fulfilment of duties was problematic against the backdrop of the formation of the Second Republic, which was grounded on a document of the Allied powers called the *Declaration of the Four Nations on General Security* or *Moscow Declaration* (Gehler, 2007a, pp. 626-627). This paper was created during the Second World War in the Foreign Office in London and was approved at the Moscow Conference in 1943. The Declaration contains a statement of the United Kingdom, the Soviet Union and the United States on Austria. Its aim was to mobilize and strengthen the resistance against the Nazi regime in the Alps and the Danube region. The paper was dropped from planes on German and Austrian territory (Gehler, 2005a, pp. 24-25) and contained the following:

> *"The governments of the United Kingdom, the Soviet Union and the United States of America are agreed that Austria, the first free country to fall a victim to Hitlerite aggression, shall be liberated from German domination.*
>
> *They regard the annexation imposed on Austria by Germany on March 15, 1938, as null and void. They consider themselves as in no way bound by any charges effected in Austria since that date. They declare that they wish to see re-established a free and independent Austria and thereby to open the way for the Austrian people themselves, as well as those neighboring States which will be faced with similar problems, to find that political and economic security which is the only basis for lasting peace.*
>
> *Austria is reminded, however that she has a responsibility, which she cannot evade, for participation in the war at the side of Hitlerite Germany, and that in the final settlement account will inevitably be taken of her own contribution to her liberation"* ("Declaration of the Four Nations on General Security," 1943).

With reference to the Moscow Declaration, Austrian politicians in 1945 proclaimed the state within its borders of 1937 (Gehler, 2005a, p. 25). According to Bischof's (1993) analysis of this text, it contains four clauses: *the clause of liberation, the clause of voidness, the clause of responsibility or complicity and the clause of contribution.* Gehler (2005a, pp. 25-26) states that diplomats in the first years of the Second Republic focused on the Moscow Declaration and interpreted it, together with experts on international law, against the backdrop of an *Okkupationstheorie (occupation theory).* This was based on the assumption that Austria, as a subject of international law, continued to exist after its annexation, but had no legal capacity. From this point of view, the Second Republic of Austria was no legal successor of the Third Reich and could not have been prosecuted for the crimes of the Third Reich during the Second World War. Hence, victims of these crimes were not able to claim payments of compensation from the Second Republic of Austria.

Austria's victim thesis is a controversial issue. Its construction was condoned by the Allied powers and had also been supported by narratives arising during and after the Second World War with regard to the First Republic of Austria. By 1940, Austrian historian Reinhold Lorenz published a book on the post-war period after the end of the Austrian-Hungarian monarchy named *"Der Staat wider Willen"*, a title that indicates that the remaining part of the monarchy became a state against its will. Despite the pro-national socialist orientation of the author, this title became associated with the fate of the First Republic of Austria in the historiography after the Second World War (Reisacher, 2010, p. 39; Stangl, 2014). By 1962, journalist Hellmut Andics published a book on the First Republic entitled *"Der Staat, den keiner wollte"* (The state nobody wanted). This book became a bestseller in 1963 and the title was nearly used synonymously to the term First Republic (Reisacher, 2010; Stangl, 2014). In referring to doubts on the viability of the successor state of the Austrian-Hungarian monarchy, Andics paved the way to further legitimize the lack of comprehensive resistance against Austria's annexation by Germany in 1938. His elaboration was heavily criticised, but the book was a big success and had a distinct impact on the historical perception of the First Republic for several decades and also influenced the self-perception of Austrians in the Second Republic. It took until into the 1990s to see more differentiated perspectives on the First Republic in public discourse (Stangl, 2014).

When referring to the post period of the Second World War in Austria, Gehler (2005a, pp. 27, 44) is of the opinion that Austrian politicians of that time were primarily driven by the objective to uphold Austria's unity and achieve its liberation of occupation. The victim thesis was a useful tool to pacify the young republic and to grant it a less problematic restart within the new world order, but it also hindered the country to come to terms with its past. The Waldheim affair was an expression of this neglect in two ways, represented by the person Kurt Waldheim and his reaction to the accusations and represented by the reaction of the Austrian population and Austrian media. The assaults of the WJC, which sometimes got over the target (Lehnguth, 2013, p. 94), led to a wave of solidarity for Waldheim in Austria and also promoted anti-Semitic attitudes in the country (Gehler, 2007a, pp. 627-629). In the end Waldheim won the election in the second round.

The Waldheim affair had multiple effects on the Second Republic of Austria. Concerning foreign policy, it cost lasting damage to Austria's international reputation and led the country to international isolation for several years. Waldheim was put on the *Watch List* for Nazi war criminals of the US Ministry of Justice in 1987 and therefore he was refused to enter the United States (Gehler, 2007a, pp. 630-635). Long-term Chancellor Bruno Kreisky, who was one of the most active foreign policy personalities of the Second Republic and who had a strong impact on the Republic's new emerging international image, stated that he was faced with the ruins of his lifework (Gehler, 2007a, p. 639).

Gehler (2007a, pp. 664-665) describes the Waldheim affair as an entirely escalated campaign, which led to the most severe crisis of the national self-conception of the Second Republic of Austria. Therein, it was less a question of Waldheim's actual perpetration, than a question of his handling of the past. The Waldheim affair was pushed by several aspects of domestic policy, foreign policy and international relations. Gehler (2005b, p. 563) thereby especially concentrates on one aspect in the Second Republic's foreign policy. According to him, the Waldheim affair should not be illustrated without referring to its linkage to Kreisky's Middle East policy.

Middle East Policy

The sensitive relation between Israel and Austria during the first decades of their existence mainly resulted from the circumstance that both nations built their national identity upon a victim thesis. Austria declared itself as first victim of the Third Reich and the population of Israel identified itself as victim of the Shoah. These contradictory constructions of types of victims led to a strained relation between the two nations (Embacher & Reiter, 1998; Gehler, 2005a, p. 388). It was the Moscow Declaration that enabled Austria to claim the victim status and this status was intensively promoted by post-war politicians in order to facilitate a unified and independent start for the new republic. The victim thesis, however, inhibited a profound examination of the individual responsibility of Austrians in crimes of the NS regime and also inhibited restitution. The acknowledgment of the Moscow

Declaration by Israel and Israel's differentiated view on Austria and Germany concerning war responsibility supported the victim thesis (Pleinert, 2002, p. 769; Gehler, 2005a, pp. 388-389). Gehler (2005a, p. 389) illustrates the ambivalent relations between Israel, Austria and the Federal Republic of Germany (FRG) by the example of diplomatic relations. Israel conducted no diplomatic relations with the FRG until 1965 although the FRG agreed on restitution. Diplomatic relations to Austria however were first established in 1950 and Chancellor Figl, as well as Foreign Minister Gruber, both of whom had been in opposition to the NS regime, deliberately choose diplomats for certain positions, who had been in resistance against the regime or had been victims of the regime. Such action served to substantiate the victim thesis.

Despite the promotion of the victim thesis and the *Okkupationstheorie (occupation theory)*, which was based on the assumption that the Second Republic of Austria was no legal successor of the Third Reich, the Austrian government was aware of the fact of complicity of Austrian citizens in NS crimes. The Austrian government engaged in talks with the Committee for Jewish Claims on Austria between 1953 and 1955. In 1955, Austria agreed on the establishment of a 22-million-dollar fund. In the same year, the State Treaty with the omission of an Austrian responsibility for the Second World War was signed and was not contested by any state (Pleinert, 2002, p. 768). Consequently, Austria's status as a victim was approved (Gehler, 2005a, p. 391). But the population of Israel, contrary to its government, did not unanimously accept Austria's attitude to stress the position of a victim of Hitler-Germany. Israeli media for example called attention to anti-Semitic incidents in Austria several times after 1945 (Embacher & Reiter, 1998, p. 58; Gehler, 2005a, p. 389). Nevertheless, bilateral relations between Austria and Israel developed well in the 1950s and 1960s, thanks to diplomatic efforts and cultural exchange (Gehler, 2005a, pp. 391-393).

When Bruno Kreisky, himself of Jewish origin, became chancellor in 1970, the mood in Israel was optimistic, although Kreisky already caused attention during his term as foreign minister, because he was the first Western politician to visit President Nasser in Cairo (Gehler, 2005a, p. 393). The dispute between Kreisky and Simon Wiesenthal in 1975, in which Kreisky made a controversial statement on the Jewish population, led to further resentments. In this incident, Kreisky's anti-Zionist and pro-Palestine attitude, which directed his Middle East policy during the next years, became apparent. According to Gehler (2005a, p. 394), Kreisky was not anti-Semitic, but his concept of *positive neutrality* overcame the Eurocentric and transatlantic-oriented approach that had been implemented by former Austrian foreign ministers. To him, establishing peace in the Middle East had to include the Arabic population. Therefore, his approach was detached from US foreign policy and was sometimes even critical of it. Beyond that, Kreisky was particularly harsh in criticism of Israel and Israeli politicians, which soon made him into persona non grata in Israel. Due to his Jewish origin, the Israeli press and population treated him differently than anti-Zionists from other backgrounds. He was named as *renegade* and blamed for Jewish self-hatred and anti-Semitism. Kreisky never called the legal existence of Israel into question, but his sympathy with the Palestine Liberation Organization (PLO) and his criticism of Israel's policy, against the backdrop of his Jewish origin, obviously challenged the Israeli identity and led to intense reactions on both sides (Embacher & Reiter, 1998, pp. 178-183). Kreisky believed that his religious origin did not bind him to a certain ideology. It is also obvious that Kreisky would not have been able to take such strong positions against Israel's policy without he himself being Jewish (Röhrlich, 2009, p. 301).

Kreisky's Middle East activities were closely connected to the Socialist International (SI) (Thalberg, 1983, pp. 294-295; Höll, 1994, p. 44). In 1973 Kreisky attended a SI-Party Leaders Conference on the issue of the *"legitimate rights of the Palestinians"* (Höll, 1994, p. 44) and he proposed to send a SI-fact finding mission under his guidance, which visited the Middle East in 1974, 1975 and 1976 (Thalberg, 1983, pp. 304-312). This mission came to the result that a Palestine state in Gaza and the Westbank should be supported and the PLO should be recognized (Bunzl, 1991, p. 47; Höll, 1994, p. 44). Indeed it was Austria that first recognized the PLO in March 1980, a step that had been controversially discussed in the international arena (Höll, 1994, p. 44). Kreisky's line of action in the previous years had already shown that Austria was about to open up to the PLO. Kreisky welcomed PLO-leader Jassir Arafat in the name of the SI in Vienna in 1979. In 1977 the PLO was allowed to establish an office in Vienna in order to conduct relations with international organizations in the city (Gehler, 2005a, pp. 400-401). At that time, the SI was not unified anymore in the question of the Middle East (Gehler, 2005a, p. 399) and Kreisky continued his policy in the framework of the Austrian government (Höll, 1994, p. 44). The aim of Kreisky's Middle East initiatives was to dissuade the PLO from terrorism and to dissuade it from the idea of destroying Israel, what should have been achieved by legitimizing the PLO (Gehler, 2005a, p. 401).

Austria had been a scene for terrorist action conducted by pro-Palestine terrorist organizations several times. In 1973 for example, Soviet Jews, immigrating to Israel, were kidnapped on their way to the Austrian transit camp Schönau. Palestine terrorists took them to the airport and claimed to fly to an Arabic country, from where they wanted to exchange their hostages against Palestine prisoners in Israel. Kreisky as well as the ambassadors of Egypt, Libya, Lebanon and Iraq negotiated with the kidnappers. In the end, the Austrian government promised to close the transit camp Schönau and the hostages came free. Despite heavy criticism from Israel and Western countries for Kreisky, because he accepted the claims of terrorists, Schönau was closed (Gehler, 2005a, p. 407; Röhrlich, 2009, pp. 303-305).

In connection with other terrorist attacks in the following years, Kreisky's critics blamed his engagement in the Middle East as being responsible for the rising terrorist threat in Austria. Gehler (2005a, p. 407) however does not ascribe the terrorist attacks to Kreisky's international activism because Kreisky represented an open-minded approach on the issue of Palestine. He rather ascribes the decision for Austria as scene for terrorist attacks to its neutral status, as on the one hand, a military reprisal of a neutral state appears rather unlikely and on the other hand, attacking a neutral state gains more attention - especially if the state, like Austria, hosts several international organizations. Kreisky himself, contrary to the opposition, was of the opinion that his appreciative interaction with representatives of the Arabic world helped to contain terrorist action in Austria because the country had the image of being a supporter of Jewish emigrants (Gehler, 2005a, p. 407).

Kreisky's chancellorship was a challenging period for the relations between Austria and the Jewish world. Gehler (2005b, p. 563) suggests considering the Waldheim affair in this context because Kurt Waldheim was UN secretary general during Kreisky's chancellorship. Gehler as well as Embacher and Reiter (1998, pp. 256-257) state that Waldheim supported Kreisky's pro-Palestine policy. By 1974, Jassir Arafat for example had the opportunity to speak in front of the UN and in 1975, resolution 3379 was passed, in which Zionism was condemned as racism. In summary, the Western dominance in the UN diminished during Waldheim's term as secretary general. Gehler (2005b, p. 563) observes a possible connection between Waldheim's support of Kreisky's Middle East policy and the international dimension the scandal around Kurt Waldheim took.

The relations between Austria and Israel started to ease in the early 1990s, when several government representatives repeatedly hinted at the responsibility of Austrians in war crimes during the Second World War (Gehler & Bischof, 2006, p. 5).

The following section reflects on how the developments illustrated in this chapter influenced the evolvement of Austria's foreign policy identity.

An Ambivalent Foreign Policy Identity

Several incidents in the formation and development of the Second Republic of Austria led to ambivalence in its foreign policy identity. In referring to the experience of civil war in the First Republic, leading politicians primarily followed the aim of keeping the young state unified at the beginning of its formation (Gehler, 2005a, pp. 27, 44), which prevented the country from coming to terms with its past. The Second Republic's territorial identity was challenged by the undecided future of Germany and potential impacts on Austria, as well as the unsolved issue of South Tyrol. However, the objective to achieve a solution for South Tyrol and its German-speaking minority supported the further development of Austria's national identity. The aim to unify the young republic had been supported by the thesis of Austria being the first victim and thus, no legal successor of Nazi Germany.

Instead of referring to its immediate past, the Second Republic rather turned towards more glorious times when it started to promote its image in the world. Rathkolb (2011, p. 37) speaks of an *"Austrianization"* of the cultural heydays of the Habsburg monarchy. In the process of *"Austrianization"* attractive elements of the Habsburg monarchy were transformed to the history and culture of the Second Republic, without taking the territorial size and cultural diversity of the environment into account, in which these cultural achievements developed. Bruno Kreisky in particular had a sense for the mythical power of the Habsburg monarchy and made use of it in foreign policy terms, for example in promoting Vienna as site for international conferences in referring to the famous congress of 1815 (Röhrlich, 2009, p. 153). Although Kreisky's foreign policy generally followed a modern approach, he did not only build up Austria's foreign policy and diplomatic identity on the creation of the image of a modern young republic with efforts to contribute to the international community, but complemented this image by traditional and cultural elements, stemming from the monarchy's imperial heritage (Röhrlich, 2009, p. 154). The successful promotion of this image, the status of permanent neutrality and Kreisky's Jewish origin, although he supported the Arabic world, protected Austria from critical examinations of its role in the Third Reich for a long time. In the context of the

Waldheim affair, Bruno Kreisky spoke of the ruins of his lifework. Indeed, as mentioned before, Höll (1994, p. 53) concluded as early as 1994 that there is nothing remaining from the era Kreisky in Austria's foreign policy. However, this does not necessarily apply to Austria's foreign policy identity. The Waldheim affair heavily damaged the thoughtfully constructed global image of the Second Republic. Austria came to terms with its past rather late and electoral successes of right wing parties still produce international headlines time after time. However, self-perception and the promotion of Austria's image in the world are based on different ideas. Being the successor state of the Habsburg monarchy and promoting its cultural heritage remains to be a central component of the Second Republic's self-perception and therefore is a permanent element in its foreign policy and diplomatic identity. Moreover, Austria's status of neutrality became one of the most popular identity-building factors of the Second Republic (Wodak et al., 2009, p. 63). So although central ideas and topics of the era Kreisky are not the main influencing issues in Austria's foreign policy of today, identity-building measures of this time still influence Austria's national and also its foreign policy identity.

The next chapter focuses on Austrian foreign policy making in the EU, whereby the first section illustrates Austria's way into the EU, while concentrating on challenges caused by the country's status of permanent neutrality. The second section outlines how Austria's ambivalent foreign policy identity influences its foreign policy making in the EU.

Austrian Foreign Policy in the European Union

At the end of the 1980s and the beginning of the 1990s, a changing global environment altered Austria's position in the international arena. The collapse of the communist regimes in Eastern Europe, the unification of Germany, the disruption of the Soviet Union and as a consequence the end of the Cold War, challenged the foundation of Austrian foreign policy. Austria's neutral status developed in the course of the East-West conflict and therefore, to a certain degree, lost its necessity in the new emerging world order. Gehler and Bischof (2006, p. 11) argue that the full extent of the impact of these developments on Austrian foreign policy making still is about to be investigated.

The developments at the beginning of the 1990s broadened the possibilities for Austrian foreign policy making. The already existing Western-orientation had been intensified and the concept of neutrality obtained a new interpretation. In 1991/92 Austria was a non-permanent member of the UN Security Council and participated in economic sanctions against the Iraq and even granted a right of transit for war material to the US-led alliance fighting against Iraqi dictator Saddam Hussein (Skuhra, 1995; Kramer, 2006, p. 824). In this case, the Austrian government gave priority to the UN Charta before neutrality (Krüger, 2003, p. 9). A new interpretation of neutrality also became necessary in the context of Austria's rapprochement to the EU.

Accession Negotiations against the Background of Neutrality

The end of the East-West conflict also opened up the way towards European integration. A more pro-European foreign policy approach already became visible between 1983 and 1986, after Bruno Kreisky's withdrawal, when the Social Democratic Party and the Freedom Party built a coalition (Kramer, 1988, p. 821; Luif, 2000, p. 681; Kramer, 2006; Luif, 2007, p. 78). This European orientation had further been strengthened by Foreign Minister Alois Mock from 1987 on, in a coalition of the Social Democratic Party and the People's Party (Kramer, 1988; 2006, p. 821). During its time in opposition, the People's Party had heavily criticized Kreisky's approach of positive neutrality and argued in a populist manner for better support of Austrian farmers than support for Jassir Arafat (Luif, 2000, p. 680). Interests of the Austrian economy played a major role for the development towards European integration. Globalization and a liberalization trend among industrial nations created difficult conditions for Austria's economic policy making (Luif, 2007, p. 78). The growing political and economic activity in the European Community (EC), especially the project of a European Single Market, attracted attention in Austria and the Austrian government decided to draw up a request to commence accession negotiations in 1989.

Austria was the first neutral state that aimed to access the EC. Switzerland, Finland and Sweden were at that time of the opinion that neutrality would be incompatible with EC membership. The Austrian government internally discussed and proved Austria's possibility for an EC accession and came to the conclusion that accessing the EC is legitimate and compatible with Austria's neutrality. Nevertheless, the Austrian government underestimated the reservations of the EC against neutrality (Schneider, 1990, pp. 127-128). Austria's neutral status caused intense discussions in the EC and it took until 1991 for the EC Commission to give an official statement on Austria's application for accession. In this statement, the Commission argued that from an economic point of view the accession of Austria would be a benefit for the EC. However, the country's neutral status was assessed as less positive and the Austrian government was asked by the Commission to make a clear statement concerning Austria not being legally prevented from participating in future CFSP actions (Luif, 2006, pp. 872-873).

The Austrian government started confidence building measures and sent several aide-mémoires to the EC in order to verify Austria's willingness to participate in the further development and deepening of the EC (Luif, 2000, p. 696; 2006, p. 873). However, it took until February 1993 before accession negotiations together with Finland and Sweden started. In preparation on issues concerning CFSP, which had been implemented with the Maastricht Treaty in 1992, the Austrian government developed a narrow interpretation of neutrality (Luif, 2006, p. 873), according to which

> *"Austria is not obliged to participate militarily in wars, not obliged to accede to military alliances and to establish military bases of foreign states on its territory (...) Austria will actively participate in the further development of the security policy structures as provided for in the Treaty on European Union."* (printed in the Austrian newspaper "Die Presse", 10th of November 1993, translated by Luif, 2003b, p. 284)

The EU (the EC was renamed the EU in 1993) and the pre-accession countries agreed on including a clause on CFSP to the final act of the treaty of accession. Therein, the pre-accession countries declare that they will be ready and able to support the different EU policy areas at the time of their accession. Beyond that, a section was formulated according to which the pre-accession countries are obliged to adapt their legal framework to the acquis of the European Union (Joint Declaration cited by Luif, 2006, pp. 873-874). Although Austria was not explicitly mentioned in this context, Luif (2006, p. 873) is of the opinion that this was a clear reference to Austria as it was the only pre-accession country with a constitutional commitment to neutrality. Beyond that, a national referendum on EU accession had to be held in Austria, due the fact that an accession required an overall amendment of the constitution (Öhlinger, 2002, p. 83). The Austrian population approved the accession to the EU with a large majority in 1994. The voter turnout was 82.3% and 66.6% voted in favour of the EU.

However, Austria's status of neutrality has not been an untouchable issue in the context of EU accession. By 1998, the People's Party suggested to abandon Austria's neutrality in respect of EU accession. But opinion polls displayed that for the majority of Austrians the status of neutrality was of greater value than EU membership (Luif, 1995, pp. 241-242; 2006, p. 874). Consequently, neutrality had to be brought into accordance with EU membership. For this purpose, the constitution was complemented by article 23f, in which concessions to CFSP are made, while the constitutional law on permanent neutrality remained intact (Luif, 2006, p. 875). Austria, Finland and Sweden accessed the European Union at 1st of January 1995.

With the Treaty of Amsterdam, another clause had been added to the constitution that enables Austria to participate in the full range of the Petersberg tasks. This includes military action in crisis management as well as peace keeping operations. Beyond that, the term *peacemaking* is also mentioned in the Petersberg tasks. It has no official definition, but Neuhold (2003, p. 15) points out that a non-defensive use of armed force is obviously included. Still there was little debate on the Petersberg tasks in Austria. Austrian participation is dependent on a decision by the EU as well as consent of the Austrian Parliament (Krüger, 2003, p. 10). Nevertheless, involvement of the parliament does not necessarily mean involvement of the public. There is a clear gap between the foreign policy orientation of Austrian governments of the last years and public opinion. The narrow interpretation of neutrality (Luif, 2006, p. 873) and the reduction to its substance (Krüger, 2003, p. 10), implemented by the Austrian government in the course of EU accession, did not transform the broad concept of neutrality in public perception. Neutrality remains to be one of the most popular identity-building factors of the Second Republic of Austria (Wodak et al., 2009, p. 63). According to Neuhold (2003, p. 15), the continual support for permanent neutrality in public opinion is grounded in historical reasons, as he pointedly expresses:

> *"Neutrality apparently placed Austrians in the best of all possible worlds: geographically in the centre, politically and economically in the West, and militarily outside Europe, since neutrality was expected to keep the country out of armed conflict despite its vulnerable geostrategic location."*

With the end of the Cold War, the argument of a vulnerable geostrategic location lost its eligibility, as Austria is almost entirely surrounded by NATO-members (Neuhold, 2003, p. 16). The public opinion concerning neutrality remains concentrated on the assumptions that it maintains political independence and territorial integrity. Public opinion also includes the myth that neutrality was the engine for an Austrian economic success story.

The reasons why a majority of the Austrian population feels committed to neutrality are diverse and policymakers rather further undermine the concept than to make the unpopular decision of abandoning neutrality. A process that, according to Neuhold (2003, pp. 15-16), today could be conducted unilaterally, although it is based upon a contractual relationship with those states that have recognized Austria's permanent neutrality.

The question rises as to whether neutrality is of profitable value at the present time. Enos-Attali (2005, p. 2) argues that neutrality emerged in the context of the Westphalian state system, in which nation states are the main actors, territorial invasion seems to be the main threat and an interstate war is the main risk. Contemporary threats are of a different kind. Interstate invasions still happen, but countries situated in the centre of Europe in a globalized world have to face different threats, mainly of non-military kinds. Therefore, defence policy cannot be focused anymore on defence of national borders. To a certain extent, the evolution of the European Union is a response to this development. Single nation states, especially smaller nation states, are often not able to cope with new emerging threats on their own. In a globalized environment, far-reaching connections give a new meaning to security and defence, which exceeds the borders of nation states. So if the threat of conventional interstate wars decreases, the relevance of a national strategy aligned to this kind of threat decreases as well.

The reason for Austria's maintenance of neutrality is primarily the positive attitude of the population towards this status, based on the positive experience outlined above by Neuhold, and complemented by several myths. Moreover, its maintenance today is most likely also motivated by the fact that it enables Austria to elude European solidarity if precarious decisions have to be made. To gain a credible position in foreign policy, the EU would need to speak with one voice and either take action or stay out of conflicting situations. With permanent neutrality, Austria is in the position to refer to a legally binding special status in order to not participate in actions, which could be unpopular among Austrian citizens and therefore among Austrian voters (Neuhold, 2003, pp. 16-17).

Neutrality is usually an expression of "*a deep will to escape the military, financial, economical as well as social consequences of participation to a war*" (Enos-Attali, 2005, p. 3). With this background, some scholars (Kramer, 2013; Wintersteiner, 2013) are of the opinion that Austria as a neutral country could positively contribute to EU foreign policy making in the fields of conflict management and conflict resolution. This would require a revitalization of active neutrality and peace diplomacy. Such a development could hold opportunities to promote Austrian positions in EU foreign policy making, and therefore diminish the gap between the myth of Austrian neutrality and its real presence. New global conflict lines (national and cultural) define the new world order and would indeed offer possibilities for new interpretations of neutrality.

Later chapters will show how neutrality is used in Austrian diplomacy today. The next chapter focuses on the development of Austrian foreign policy making and diplomacy in the EU.

Implications on Austrian Foreign Policy Making and Diplomacy

With accession to the EU, Austria on the one hand accepted limitations of its scope of action for conducting foreign policy, while participating in CFSP on the other hand enables the country to conduct a different form of foreign policy within a broad network. This network on the one side is represented by the foreign policy system of the EU and on the other side by the network of interaction of EU member states, into which a new state is entering. Within this network, the relations of new members to other EU member states do change, as national policies intervene and form a new policy area, a sort of "*Europäische Innenpolitik*" (European domestic policy) (Höll, 2002, p. 370). The following remarks on Austrian foreign policy making in the EU are mainly based on the works of Höll, who comprehensively examined this field of research.

With accession to the EU, the foundation for Austrian foreign policy making changed on several levels. First of all, in relations to third states Austria does not only represent itself as a nation state in the course of bilateral contexts anymore, but it also represents an EU member state, which leads to new implications and ascriptions. Secondly, relations to other EU members do change, because beside bilateral relations now also multilateral EU relations are conducted between them and affect bilateralism within the EU. Thirdly, EU membership changes the inner-national organization of Austrian foreign policy and diplomacy, as the range of EU topics in this area increased. Details on this are outlined in the chapter on structural developments.

According to Höll (2002, p. 375), Austria's global foreign policy position was strengthened by the country's EU accession because the small country is now part of a powerful global player. At the same time, Austria's possibilities for individual action diminished. One of the big challenges Höll (2002, p. 377; 2010b, p. 160; 2010a, p. 367) determines, is the growing invisibility of national foreign policy in the context of EU membership, as national bargaining positions usually do not reach the public, which complicates the involvement of citizens in foreign policy making.

Concerning specific foreign policy positions, Austria went in line with the EC/EU from the beginning of the 1990s. Alecu de Flers (2012, pp. 80-81) mentions two incidents in this respect. Firstly, although Austria, as a neighbouring country, was particularly affected by the crisis in Yugoslavia in 1990/91, it rather acted in accordance with the EC's wait-and-see policy concerning the recognition of Yugoslav Republics, which had declared themselves independent. Only after the EC member states signified their willingness of recognition Austria did also make a step in this direction. The second incident concerns Austria's relationship to Russia. Austria had refused to recognize Russia as legal successor to the Soviet Union after its breakdown because the Austrian government wanted to keep Russia from making demands based on obligations in the context of the State Treaty and permanent neutrality. With EU accession, Austria had to step into line with the EU position on this issue and accepted Russia as legal successor of the Soviet Union in 1995. Russia in return assured that it would not interfere in Austria's neutrality policy (Skuhra, 2006, p. 851).

During its first years of membership, Austria showed effort to improve the efficiency of EU institutions as well as to strengthen the position of smaller member states (Höll, 2002, p. 375). The country also used its first years of membership to broaden its economic relations with partners in Asia and Latin America and acted as stakeholder in the European agreements in Central and Eastern European Regions. Austrian representatives actively took part in negotiation meetings for the preparation of the Amsterdam Treaty. Thereby, the Austrian focus aimed on topics like environmental issues, fundamental rights and equal treatment (Höll, 2010b, p. 162). Just three years after its accession, Austria held the EU presidency. The period of time for this presidency was a crucial one. In the second half of 1998 not only the third stage of the Economic and Monetary Union and the Agenda 2000 reform package had to be prepared, but also the next round of EU enlargement with a rather high number of candidate countries had to be initialized. According to Höll (2010b, pp. 162-164), Austria was able to handle the presidency without major problems, not least because the presidency was not affected by any unexpected events, like an international crisis, which may could have caused difficult situations concerning Austria's status as neutral country that time. Only three years after its accession to the EU, this circumstance had been regarded with more suspicion than it probably is today. Nevertheless, some member states criticised Austria's presidency with regard to a lack of a consistent political strategy. Beyond that, a certain ambivalent attitude of Austria towards EU enlargement was perceived by some. This ambivalence can be seen as a result of the growing influence of the right wing Freedom Party FPÖ, which has heavily criticized the EU and its enlargement efforts (Höll, Pollak, & Puntscher-Riekmann, 2003, p. 352).

Positive effects of this early presidency are to be found in domestic policy. Administrative structures had to be sufficiently adapted, in order to overcome the intense workload. The cooperation among and between ministries as well as the coalition partners had been strengthened and the involvement in the EU agenda resulted in a downgrading of hierarchical procedures, what gave a broader latitude to individual politicians (Höll, 2010b, p. 164). Höll (2010b, p. 165) concludes that

> *"the Presidency made the Austrian bureaucracy and the Austrian politicians fit for the Union, and the Austrian public more aware of the fact that Austria had become part of the European Union and was internationally more recognized and respected than in recent years".*

However, Austria's newly gained international reputation was heavily damaged again around the turn of the millennium. After the general elections of

1999, Foreign Minister and People's Party leader Wolfgang Schüssel decided to quit the long-term coalition with the Social Democratic Party in favour of a coalition with the right wing Freedom Party. The People's Party was confronted with an ongoing loss of voter support during their time as junior partner of the social democrats. In the elections of 1999, the People's Party for the first time only reached third place, behind the Freedom Party. Schüssel then abandoned the exclusion policy against the Freedom Party, previously agreed by the Social Democratic Party and the People's Party. In so doing, he was able to become Austrian chancellor in a coalition with the Freedom Party, although his People's Party was third in the elections. Since Jörg Haider became head of the Freedom Party in 1986, the party experienced an obvious swing to the right and Haider attracted attention several times with xenophobic statements and glorifying depictions of the Third Reich. The formation of this government not only split the Austrian population, but also confronted former Foreign Minister and now Chancellor Schüssel with a wave of indignation from the international sphere. After the Waldheim affair and controversial discussions on Austria's role in the Third Reich, the worldwide interest of media concerning this topic was enormous.

Austria had also been affected by the range of possibilities available within the framework of diplomacy in order to express clear displeasure with a certain development. The Israeli ambassador had immediately been recalled to his country. The ambassador of the United States was recalled as well, but returned after a few days for consultations (Höll, 2010b, p. 166). A considerable step was taken by the other EU member states. Already before the inauguration of the government, the Portuguese EU presidency informed Austria that the other member states would *"not promote or accept any bilateral official contacts at the political level with an Austrian government integrating the FPÖ"* (Statement from the Portuguese Presidency of the European Union on Behalf of the XIV Member States, 1st of February 2000, quoted by Höll, 2010b, p. 166). After the inauguration of the government, sanctions were imposed on Austria by the member states. These sanctions prevented bilateral visits on the ministerial level and only allowed ambassadorial visits on a technical level. Beyond that, EU member states would not have supported Austrian applications for international appointments during this time (Höll, 2010b, p. 166). Whether these sanctions had been a useful tool or not is a controversial issue. According to European law experts, the sanctions were not covered by EU law. Moreover, the hasty implementation had the effect that an exit strategy was missing in the sanctioning mechanism (Cede & Prosl, 2015, p. 95). The sanctions imposed on

Austria were not able to cause the resignation of the government and major parts of Austria's population perceived them as sanctions against Austria and not against the government (Höll, 2001). The sanctions were lifted six months later, after a high-level internationally staffed investigation group ("Wise Men Group") declared themselves in favour of this step. Following this, the Austrian case served as guideline for the formalization of a sanction mechanism against member states (Höll, 2010b, p. 167).

Shortly after the sanctions were lifted, the government led by Wolfgang Schüssel became active in an EU-related foreign policy field. Austria proclaimed its interest to build a *strategic partnership* with the neighbouring non-EU member countries, the Czech Republic, Hungary, Slovenia and Slovakia as well as with its *cultural neighbour* Poland. The underlying idea for this form of pre-EU regional cooperation was to find common interests and positions of the countries in this region, in order to use the advantage of such a cooperation as soon as these countries join the EU (Höll, 2010b, p. 168). Austrian foreign minister of that time was Benita Ferrero-Waldner, who had been state secretary under Wolfgang Schüssel in the MFA and later became European Commissioner for External Relations and European Neighbourhood Policy. Ferrero-Waldner was convinced of the idea that regional cooperation between small member states is a necessity in the EU, in order to establish a basis to upload common ideas and proposals to the EU-level (Ferrero-Waldner, 2002). However, neither the EU, nor the countries addressed were immediately fond of the idea of *strategic partnership* (Höll, 2010b, p. 168). Höll (2010b, footnote 23) is of the opinion that Austria made two mistakes in this case. First of all, the neighbouring countries and Poland were not involved in the development process of this concept. Second, the idea was made public too early, possibly as an act of defiance after the member states' sanctions. In the course of this *strategic partnership*, the Austrian MFA proposed to institutionalize regular meetings at the end of each EU presidency with representatives of the Czech Republic, Hungary, Poland, Slovakia and Slovenia. Furthermore, Foreign Minister Ferrero-Waldner proposed to establish an information platform in order to give the Austrian population a better idea of chances and challenges in the context of the EU's Eastern enlargement. Ferrero-Waldner invited the foreign ministers of the countries addressed, in order to discuss Austria's concept of *strategic partnership*. With the exception of Poland, all foreign ministers accepted Ferrero-Waldner's invitation. Poland had been represented by its state secretary. In the course of this conference, Austria's concept was renamed from *strategic partnership* to *regional partnership*. The participating countries agreed on enhancing the exchange of experience in all areas of public administration and decided on strengthening the cooperation in communication and information initiatives concerning the EU enlargement. However, although all foreign ministers did welcome the idea of regional cooperation, most of them were not in favour of an institutionalized regional partnership. Hungary and Poland had a rather positive attitude towards the Austrian idea, but they explicitly argued in favour of the maintenance of the Visegrád Group. Therefore, they pointed out that the Austrian project shall not have any negative effects on the structure of the Visegrád cooperation. In particular, Hungary argued for a loose and flexible form of cooperation with Austria. Severe criticism came from the Czech Republic. Its relation to Austria was strained as Austria demanded the shutdown of the ageing power plant in Temelín and the Austrian right wing Freedom Party, which now was in government criticised the so-called Beneš Decrees (Kiss, Königova, & Luif, 2003, pp. 62-65). According to Königova (Kiss et al., 2003, p. 66), the scepticism of the Czech Republic was based on the following considerations: For the Czech Republic, the Austrian concept largely overlapped with the Visegrád cooperation. If the EU's Eastern enlargement would indeed be implemented as soon as 2004, the benefit of a preceding cooperation with Austria would be rather limited. Furthermore, the role of Poland in this constellation was estimated as problematic by the Czech Republic, because of its size and its attitude to act as regional power. Beyond that, the Czech Republic perceived the Austrian initiative as a one-sided, self-serving attempt to improve its position after the end of the sanctions.

The sanctions can be seen as a turning point in Austria's partnership orientation, because the country's closest allies suddenly turned their backs (Kiss et al., 2003, p. 63). The duration of the sanctions was not foreseeable and although they only lasted for a few months, this incident had ongoing influence on the relation between Austria and the other member states. Despite the rather reluctant attitude of the candidate countries for *regional partnership*, further meetings with the aim of intensifying the political, economic and cultural cooperation took place. However, Höll (2010b, p. 168) argues that it *"still is an informal – and presently poorly working – forum for regional cooperation"*. He states that Austria is not exactly a strong networker in the EU and was not able so far to take part in, or establish a profound cooperation network, like the Scandinavian countries or the Benelux states do have.

In Höll's (2010b, p. 169) opinion, Austria did not meet the high expectations of neither well-established, nor new member states in the EU. The country was not able to position itself as a supporter for new member states and accession candidates, or as initiator of new strategies. Already in his analysis from 2002, Höll (2002, p. 382) concludes that Austrian foreign policy within the EU needs to overcome ambivalent behaviour in its positioning and needs to develop a clear foreign policy profile, in order to be perceived as reliable partner.

Generally, Höll (2002, p. 372) does not classify Austria as a powerful member in the EU, but still as an important one. Austria's foreign policy history for certain decades presents the image of an active and independent foreign policy agent. Although Austria's global image suffered when the victim thesis was called into question and the responsibility of Austrians in crimes during the Second World War became a topic of discussion, the country was able to further promote a confident foreign policy image, which does not refer to its recent past, but to its past life as a major European power, the Habsburg Empire. The geographical, political and economic dimension of the Second Republic of course does not allow a connection to the Habsburg monarchy in these terms. Nevertheless, the Second Republic did manage to present itself as successor of the Habsburg Empire in terms of national culture. The official Austria defines itself as *"small nation with a great culture"*. Therefore, it takes the position of a *"cultural middle or great power"* and it seems that this correlates with Austria's global image (Gärtner, Höll, & Luif, 2005, p. 12).

Höll (2002, p. 372) pleads for a critical examination of this outdated image, because its maintenance is no longer necessary in the framework of the EU. The country should instead concentrate on contemporary conditions for foreign and EU policy making as well as on representing Austrian interests in this context. Höll (2014, p. 84) is of the opinion that Austria has thus far insufficiently adapted to the new circumstances. According to him, the country would need to develop better networking abilities beyond regional contexts or small state relations, in order to successfully participate in coalition building processes on the EU-level. Austria would, in addition, need to change its external communication. Höll (2014, pp. 84-85) states that Austria behaves like a big member state, in which domestic policy debates dominate foreign policy making. The country instead should focus on communicating clear messages to the EU and the international sphere.

Höll (2010b, pp. 169-170) does however indicate one example in which Austria was able to position itself as powerful negotiating partner and agenda setter. In 2005, Austrian negotiators in Brussels for some days threatened to oppose the start of accession negotiations with Turkey. Austria only conceded after all member states agreed on the Austrian proposal to start accession talks with Croatia. This was not a purely altruistic act for

Croatia by the Austrian government. At the time Austria stalled the negotiation process with Turkey, provincial elections took place in Styria and 80% of the Austrian population were against Turkish EU membership, while 50% were in favour of Croatian EU membership. Austria's steadfastness in this case was appreciated by many smaller states, while bigger ones were rather resentful. A well-organized second EU presidency in 2006, with well-handled crisis management, was perceived positively by Germany and France (Höll, 2010b, p. 171).

Concerning Austria's general foreign policy orientation, Höll (2002, p. 379) determines a strong EU focus, which to him is at the expense of other foreign policy issues. He ascribes this circumstance to a lack of resources, to organizational and institutional shortcomings in Austria's foreign policy administration and also to party policy conflicts. By 2013, a new and young foreign minister, Sebastian Kurz, took office and obviously tried to capitalize on Austria's past foreign policy successes, despite the unfavourable situation of the Austrian MFA, for example by activating Vienna as diplomatic meeting point in the course of negotiations related to Iran's nuclear atomic policy, or by building a coalition with the Balkan states that facilitated the closure of the Balkan route in the refugee crisis in 2016 (Kramer, 2016, p. 56).

This outline has shown that Austria's foreign policy identity dramatically changed with its accession to the EU. In its position between two poles in a bipolar world order during the Cold War, Austria was able to follow an active and rather independent foreign policy strategy, based on its unique status within this system. Changing global conditions diminished the value of independence for a small state like Austria. Interconnectedness with others, especially in economic terms, as well as involvement in decision making processes gained importance. Austria's formerly far-reaching foreign policy focus became a European policy focus. Höll's assumptions on Austrian foreign policy making will serve as knowledge base for examining the development of Austrian bilateral diplomacy in the context of Austria's EU membership. However, these assumptions do not take the establishment of the EEAS and implications for Austria's foreign policy making into account. The EEAS had been established to support the High Representative of the Union for Foreign Affairs and Security Policy. The basis for these developments is the Lisbon Treaty, which launched major evolvements in the field of CFSP. The High Representative took over the CFSP tasks of the rotating presidency, presides over the Foreign Affairs Council of Ministers and exercises authority over the EU delegations, which previously represented the EU Commission, and now represent the EU in its entirety. The

EEAS operates in a broad variety of foreign and security policy areas. Peace building, neighbourhood policy, EU enlargement, foreign trade, development aid, protection of human rights, crisis response, humanitarian aid, climate change and United Nations policy are mentioned as tasks and fields of operation (EEAS, 2017b).

The implementation of the EEAS and its onward development will further transform the member states' manner of conducting foreign policy. The EEAS' concept of staff development is of particular interest in this context. By the time the EEAS has reached its full capacity, one third of EEAS staff should be represented by diplomats from the member states and they shall be treated as equals to EU officials (European Council, 2010). Some members of the Austrian national diplomatic service are already part of the EEAS network, either in Brussels or in one of the EU delegations or in representations to international organizations. The question of how this development changes the national Austrian diplomatic service is part of the investigation in this work. Beyond an exchange of personnel, also the manner of interaction between the Austrian MFA and the European Union changed with the implementation of the EEAS. The same applies to the work of Austrian embassies in third countries, due to the modified status of EU delegations. However, not only the field of relations to third states is subject to changes caused by Austria's EU accession, but also the field of inner-EU bilateral relations is affected, as outlined in the chapter on changes in bilateral diplomacy.

This investigation focuses on both areas and thereby concentrates on the most traditional actor within the field of modern diplomacy, the MFA. Investigating changes and adaptations within the framework of this well-established diplomatic actor, caused by the appearance of a new actor in diplomacy, the EU, enables the gleaning of profound insights into the development of diplomacy. In order to do so, central issues of the MFA must be considered, with the aim to illustrate its organizational character. Therefore, the next chapter gives insights to relevant aspects of the historical development of the Austrian MFA, its legal framework, current strategic focus and organizational set-up.

The Austrian Ministry of Foreign Affairs as Diplomatic Actor

At the beginning of the previous chapter on the foundations of Austria's foreign policy it was mentioned that the terms foreign policy and diplomacy cannot be equated, although they are used synonymously in some cases. Watson (1984, p. xvi) distinguishes between foreign policy as the *"substance of state's relations"* and diplomacy as a *"process of dialog and negotiation"*. In the context of the understanding of diplomacy as an institution, foreign policy has to be seen as a part of the organizational basis of diplomacy, rather than a part of its core purpose or function, which according to Bátora and Hynek (2014, p. 50) is mediation. Jönsson and Hall (2005, pp. 25-26) define diplomacy as an institution and describe the MFA is an organization within this institution. Observing changes in the organizational basis of diplomacy therefore requires an intense investigation of structures and practices as well as identities within the MFA, what also considers the impact of a country's respective foreign policy position. In order to do so, not only the organizational set-up, the historical development and legal framework of the MFA have to be taken into account, but also its strategic focus and the underlying foreign policy orientation. The following chapters will concentrate on these issues.

Historical Development

Although the post of minister of foreign affairs was first established during the Habsburg monarchy in 1720, the historical focus of this work is limited to the Second Republic of Austria because the current structures and practices in the Austrian MFA predominantly developed after 1945. However, preceding incidents of course influenced the development of the MFA in the Second Republic. The MFA of the First Austrian Republic for instance had been integrated to the Federal Chancellery in the year 1923, only three years after its foundation in 1920. This condition had been retained after the end of the Second World War in 1945 when a provisional government had been established. Consequentially, foreign affairs were governed by State Chancellor Karl Renner. Foreign Minister Karl Gruber acted as under secretary in the State Chancellery.

The First Republic of Austria was represented by 28 diplomatic missions before it was integrated to Hitler-Germany in 1938. By 1947, Austria, still under occupation, was represented by 15 missions (Gesandtschaften) located in Ankara, Bern, Brussels, Budapest, at the Holy See, London, Moscow, Paris, Prague, Rio de Janeiro, Rome, Stockholm, The Hague, Washington and Warsaw. In the following years, the number of Austrian representations more than tripled and increased to 55. By 1959, Austria was represented with 38 embassies, 5 permanent representations and 12 consulates (BMAA, 1987, pp. 324-325). In the same year, Bruno Kreisky became foreign minister and insisted on the establishment of an independent MFA. Thus, not only Austria's foreign policy profile was intensively shaped by Kreisky's initiatives, but also the establishment of the MFA as an organization was influenced by his ideas.

According to research conducted by Röhrlich (2009, pp. 152-156), Kreisky started to modernize the traditional working procedures in the Austrian diplomatic service, especially concerning the task of political reporting whereby he established close connections to the press. Although Kreisky was deeply rooted in the social democratic tradition, he did not refrain from the possibility to use Austria's monarchic image to build up a diplomatic identity and he also had no reservations towards aristocratic elements in the diplomatic corps. Nevertheless, he used the establishment of an independent MFA for the implementation of a new staff policy. Traditionally, party affiliation was considered to be the main selection criterion for filling vacancies in the Austrian diplomatic service. The dominance of members of the catholic student league CV in the Austrian diplomatic corps was perceived negatively by Kreisky. He therefore tried to open up the diplomatic service by promoting the possibility to participate in the MFA's selection procedure via the press. Due to the fact that mainly supporting social democrats would may have caused reproaches, Kreisky used his affinity for the aristocracy and reinforced the old tradition of hiring non-party affiliated aristocrats for the diplomatic service.

Moreover, Kreisky re-established Austria's diplomatic academy in 1964. The academy had been founded earlier, in the 18th century, but was shut down during the Second World War. Historian and former attaché in the MFA Gerald Stourzh (2004, pp. 183-189) documented a meeting between Kreisky, high-level diplomats and university professors on the issue of the conceptualization of a diplomatic academy. In this meeting, the structural orientation and the contents of the curriculum of the diplomatic academy had been discussed. With regard to the curriculum of the future academy, four aspects were central in this talk: issues of political science and international relations, economic subjects, legal subjects as well as linguistic competences.

In the field of political science and international relations, Kreisky argued for specifying the scope in order to meet the special needs of Austrian foreign policy. Thereby, he suggested not only teaching foreign policy strategies of great powers, but also of other neutral and other non-aligned countries. Among the bigger states, the foreign policy of Germany, France and Italy was an important aspect for Kreisky to be considered in diplomatic training in Austria. Concerning economic subjects, international trade policy, international financial policy, economic problems of European integration, economic geography and economic growth in developing countries were central issues. Concerning legal subjects, the discussants agreed to consider the law of neutrality, private international law, comparative constitutional law, consular matters, nationality law as well as the law of diplomatic relations and consular relations, according to the Vienna Convention. Regarding linguistic competences, Kreisky especially mentioned the importance of shaping linguistic intuition. Thereby, expressive skills should not only be trained in foreign languages, but also in the mother tongue. Kreisky proposed to let students analyse journalistic articles in regard to their linguistic quality, in order to train their linguistic competence. A further topic brought into the discussion by Kreisky was the issue of public relations. He pointed out that this aspect has to be brought to the curriculum of the diplomatic academy with the broad variety of its effects. Examples of other countries handling this issue should be presented, and knowledge about the phenomenon of mass media should be imparted. Kreisky proposed exercises in which future diplomats should analyse the coverage of a particular event in different newspapers, in order to get to know certain tendencies of articles. Beyond that, a visit of a newspaper publishing company was also discussed. Hans Thalberg, that time head of the press office in the Austrian MFA, emphasized that future diplomats have to be prepared to represent and promote Austria's image in the world. According to Stourzh (2004, p. 192), these enthusiastic plans concerning the curriculum of the diplomatic academy have not been fully implemented. Nevertheless, this documentation does give informative insights to Kreisky's priorities in the development of the Austrian diplomatic service. Thereby, the establishment of the diplomatic academy was one of Kreisky's favourite projects (Rathkolb, 2004) and it was closely connected to the MFA, as the foreign minister and high-level representatives of the MFA were in the leading committees of the diplomatic academy (Stourzh, 2004, pp. 191-192). Today, the diplomatic academy still focuses on multidisciplinary training and multilinguism, in order to prepare its students for international careers. However, beside the professional field of diplomacy, the academy now also focuses on preparing its students for positions in economy (Diplomatische Akademie Wien, 2018).

Kreisky took one of the most influential roles in the establishment of the contemporary Austrian diplomatic service as he deeply influenced its constitution on several levels. The separation of the foreign service from the Federal Chancellery and the establishment of an own MFA brought changes and alterations on the structural level and certainly this independence also brought more confidence to the diplomatic service. Kreisky immediately started to implement adaptations on the level of practices. He, for instance, modernized the procedure of diplomatic reporting. Moreover, his sensitivity for the necessity of public relations and media contact gave a new image to foreign policy and his new approaches in human resources policy, as well as his venture in the education of diplomats opened up the diplomatic corps and brought new concepts and ideas to the self-image of diplomats, what consequently affected professional identities in Austrian diplomacy (Röhrlich, 2009, pp. 151-158). Bruno Kreisky influenced the Austrian diplomatic service during three decades in the positions of state secretary for foreign affairs, foreign minister and chancellor.

By the end of the era Kreisky in 1983, the organizational set-up of the Austrian MFA had a bilateral and a multilateral dimension, including topics like security policy, foreign trade policy as well as external cultural policy. Multilateral cooperation at that time mainly concentrated on the work within international organizations (Kneucker, 1983, p. 41). In his analysis of the organizational set-up of the Austrian MFA from 1983, Kneucker (1983, p. 41) already stated that on the multilateral level a new form of transcultural cooperation is about to develop, with the aim to cope with problems emerging in the context of globalization. He further pointed out that this new form of transcultural cooperation is going to play a significant role in the future management of external relations.

So already by 1983, growing interconnectedness on the multilateral level had been perceived as a driver of change in the organizational set-up of MFAs, although the EC had not reached the degree of integration the EU displayed later on.

At the end of the era Kreisky in 1983, the organizational set-up of the Austrian MFA was divided into six divisions:

Central Affairs	Political Division	Economic Policy Division
I.1 Protocol I.1a Medals, Decorations I.1b Privileges, Immunities I.1c Events I.2 International Law Office I.2a General International Law I.2b International Economic Law, Human Rights, Ethnic Minorities I.2c Notary of State I.3 Press and Information I.3a Documentation I.4 International Conferences, Issues of International Organizations I.5 Security Issues I.6 Coordination of Multilateral, Social and Special Other Issues	II.1 Department of Western Affairs II.2 Department of South Tyrol and Southern Europe II.3 Department of Eastern Affairs II.4 Africa, Asia, Oceania II.5 International Organizations II 5a Coordination of the Foreign Policy Report and the Foreign Policy Council II.6 Council of Europe, Cosmic Space, Nuclear Power, Office of the Parliamentary Delegation to the Council of Europe II.7 Security Policy II.8 Arms Limitation, Disarmament	III.1 Bilateral and General Economic Policy Issues III.2 Economic Integration III.3 Multilateral Economic Policy Issues III.4 Development Aid III.4a Office of Experts III.5 Transport Issues III.6 ECE, Energy, Environmental Protection, Regional Development

Legal and Consular Division	Division of Cultural Policy	Administrative Division
IV.1 Legal Protection, Judicial and Administrative Assistance IV.2 Touristic and Border Traffic, Citizenship IV.2a Passport and Visa Issues IV.3 Social Policy and Investment Affairs IV.3a Social Policy Affairs	V.1 Bilateral and General External Cultural Issues V.1a Science and Education V.2 Multilateral External Cultural Issues V.2a Council of Europe, EC V.3 Administrative Issues of Foreign Cultural Policy V.4 Exhibitions and Film V.4a Organization of Exhibitions abroad Contact Point	VI.1 Human Resources VI.1a Public Services Law VI.1b Personnel Measures VI.2 Salary and Social Security Legislation VI.2a Social Security Legislation, Additional Fees VI.3 Budgetary Matters VI.3a Official Journeys and Relocations VI.3b Estimate, Credit Management VI.4 Facilities and Equipment VI.5 Organization VI.5a Courier Service VI.6 Telecommunication VI.6a Training Programmes

Figure 1: Organizational Chart of the Austrian MFA 1983
(Source: Own translation based on Kneucker, 1983, pp. 44-46)

Bilateral and multilateral relations were divided between division II and III in the MFA's organizational set-up. Due to the fact that relevant actors on the international stage multiplied and the number of states in the international system increased, the MFA had to prioritize its bilateral relations and cluster them in organizational terms, based on groups of states or regional clusters.

It must be considered that the set-up of an organization is not the result of rational considerations and theoretical reasoning, but it is also based on goals and expectations as well as norms, values and traditions (Kneucker, 1983, p. 44). In the case of the Austrian MFA, one example in particular makes this apparent. As outlined in the chapter on the foundations of Austrian foreign policy, South Tyrol had been a major foreign policy issue in the first years after the emergence of the Second Republic. Therefore, South Tyrol together with Southern Europe was granted its own department. On the multilateral level, the increasing number of associations and a growth in regional cooperation led to a diversification of responsibilities within the divisions of the MFA. Issues of multilateral relations were handled in division II, III, IV and V. Thereby, international organizations and the European Council were treated separately and some of these departments also were in charge of other matters of multilateral relations. Division I and VI were responsible for internal and administrative issues as well as specific central issues (Kneucker, 1983, p. 46). Kneucker (1983, p. 46) points out that the distribution of administrative and organizational tasks into two divisions is not rational, but historically grown. Matters of training, organization and telecommunication could have also been integrated to division I, which deals with central affairs. According to him, it is further notable that two other topics of foreign policy, mainly situated in the field of bilateral diplomacy, are treated separately from others and within their own divisions: economic policy and cultural policy.

Kneucker (1983, p. 41) also concentrates on the interaction between domestic and foreign policy and points out that the federal structure of Austria makes it necessary to consider the interests of the nation state as well as the interests of the nine federal states. In his outline of the organizational dimension of Austrian foreign policy from 1983, Kneucker (1983, p. 42) describes different aspects of foreign policy, following different backgrounds and time horizons. He draws a line between foreign policy in the interaction with the international system, concerning global issues, international organizations, multilateral issues as well as bilateral issues; and foreign policy in the interaction with domestic policy, regarding national interests and interests of the federal states. Specific and factual issues of foreign policy usually encompass several of these dimensions. However, Kneucker's (1983, p. 46) organizational dimensions concerning relations to the national and provincial governments are not to be found in the organizational set-up of the Austrian MFA of 1983. He is of the opinion that these aspects are covered by each division and each department in the course of normal, everyday work.

Kneucker (1983, p. 47) describes the structure of the Austrian MFA as unconventional. It had not been set up at once, but is a compound of older structures and new functions. Classical and traditional tasks conducted by MFAs were all situated in the departments of division II and division IV by 1983. In the course of the development of the organizational set-up traditional elements were adjusted by new ones. Own administrative sections were created in the form of division I and VI and the increasingly important fields of economic and cultural policy were covered by own divisions, which had to be added to the existing organizational form. Hence, at the end of the era Kreisky, the organizational framework of the Austrian diplomatic service was characterized by four topics: general issues, political issues, economic issues and cultural issues. According to Kneucker (1983, p. 47), this is a typical development in foreign services in industrial countries after the Second World War.

Considering the role of the Austrian MFA in the Second Republic's federal administration network, Kneucker (1983, p. 47) refers to an unpublished study conducted by Schattovits (results published in 1986) on organizational developments in Austria's federal administration. Data for this study were collected from 1980 to 1982. The results showed that external relations were the second most growing organizational field, after economy, in the structure of the Austrian administration framework. The number of personnel in the Austrian federal administration quadrupled between 1954 and 1978. Thematically, the growth in external relations referred to the fields of culture, economy, including external trade, as well as European integration and customs matters. The major part of this growth however did not occur in the organizational structure of the MFA, but in other ministries (Schattovits, 1986). Hence, the attempt of other ministries to conduct external relations is not a phenomenon that evolved in the rise of Austria's EU accession, but a phenomenon that started to appear in Austria's foreign policy system already before, caused by the demands of an evolving international system. This observation corresponds with Hocking's (2013) perception of MFAs not representing the national diplomatic system, but a subsystem of the national diplomatic system.

By the end of the era Kreisky in 1983, this subsystem encompassed a wide network of representations, compared to the initial situation at the end of the Second World War, when Austria had been represented by just 15 missions.

By 1983 Austria was represented abroad by:

68 Bilateral Embassies accredited in 116 States
5 Permanent Representations at International Organizations
16 Consulates General
10 Cultural Institutes
1 Delegation in Berlin

100 in total (BMAA, 1983, p. 220)

Furthermore, in 1983 the Austrian MFA had a network of 181 honorary consulates. According to the Foreign Policy Report of this year, the expansion of Austria's diplomatic network had been considered to be completed at this stage. It is mentioned that after an extensive expansion in the previous years, further openings of representations are restricted. In 1983 the Austrian MFA had employed 1 453 persons, 360 of them in the diplomatic service (BMAA, 1983, pp. 220-221).

Considering its bilateral relations, the MFA's Foreign Policy Reports in the last years of the Kreisky era highlight the importance of maintaining and developing relations to Austria's neighbouring countries, regardless of the respective political order. Moreover, a clear commitment towards European cooperation and integration was made in these years (BMAA, 1979, 1980, 1981, 1982, 1983).

Considering the MFA's structural set-up, a major development occurred by 1983, when a General Inspectorate had been established as independent organizational unit under the direct authority of the MFA's Secretary General. This unit is responsible for inspections in the MFA as well as in representations abroad (BMAA, 1987, p. 334). By 1985, after an amendment of the Federal Ministries Act, development aid competences, which had been divided between several governmental institutions, were pooled in the MFA. Therefore, a seventh division had been added to the organizational set-up, namely the Division for Development Aid, which combined the former Development Aid Department of the Federal Chancellery and the Development Aid Department of the MFA. This new division covered four departments: General Affairs, Technical Development Aid, Financial Affairs and Multilateral Development Aid. Therein, the MFA also assumed the responsibility for the annual update of Austria's three-year development aid programme, which defined Austria's mid-term orientation in development aid policy. Specific priorities were rural development, development-oriented education and technology development, health and social affairs, development of a physical infrastructure, development and utilization of natural resources and the promotion of production capacities in the modern sector. Less developed countries, especially in the Sahel Zone, in Eastern Africa and selected countries of Southern Africa as well as certain Asian and Latin American countries were the focus at that time (BMAA, 1984, pp. 198-200; 1985, pp. 180-183).

In the government declaration of 1987, the Austrian government targeted an increase in the efficiency of public administration. Therefore, the MFA also had to evaluate its administrative system. According to the Foreign Policy Report of 1989, in the preceding two years all internal regulations had been examined in order to prove whether they are still appropriate and economically viable. Regulations which did not meet these requirements were abandoned. Regulations that had been proven appropriate, but were identified as labour-intensive were abandoned as well. It is noted that new means of data processing and new communication tools brought an enormous rationalization effect. Furthermore, the Austrian government initiated an administration management project. In the course of this initiative, an international consulting company underwent an investigation of the MFA's administration and determined a potential for increased efficiency of about 4.5%. This figure is calculated from a saving potential in the headquarters in Vienna of 3% and potential higher efficiency in representations abroad of about 4% as well as in the headquarters of about 1.8%. According to the Foreign Policy Report of 1989, this low percentage is due to the already implemented initiatives of the MFA concerning the rationalization of administrative regulations. In this report, the MFA points at the fact that the improvement suggestions of the external consulting company will be taken into account, but cannot be implemented without amending a higher number of laws and regulations (BMAA, 1989, pp. 471-472). In the following year, the MFA focused on the improvement of efficiency by the expansion of computer systems and communication technology. By the end of 1990, the headquarters in Vienna had 79 computer workstations; 80 Austrian representations were equipped with fax machines and 28 with PCs.

However, the political upheavals at the beginning of the 1990s caused an increase of workload in the MFA that could not be covered by the relief brought by new technologies. By 1990, Foreign Minister Alois Mock submitted a report to the Foreign Affairs Committee of the Austrian parliament which outlined the new emerging tasks of the Austrian MFA and the MFA's difficulties to fulfil these tasks against the background of rationalization efforts. According to this report, new tasks emerged in the course of European integration, changing conditions in Eastern Europe, enhanced regional co-operation, increased efforts to protect human rights and to protect the environment, enhanced scientific cooperation, additional peacekeeping missions, new tasks in consular services as well as the expansion of cultural contacts. The report criticised that despite this number of new tasks, the MFA's proportion of the total budget decreased from 0.34% in 1980 to 0.25% in 1990. Furthermore, the report compares the situation of the Austrian MFA with neighbouring countries and concludes that in comparison with the Federal Republic of Germany and Switzerland, the Austrian foreign service is underfinanced. Germany spent 1% of its budget on foreign affairs that time, while Switzerland even spent 1.45% of the national budget on foreign affairs. Additionally, the report noted that only the high personal commitment of people working in the Austrian foreign service enabled the MFA to overcome the difficult situation caused by efficiency and budgetary pressure. Thus, the report speaks of a dramatic change in the occupational image of diplomats in the Austrian MFA from being a *"saloon diplomat"* to becoming an *"allround manager"* – a change that, according to the report, remained unnoticed by the public. In particular, in the field of human resources the report detects severe problems, because the competitiveness of the public service is rather low compared to private business. Furthermore, the report refers to an opinion poll, which indicates that the social prestige of the profession of diplomats was about to decline, which reduces compensatory effects that covered the inconveniences of the profession. Subsequently, the report demands for the improvement of labour and life conditions of the staff working in the Austrian diplomatic service. As a result, Foreign Minister Alois Mock commissioned the elaboration of a federal law for the Austrian foreign service (BMAA, 1990, pp. 474-476). At the beginning of 1991, a working group of members of the personnel administration and the staff association, members of all divisions of the MFA as well as members of the Public Service Union was built. This working group developed a draft version of a federal law. In autumn 1991, a first public debate on the creation of the federal law for the Austrian foreign service was held. The law should contain regulations on the specific requirements of the diplomatic service, like mobility, flexibility and rotation of staff as well as on specific duties and tasks to be undertaken abroad (BMAA, 1991, pp. 507-508). In 1992, the draft version of the federal law had been complemented by suggestions from Austrian representations as well as from individual members of the Austrian diplomatic service. However, concerning this matter, the Federal Chancellery as well as the Ministry of Finance pointed to initiated preliminary work completed for a reform of salaries in the public service, which ought to cover these demands. Still, the MFA furthermore insisted on the implementation of a federal law for the Austrian foreign service, because a reform of salaries in the public service does not consider certain specialities of the diplomatic service, like world-wide mobility and its consequences for family life (BMAA, 1992, p. 550). However, the federal law on the Austrian foreign service had been put on hold in 1994. Instead the reform of salary in public administration was pushed forward by the Austrian government. In the course of this reform process, the MFA had the chance to illustrate the special situation of employees in the diplomatic service and was able to achieve special regulations for its staff members (BMAA, 1994, p. 436).

Based on changing conditions in the diplomatic service, the Austrian MFA commissioned two scientific studies in order to evaluate the situation of the MFA. Outcomes of these studies are illustrated in the Foreign Policy Report of the year 1992 (BMAA, 1992). The first one was conducted by Neuhold, who investigated international developments, which influence the workflow in the MFA. Proceeding from the results of this study, he formulated several suggestions for the MFA to better adjust to new challenges. Namely, Neuhold suggested a modernization of the MFA's office and communication infrastructure and to increase the number of employees with selective specialization. The second study had been conducted by Titscher and Wille-Römer. The aim was to determine personal attitudes of staff members towards their occupation. The situation of partners of staff members was also considered in the study. According to this, wives of diplomats suffer from the difficulty of pursuing a working career, due to the frequent changes in location. They also suffer from the issue that there is no compensation per se for this loss of professional identity. After the presentation of these studies, Foreign Minister Alois Mock initiated a commission to analyse the outcome of the studies and to propose improvement suggestions. For certain issues with special need for action, working groups were established in order to increase the transparency and predictability in human resources management, with the aim to increase the life quality of employees. But within this working process, it became obvious that the integration of new standards into the historically grown structure of the Austrian MFA was especially difficult (BMAA, 1992, pp. 547-549).

Meanwhile, further specialization of tasks in Austrian diplomatic missions led to an increased use of staff from other Austrian institutions. By 1991, 4 members of other ministries and 6 members of Austrian advocacy groups worked at Austria's Permanent Representation in Brussels. Additionally, one member of the Austrian Ministry of the Interior worked at the

Austrian embassy in Bucharest in order to deal with migration issues, and one member of the Austrian Ministry of Defence worked at Austria's mission in Geneva in order to deal with disarmament affairs (BMAA, 1991, p. 496).

Also the diplomatic academy had to adapt to a changing international environment. By 1988, the courses of the diplomatic academy consisted of six thematic teaching fields:

> History and Geographical Basics of International Relations
>
> International Relations and Politics, Theory and Practice of International Organizations
>
> International Law and Private International law
>
> International Economic Relations
>
> Special Skills, Personality Development and Public Relations
>
> Language Skills (BMAA, 1988, p. 401)

The diplomatic academy reacted to the political upheaval at the end of the 1980s and the beginning of the 1990s with special courses for young diplomats from countries in Central and Eastern Europe. In 1990, 14 diplomats from Bulgaria, Czechoslovakia, Poland, Rumania, Hungary and the Soviet Union took part. Furthermore, the offer of languages taught had been adapted to the new circumstances. Alongside the compulsory languages of the academy, German, English and French, as well as the working languages of the UN, Arabic, Chinese, Russian and Spanish, now courses in Serbo-Croatian, Slovenian, Czech and Hungarian were offered (BMAA, 1990, pp. 482-483). This development already indicated the close diplomatic connection Austria maintains to its Eastern neighbours and the Balkan region today.

In summary, it can be said that the development of the organizational set-up of the MFA as well as its staff composition and the educational preparation of its personnel were heavily influenced by the era Kreisky in its beginnings. Although Kreisky's foreign policy efforts were grounded upon a modern approach, based on the idea of positioning Austria as an active neutral country in the international system, he also was well aware of the mythical strength of the Habsburg monarchy and allowed it to become a part of Austria's diplomatic identity (Röhrlich, 2009, pp. 152-156). The economic upturn in Kreisky's term as foreign minister and during his chancellorship allowed to organize the diplomatic service, the MFA as well as the diplomatic academy without cost pressure. Certainly cost pressure became a central issue in the following years. Efficiency efforts and a changing international environment challenged Austria's foreign policy orientation and therefore the basis of the conduct of diplomacy.

Beside the international surrounding, the duties of a MFA are also defined by circumstances in the national administration framework. A fundamental aspect of a ministry's remit is the legal basis that defines tasks and obligations and therefore embeds the ministry to the nation's public administration framework.

Legal Framework

The Austrian MFA is subject to the Federal Ministries Act of 1986. According to this act, the MFA is responsible for foreign affairs, as long as these affairs are not part of the responsibilities of other ministries. The following duties are explicitly defined for the MFA in the Federal Ministries Act:

- Issues of foreign policy in all areas of the state's jurisdiction
- Issues of international law
- Negotiation of state treaties
- Representation of the Republic of Austria in foreign states and other subjects of international law including international organizations
- Other issues of international organizations
- Issues of foreign representations in Austria and issues of members of foreign representations in Austria as well as issues of Austrian representations in foreign countries
- Issues of diplomatic passports
- Issues of protocol
- Issues of honours for foreign citizens as well as issues of foreign honours and titles
- Protection of Austrian citizens and their assets abroad
- Providing judicial and administrative assistance
- Issues of economic integration
- General law issues concerning the European Union with the exception of the representation of the Republic of Austria at the Court of Justice at the European Union
- Coordination of issues concerning the European Union

- Coordination of issues concerning Middle and Eastern European countries as well as new independent states
- Issues concerning the International Atomic Energy Agency (IAEA)
- Issues of cultural foreign relations
- Issues concerning the diplomatic academy
- Issues concerning consular fees
- Administration of all buildings and properties of Austrian representations governed by the Austrian MFA
- Issues of development cooperation and coordination of international development policy
- Issues of cooperation with the United Nations High Commissioner for Refugees (UNHCR) and the International Committee of the Red Cross (ICRC)
- Issues of integration policy, especially concerning social integration and the coexistence of persons with and without migration background, coordination of general integration policy, coordination of expert groups for issues of integration as well as coordination of grants in the field of integration including funds and foundations (BKA, 1986; Part 2/B).

Furthermore, all Austrian ministries are obliged to support other federal bodies in issues concerning their specific field of operation if it is set by law. Austrian federal ministries must support the federal government in handling its tasks; they have to prepare submissions of the government to the national council as well as regulations and announcements of the government if they are part of the operational field of the respective ministry. Beyond that, federal ministries must implement decisions of the federal government within their respective field of operation. Additionally, ministries are obliged to manage their duties in a proactive and efficient way, in terms of appropriateness and economic balance. Therefore, they have to consider all aspects that are of relevance within the scope of the state, especially with regard to legal issues, issues of administration and economic issues. Results of these investigations must be provided to the federal government as well as to the federal ministers and must be utilized in an appropriate manner when executing the respective tasks. Furthermore, ministries are obliged to consider the role of the nine Austrian federal states in the coordination and execution of their tasks (BKA, 1986; §3).

Moreover, Austrian foreign service institutions and their staff are governed by the Federal Act on the Functions and Organization of the Foreign Service, passed by parliament in 1999. The federal act defines the professional roles of the minister, the secretary general, the general inspectorate, the heads of missions as well as the role of honorary consuls. It also determines the legal framework for serving in the Austrian foreign service, regulates the selection procedure to enter the diplomatic service and also regulates the management of properties in receiving countries (BKA, 1999).

Beside the legal framework, a strategic focus, specified according to foreign policy goals, defines the MFA's remit.

Strategic Focus

In the Federal Finance Act of the Austrian Ministry of Finance (BMF, 2014, 2015, 2016), five foreign policy outcome goals are defined, which encompass the areas of citizen service, integration of migrants, foreign cultural policy, asserting Austrian interests in the fields of foreign policy, security policy and economy as well as the protection of human rights, the improvement of life conditions in developing countries and the protection of the environment.

The first defined outcome goal aims to optimize the assistance for Austrian citizens who are in a situation of emergency abroad, as well as the support for Austrian citizens who are resident in foreign countries. The Austrian MFA broadcasts the slogan *"Worldwide at your service"* and the protection of Austrian citizens, the protection of the property of Austrian citizens in foreign countries as well as judicial and administrative assistance have priority. It is mentioned that the increasing mobility of Austrians also increases the necessity of consular work. According to this paper, Austrian citizens go on 10 million trips per year and 450 000 Austrian citizens are on long-term stays in other countries.

The objective of supporting Austrians shall be achieved by providing significant information to Austrian citizens travelling abroad by means of new technologies and new media (BMF, 2014, p. 120; 2015, p. 116; 2016, p. 116). The Austrian MFA indeed developed supportive tools. The so-called *Foreign Service App* (BMEIA, 2017a) had been launched, which offers information on travelling destinations with special focus on the services Austrian representations do provide in the respective destination. Beyond that, the so-called *Travel Registration* (BMEIA, 2017d) had been launched. This platform offers the possibility to register at the MFA before starting a journey. The aim is to give embassies the opportunity to contact Austrian citizens who are travelling in a certain country, if the security situation changes and also to be better prepared if an Austrian citizen contacts the embassy in a case of emergency.

Furthermore, the first outcome goal also includes intensified support for Austrian citizens imprisoned abroad. The foundation of so-called *Haftdepots*, which offer the possibility for relatives of detainees to support them with foodstuff or other facilities, what can especially be important in states with poor prison conditions, shall guarantee better support for Austrian citizens in prison abroad.

The area of crisis and disaster management shall also be optimized, for example by a closer cooperation with EU partners, the expansion of training programs in the consular field and through the optimization of emergency preparedness plans (BMF, 2014, p. 120; 2015, p. 116; 2016, p. 116).

The second defined outcome goal is to ensure Austria's foreign and security policy interests as well as its European and economic interests. Vienna's position as conference venue and official seat of various institutions shall be strengthened and the cooperation with international organizations shall be intensified. The further development of peace and security as well as the observance of human rights are declared goals in this context.

This is followed by a clear commitment to multilateral cooperation, EU membership and further development of the European integration process. Austria's position in the EU shall be strengthened and its international competitiveness shall be fostered (BMF, 2014, p. 121). In the Federal Finance Act of 2015 and 2016, the strategies to achieve the second outcome goal are even stronger connected to Austria's EU membership. It is explicitly mentioned that the opportunities offered through EU membership shall be used in an optimum manner (BMF, 2015, p. 117; 2016, p. 117). For 2014, several approaches were mentioned to pursue these goals. First of all, Austria's bilateral and multilateral relations should be further developed, which includes contractual relations and regular meetings on the political level as well as on the level of civil servants. Secondly, Austria shall actively participate in CFSP activities, in activities of the Common Security and Defence Policy (CSDP) as well as peace keeping missions of the UN. Thirdly, Austrian interests shall be represented on all levels of the European decision making process, especially in relevant bodies in the European Council. Public relations as well as the dialog with Austrian citizens concerning EU issues shall be intensified. Fourthly, institutions and projects that support the implementation of European, foreign, economy and security interests shall be promoted. Fifthly, Austria's interests as a host country vis-à-vis international organizations shall be actively represented, especially regarding the availability of conference rooms and the maintenance of the VIC. Finally, conferences with the aim to further develop foreign policy priorities related to security policy, energy policy, protection of human rights and interreligious dialogue shall be supported and organized (BMF, 2014, p. 121).

Concerning the achievement of these goals, concrete numbers are defined in the Federal Finance Act. This outline contains the current state from 2012 and earlier as well as the target state for the years 2013 to 2017. In 2012, the MFA organized 311 state visits and working sessions. For 2014, 2015 and 2016, the target state was 327 state visits or working sessions. For 2017 the number was lowered to 302 visits or working sessions. In 2014, 287 Austrian initiatives were set in European and international fora. The defined target for 2015 and 2016 was 250 initiatives, and 270 initiatives for 2017. In 2014, 41 initiatives to foster human rights, especially the rights of woman and children were set, but in this area no further expansion is planned. The defined target for 2016 and 2017 declined to 35. 1838 initiatives to support Austrian economic interests in third countries were set in 2014. The targets for the following years were 1300 in 2015, 1100 in 2016 and 1350 in 2017.

In the last examples the numbers displayed for 2014 are higher than the targets defined for the following years. This is explained by the fact that the target state is adjusted to the expected budgetary and staff situation (BMF, 2014, pp. 121-122; 2015, pp. 117-118; 2016, p. 118).

The third outcome goal (BMF, 2014, p. 122; 2015, p. 118) can be neglected at this point as it refers to the integration of migrants in Austria, which cannot be categorized as classical foreign policy issue, but rather as an issue of domestic policy. The field of integration policy has been transferred from the Austrian Ministry of the Interior to the MFA, due to political reasons. After general elections in 2013, the grand coalition continued its work, but the cabinet had been reshuffled. The state secretary for integration in the Ministry of the Interior, Sebastian Kurz, became foreign minister and transferred his division to the MFA. Nevertheless, in the system of Austrian foreign policy making and diplomacy this topic remains at an outside position and therefore is not taken into account in this investigation.

The fourth outcome goal refers to the sustainable reduction of poverty, the consolidation of peace and security and the preservation of the environment in bilateral and multilateral development cooperation. Special attention is paid to gender equality as well as to the requirements of children and individuals with disabilities (BMF, 2014, p. 123; 2015, p. 119; 2016, p. 119).

The fifth outcome goal refers to the development of an innovative and creative image of Austria in the course of foreign cultural policy. Special attention thereby is paid to the European principle *"unity in diversity"*. Austrian foreign cultural policy shall present contemporary aspects of Austria's science and culture in order to add a new perspective to Austria's global image. The country shall not only be perceived as a nation with a rich history and culture, but also future-oriented developments in Austria should be noticed internationally. Taking part in cultural projects with European partners is a declared aim. Furthermore, Austrian cultural initiatives shall promote peace and security and support interreligious and intercultural dialogues. Measures to implement these goals include the development of Austrian cultural networks and the support of cultural and scientific projects. Austria also concentrates on special thematic and geographical foci (BMF, 2014, pp. 124-126; 2015, pp. 120-121; 2016, p. 121).

Relating these outcome goals to the role of the MFA and the diplomatic service in Austria's public administration framework offers interesting perspectives. First of all, despite the fact that further development of Austria's bilateral and multilateral relations is mentioned in the context of the second outcome goal, bilateralism plays an insignificant role in the foreign policy goals. Most remarks refer to multilateral cooperation. Only in the fifth outcome goal on cultural foreign policy bilateral elements are to be found. This speaks for a diminishing role of bilateral diplomacy in the diplomatic framework.

Such a development had already been predicted for inner-EU diplomacy (Keukeleire, 2003), but also in a wider international context multilateralism is about to take the central position in diplomacy. Former Austrian diplomat Thomas Nowotny therefore advises MFAs to shift resources from bilateral to multilateral diplomacy:

> *"Multilateral diplomacy was once considered a mere adjunct to bilateral diplomacy. Now it should be the other way round. Bilateral diplomacy should have its function in support of multilateral diplomacy mainly."* (Nowotny, 2011, p. 273)

Empirical findings of this investigation and the display of results will give insights on the relevance of Austrian bilateral diplomacy for the country's diplomatic work as well as for multilateral cooperation.

A second interesting aspect of the foreign policy goals defined for 2014, 2015 and 2016 is the fact that service for Austrian citizens takes the first rank in these outlines. The Austrian MFA offers several features for Austrians travelling abroad that shall support the interaction between travellers and the MFA or the embassy responsible for the respective destination. The MFA also developed a new public relations strategy that encompasses the regular use of several social media channels and also supports individual diplomats in using social media when promoting their work. Such an approach cannot necessarily be classified as public diplomacy in its original sense. Public diplomacy describes the promotion of own national interests in the receiving state. Here, the aim is to reach Austria's own population, which might be better labelled with the term public relations. Further steps towards strengthening this service orientation have been taken in the course of the MFA's modernization strategy in 2015 (BMEIA, 2015c). This modernization strategy will be depicted in detail in the chapter on structural developments. The next chapter illustrates the current structural constitution of the Austrian MFA.

Organizational Set-up

By 1983, at the end of the era Kreisky, when the expansion of the Austrian MFA and the diplomatic service had been considered to be completed (BMAA, 1983, pp. 220-221), Kneucker (1983) published a comprehensive outline on organizational and institutional aspects of Austria's foreign policy. He indicates that organization theory classifies ministerial administration as a bureaucratic form of organization (Kneucker, 1983, p. 53). Thereby, he distinguishes between Max Weber's (2006, pp. 1046-1092) ideal-type of bureaucracy and a real-type of bureaucratic organization. The latter one is based on empirically gained insights to organizations, while Weber's ideal-type can rather be seen as a reference point in order to understand underlying intentions of an investigated phenomenon. Kneucker (1983, pp. 54-55) emphasizes that Weber's essential contribution to the understanding of bureaucratic organizations was to demonstrate that the development of bureaucracy is closely linked to the development of the modern state, industrialization and mass society, as well as to demonstrate that bureaucratic organization represents the purest form of legal authority.

Weber (2006, pp. 218-247) distinguishes three ideal types of legitimate authority and domination with different sources of legitimacy. The first type, charismatic authority, is based on the belief of the holiness, heroism or excellence of a person. Hence, not an office or a status granted to a person is the source of legitimacy here, but the person itself and his or her personality. The second type, traditional authority, is based on the belief in the validity of traditions or customs and the legitimate authority of persons, who come to power on the basis of rules and norms related to these traditions and customs. The third type, legal authority, is based on the belief in modern law and regulations. Here, the authority of persons or institutions is linked to the legal office they hold. In Weber's view, the purest form of legal authority is to exercise power via a *"Verwaltungsstab"* (administrative staff). According to Kneucker (1983, p. 55), Weber shows that this form of organization was able to promote progress on a large scale, as it is formally and technically universal and therefore applicable to a wide range of assignments. However, Kneucker (1983, p. 55) also points out that the efficiency of a bureaucratic organization depends on certain conditions and bureaucratic organizations can become dysfunctional. This ideal-type model serves as guiding principle in Kneucker's classification of the organization of the Austrian foreign service. He uses the ideal-typical features of bureaucratic organizations defined by Weber: regularity, hierarchy, division of labour, division of responsibilities, scribality and officialdom. In his investigation of the MFA, Kneucker (1983, p. 54) also refers to the real-type form of bureaucratic organization. He emphasizes that organizations and particularly ministries are characterized by specific details, like an own organizational identity, specific working methods, learning processes and something he describes as the organizations own *"life and atmosphere"*. He perceives a tendency in Austria to overestimate organizational goals and formal structures, whilst little attention is given to the importance of other aspects that shape an organization, like certain styles and traditions in staff development, leadership, training, informal relations and well-practiced behaviour.

Kneucker (1983, pp. 55-56) assumes that the Austrian MFA is a more classical representation of a bureaucratic organization than other ministries in Austria. The organizational form developed as line organization and thereby followed a regular structure of divisions, departments and units. The underlying idea of a line organization is to clearly define areas of responsibility and competence and clearly define hierarchies and working flows. However, in 1983, at the time of Kneucker's investigation, adaptations to this traditional form of organization were already visible. First and foremost, a tendency towards project management, where staff members from different organizational units are working together on a specific topic, announced a softening of the line set-up.

Today the principle set-up of the Austrian MFA still follows the set-up of a line organization. The MFA is divided into eight divisions with several departments. On top of the divisions the Cabinet of the Foreign Minister as well as the Office of the Secretary General are located. Beyond that, a General Inspectorate exists on the level of the eight divisions.

I Central Affairs	II International Affairs	III Europe
I.1 Protocol I.A International Law Office I.2 Public International Law I.3 Press and Information I.4 European Law I.5 Organization of International Conferences and Matters relating to International Organizations in Austria I.7 Human Rights, Minority Issues I.9 Security Affairs	II.1 Common Foreign and Security Policy (CFSP) General Policy Issues II.2 Security Issues, Common Security and Defence Policy (CSDP) II.3 Eastern Europe, South Caucasia, Central Asia, Central European Initiative, Eastern Neighbourhood Policy of the EU , Eastern Partnership II.4 Near and Middle East, Southern Neighbourhood Policy of the EU II.5 International Organizations II.6 Sub-Saharan Africa, African Union (AU) II.7 Organization for Security and Co-operation in Europe (OSCE), Council of Europe II.8 Arms Control, Disarmament, Non-Proliferation II.9 The Americas, Organization of American States (OAS) II.10 Asia, ASEM, ASEF, ASEAN, SAARC, ARF	III.1 General EU Matters and EU Institutions III.2 Coordination of Matters relating to COEREPER II, European Council, General Affairs Council, ECOFIN, Justice and Home Affairs Council, Economic and Monetary Union III.3 Multilateral External Economic Relations, Common Commercial Policy of the EU (i.a. Trade Policy Committee), Export Promotion, Investment Protection, International, Financial Institutions, Macro-regional EU Strategies, Central European Initiative III.4 West Balkans, EU Enlargement, Twinning III.5 Coordination of Matters relating to COEREPER I, EU 2020 Strategy, Singe Market, Industry, Science, Employment Policy, Social Policy, Health Policy, Consumer Protection, Education, Youth, Culture and Sport, Agriculture and Fisheries III.6 Environment, Energy, Transport and Telecommunication III.7 South Tyrol and Southern Europe III.8 Middle, West- and Northern Europe
IV Service	**V Culture**	**VI Management**
IV.1 Legal Protection, Legal and Administrative Cooperation, Legal Affairs IV.2 Tourist and Cross-Border Traffic, Citizenship, Residence Matters, Combating Trade in Human Beings, Refugees and Migration IV.3 Austrians Abroad, Powers of Protection, Social Policy and Investment Policy Affairs, Citizenship Matters IV. 4 Service for Enterprises IV.5 Citizen Service, especially Information Service concerning Consular Affairs, Assistance, Protective Measures in Conflict Areas, Attesta-tions	V.1 General and Legal Issues, Cultural Agreements, Coordination, Budget and Evaluation V.2 Organization of Cultural and Scientific Events Abroad V.3 Scientific Cooperation, Dialog of Cultures and Religions V.4 Multilateral Issues of Foreign Cultural Policy and Sport	VI.1 Human Resources and Organization Management, Accreditation, Notification VI.2 Compensation and Allowances, Reimbursement of Costs, Social Insurance VI.3 Budget and Controlling VI.A Property Management, Facilities and Equipment VI.4 Matters of Facilities and Equipment, Legal Affairs including Procurement, Courier Service, Property Management, Federal Employee Protection Law and Fire Protection VI.5 Construction Affairs, Project Management,

		Facility Management, Real Estate Controlling, Procurement VI.7 Information Technology VI.8 Information, Documentation, Knowledge Management
VII Development	VIII Integration	
VII.1 Multilateral Development Cooperation VII.2 Development Policy, Strategy and Evaluation VII.3 Humanitarian Aid, Food Aid, Foreign Disaster Relief Fund, Development Policy Aspects in the Area of Environment and Sustainability VII.4 Development Cooperation and Cooperation with Eastern Europe, Coordination in Austria, Information VII.5 Planning and Programme Matters concerning Development Cooperation and Cooperation with Eastern Europe	VIII.1 Matters of Integration VIII.2 Integration Coordination VIII.3 Funding in the Area of Integration	

Figure 2: Organizational Chart of the Austrian MFA 2017
(Source: Own translation based on the German version of the MFA's organizational chart, status of January 2017 (BMEIA, 2017c))

The MFA's organizational set-up had been modified by 2015 in the course of a modernization strategy. Details on this process are found in the next chapter on structural developments. When considering the MFA's current organizational set-up against the backdrop of the foreign policy goals defined in the Federal Finance Act (BMF, 2014, 2015), which were outlined in the last chapter, it becomes obvious that here traditional bilateral issues are also in decline. Multilateral elements are predominantly represented in the organizational set-up, especially concerning political work. A dominance of bilateral elements instead is to be found in other areas: culture and service, for example. The dominance of aspects other than bilateralism in the MFA's organizational set-up indicates that the organization of bilateral diplomacy and the work done by bilateral missions rather is planned and organized in the respective missions than in the Viennese headquarters.

By 2015 Austria was represented abroad by

79	Bilateral Embassies
5	Permanent Representations at International Organizations
8	Consulates General
6	Independent Cultural Fora
1	other Representation
99	in total (BMEIA, 2015a, p. 309)

These missions, most of them representations of bilateral nature, represent the biggest item in the MFA's budget. For the year 2015 the budget of the Austrian MFA was set at 409,1 million euros, divided as follows:

163,9 million	Austrian Representations abroad
65,4 million	Austrian Development Agency and Disaster Relief Fund
80,6 million	Contribution to International Organizations
69,6 million	Head Office
22,2 million	Subsidies for Integration Activities
5,6 million	Cultural Projects
1,7 million	International Conferences (BMEIA, 2015a, p. 306)

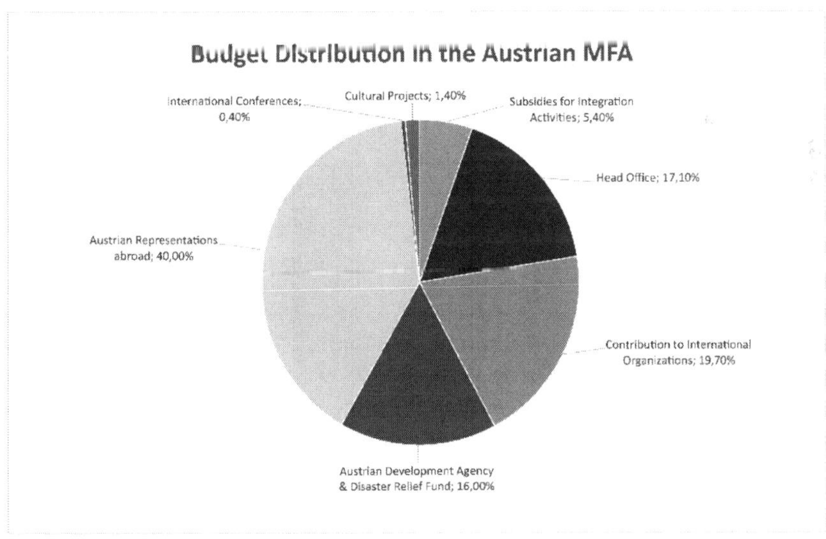

Figure 3: Budget Distribution in the Austrian MFA 2015
(Source: Own diagram based on data from the Foreign and European Policy Report 2015, p. 306)

The major part of the MFA's employees works in diplomatic representations, where most of them are of bilateral nature. By the end of the year 2015, 1 149 persons had been employed with the Austrian MFA. Of this figure, 567 employees (49%) worked in the Viennese headquarters and 582 employees (51%) worked in Austrian representations in the EU, in third countries and at international organizations (BMEIA, 2015a, p. 304) . The following table shows the distribution of employees according to their position.

Position	Inland	Abroad	Total
Diplomatic Staff	217	207	424
Consular Administrative Staff	109	121	230
Technical Staff and Qualified Support and Office Staff	224	254	478
Auxiliary Service Staff and IT-Specialists	17	0	17
Total	567	582	1149

Figure 4: Distribution of Staff in the Austrian MFA 2015
(Source: Foreign and European Policy Report 2015, p. 304)

Beyond that, 723 persons are employed as local staff, working in representations abroad. These persons are employed according to the labour regulations of the respective country (BMEIA, 2015a, p. 304).

Besides the employees of the Austrian MFA, several special attachés of other ministries and institutions than the MFA work in Austrian representations in their respective area of jurisdiction. Considering practices and working methods, their field of operation is similar to the fields of diplomats posted by the MFA. But considering the content of their work, special attachés are restricted in their field of operation to their respective specification. They are also not suspect to the rotating principle like diplomats posted by the MFA. Hence, they do not have to change their post after around four years of service, but can serve at the same representation abroad for a longer period of time. Special attachés usually also obtain diplomatic status (BMEIA, 2008, p. 214). In this context, a second major player beside the Austrian MFA in Austria's national diplomatic network should be mentioned. The Austrian Federal Economic Chamber provides its own network of representations with special focus on Austrian foreign trade. This network is of similar size to the diplomatic network of the Austrian MFA. The Federal Economic Chamber provides a network of 77 Austrian Foreign Trade Centres. Under international law, these Foreign Trade Centres belong to Austrian embassies and trade commissioners working in Foreign Trade Centres are accredited as diplomats. The network of representations of the Austrian Federal Economic Chamber primarily supports Austrian companies in their export and internationalization efforts. The main tasks are (WKO, 2015)

- support of Austrian companies in market cultivation, establishing business partners and finding business opportunities
- establishing business contacts between domestic and foreign companies
- services for supporting company establishments in the host country as well as in Austria
- marketing and public relations for Austrian products
- information and reporting on foreign market issues
- publication of an economy bulletin with current offerings from Austria
- participation in trade fairs and events with an Austrian exhibition stand
- representation of Austria in international organizations (WKO, 2015)

Details on the form of cooperation between Foreign Trade Centres and Austrian embassies in receiving countries are illustrated in the chapter on economy in Austrian bilateral diplomacy.

The preceding sections outlined the historical development of the Austrian MFA in the Second Republic before EU accession, its legal framework and the strategic focus its work is based on, as well as the MFA's organizational set-up. The following sections will close the gap between the MFA's pre-EU-status and the current status-quo on several levels. Developments on the structural level are presented first, regarding effects of Austria's EU membership on the organizational development of the Austrian MFA, followed by a representation of developments in bilateral diplomatic work inside and outside the EU as well as in the MFA, and finally followed by a depiction of developments concerning the occupational image of Austrian diplomats.

Europeanization Tendencies in Austrian Bilateral Diplomacy

Structural Developments and Changes

Austria accessed the EU in 1995. Already in the pre-accession period, the MFA started to adapt its mode of operation and its structure to the demands an EU membership would entail. By 1992, division III of the Austrian MFA had been supplemented by a further department, dealing with issues of European integration and the division had been renamed from Economic Policy Division to Economic and Integration Policy Division (BMAA, 1992, p. 552). At the same time, the number of political visits of Austrian delegations to Brussels increased and the Austrian government started an EU-information initiative. In the course of this initiative, the MFA intensified its information activities concerning the integration process. A monthly Newsletter outlined the negotiation results, and the MFA's so-called *European Hotline*, which had already been established in the year 1989 in order to inform citizens on EU issues, recorded an increasing amount of calls. Austria's EU accession efforts not only changed the remit of the Viennese headquarters, but also Austria's Permanent Mission in Brussels had to deal with new circumstances in interacting with the EU, caused by the status of being an accession candidate.

Being a possible future EU member first of all affected the political interaction process on the Brussels-level, but also created growing interest among Austrian citizens and Austrian organizations regarding the structure and tasks of EU institutions. Hence, political visits increased and Austria's Permanent Mission in Brussels also recorded a rise of group visits by Austrian organizations and citizens interested in the work of the EU (BMAA, 1993, pp. 44-48). Consequently, the necessity for providing information on the EU in an understandable way made EU-related public relations a new central task within the MFA's organizational framework. After the national referendum on EU accession, the MFA obtained another central task in this field. The Austrian government initiated a *White Paper*-project. The *White Paper* should inform Austrian citizens on topics of EU policy and should also give information on new tasks for Austria in the context of European integration. The preparation process for this paper was led by the Federal Chancellery as well as the MFA and also involved other ministries, social partners and interest groups. Within this grouping, essential areas of Austrian EU involvement were identified and Austrian EU positions were outlined, in order to serve as a basis for discussion with the public (BMAA, 1994, pp. 12-13).

However, growing importance of ministries and governmental organizations other than the MFA in the context of interaction with the EU and European integration already became visible in the year 1991. In this year, the Austrian government developed a human resources development concept with the aim to cover the increased demand of high qualified personnel in the context of European integration. In the course of this initiative, 250 positions for the execution of integration-specific tasks in Austrian ministries were created. (BMAA, 1993, p. 48) In a parliament session, the State Secretary for European Issues at that time, Peter Jankowitsch, a post aligned to the Federal Chancellery, mentioned that positions in this pool are only appointed to integration policy issues, which should on the one hand support Austrian institutions in European integration and should on the other hand provide future human resources for the EC, later EU, and its institutions (Österreichisches Parlament, 1991, p. 4176). From the 250 positions created in the course of this initiative for the execution of integration-specific tasks in Austrian ministries, only nine were allocated to the MFA (BMAA, 1993, p. 48). Therefore, with regard to its human resources, the Austrian MFA did not experience a severe change in the context of beginning European integration, but its organizational set-up had continuously been adapted. In the years after EU accession, division III of the MFA, which was responsible for integration and economic policy, had been re-structured several times. At the end, division III fully turned its focus to EU integration. By 1995, two departments of this division were in charge of COEREPER issues and four departments remained for non-immediate EU related issues (BMAA, 1995, p. 372). By 1996, only one department remained with a non-immediate EU related focus (BMAA, 1996, p. 208). This indicates high pressure to adapt to the new circumstances. A fundamental step towards European integration had been taken by the MFA in 2007. After 12 years of EU membership, the MFA was renamed from Ministry of Foreign Affairs to Ministry for European and International Affairs. At that time, Foreign Minister Ursula Plassnik explained this renaming by arguing that Europe is nothing foreign, but we are Europe (Der Standard, 2007). On the one hand, this step marks a pro-active attitude towards challenges arising for the MFA in the context of Austria's EU membership. On the other hand, this step also indicates a form of strategic positioning of the MFA as the main Austrian actor in European affairs. The MFA was renamed once again in 2014, in the context of a shift of competences from the Ministry of the Interior to the MFA concerning the integration of migrants. The term Europe, however, remains part of its label.

With Austria's accession to the EU, only certain parts of the MFA had to be re-structured. Austria's Permanent Mission in Brussels gained importance, took new tasks and responsibilities and was staffed differently. A significant amount of new tasks emerged within the Committee of Permanent Representatives. Furthermore, the composition of staff in the Permanent Representation changed, because a tradition, which had been established during the period of accession negotiations, had been retained. Not only staff members of Austrian ministries were represented at Austria's Permanent Representation in Brussels, but also envoys of the federal states, the social partners, the Austrian National Bank, as well as the Austrian Association of Cities worked in Brussels. A significant effect of European integration is visible here, because this form of multilevel cooperation was not limited to Brussels. At the inner-state-level, EU accession had the effect of closer cooperation between several institutions. Under the direction of the Federal Chancellery and the MFA a coordination mechanism was established in order to formulate common positions. This forum included weekly meetings with representatives of other ministries, but also with representatives of the social partners, the Austrian National Bank, the Industry Association and representatives of the federal states and of communities (BMAA, 1995, pp. 8-9). This development displays that Austrian EU policy making from the beginning had not been perceived as a part of foreign policy making in its structural and processual dimension, but as a process with comprehensive implications for several aspects on the domestic policy level. Adapting the staff composition of Austria's Permanent Mission in Brussels with experts from several Austrian institutions and different policy fields supports Hocking's (2013) assumption of the MFA not representing the national diplomatic system, but a subsystem of the national diplomatic system. However, the example of the Permanent Representation is certainly more related to multilateralism than to bilateral diplomacy. When concentrating on the impact of EU integration on the bilateral dimension of Austrian diplomacy, it is of special interest to have a look on how the network of bilateral representations developed after Austria's EU accession. An observation of this kind allows the drawing of conclusions concerning possible connections between developments in Austrian bilateral diplomacy and Austria's EU membership.

When Austria accessed the EU in 1995, the country had a network of 117 representations, divided into:

80	Bilateral Embassies
7	Permanent Representations at International Organizations
18	Consulates General
11	Independent Cultural Fora
1	Information Office
117	Representations (BMAA, 1995).

The number of representations was reduced from 117 to 99 between 1995 and 2015 (BMEIA, 2015a, p. 309). Thereby, the number of embassies remained relatively stable at around 80, while the number of consulates general declined on a large scale. Relative stability in the number of embassies does not mean that the Austrian MFA operates with an unchanged network of embassies. To the contrary, there have been several closures and openings since Austria's EU accession in 1995. It becomes obvious that, in fact, more embassies have been opened than closed in this period. The general stability in the number of embassies results from the fact that temporary closures, in most cases due to security reasons, and re-openings are also taken into account in the annual display of the number of embassies of the Austrian MFA.

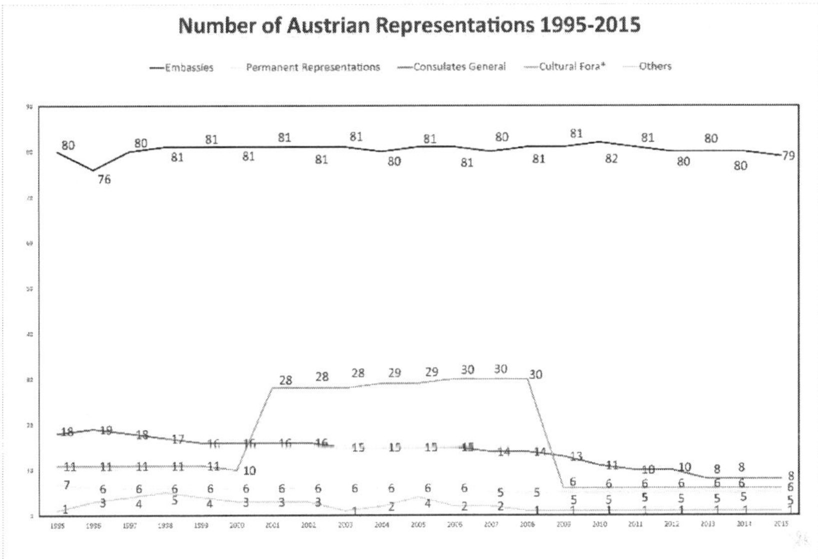

Figure 5: Number of Austrian Representations 1995-2015
(Source: Own diagram based on data from the Foreign Policy Reports 1995-2015)
*numbers differ significantly due to different counting methods in the periods of 1995-2000, 2001-2008 and 2009-2015

By 1996, several Austrian embassies in the Middle East had to be closed owing to security reasons. This affected Algiers, Bagdad, Beirut and Kinshasa (BMAA, 1996, p. 200). By 1997, the Austrian MFA started to expand its network of representations in Eastern Europe and opened embassies in Riga, Skopje, Tallinn and Vilnius (BMAA, 1997, p. 231). In addition, a new embassy in Hanoi had been opened (BMAA, 1998, p. 259). Since the end of the 1990s, temporarily closed embassies in the Middle East gradually started to re-open, while two representations in the EU were closed at the turn of the millennium: the consulate general in Frankfurt, (BMAA, 1999, p. 246) as well as the Austrian consulate in Düsseldorf (BMAA, 2000, p. 247). In this period the Austrian Cultural Institute in Teheran as well as the Austrian Information Office in Washington had been integrated to the respective embassies at these locations (BMAA, 2000, p. 247).

The huge growth in the number of Austrian cultural fora between the year 2000 and the year 2001 had been caused by an MFA initiative to restructure the handling of its foreign cultural policy, regarding content, structure and practices. This process included the implementation of a corporate identity for all existing offices which represent Austrian cultural policy. In the course of this initiative, previously existing offices dealing with cultural foreign policy were integrated to the network of Austrian cultural fora, which explains the significant increase in this year. Three new cultural fora were opened in Belgrade, Cairo and Mexico. Thus, by 2002, the Austrian MFA had 28 offices worldwide labelled as cultural forum. The strategic focus of this new cultural policy orientation was set around the two concepts *Global Cultural Centres* and *Cultural Neighbours*. The first term includes the representation of Austrian culture in traditional hot spots of the cultural scene like London, New York, Paris, Rome or Tokyo. The second term focuses on regions to which Austria traditionally has had a cultural connection, such as countries in South East Europe, neighbouring countries or Israel (BMAA, 2001, pp. 218-219). By 2003, Austria's cultural foreign policy was represented by cultural fora in Belgrade, Berlin, Bern, Bratislava, Budapest, Bucharest, Brussels, Cairo, Istanbul, Kiev, Krakow, London, Ljubljana, Madrid, Mexico, Milan, Moscow, New York, Ottawa, Paris, Prague, Rome, Teheran, Tel Aviv, Tokyo, Warsaw, Washington and Zagreb (BMAA, 2003, p. 252).

In 2003, the Austrian Trade Council in Abu Dhabi had been transformed to an Austrian embassy. In the same year, the Austrian consulate general in Trieste was closed, while one embassy had to be closed temporarily again (BMAA, 2003, p. 252). In 2004, Austria opened its 29th cultural forum in Beijing (BMAA, 2004, p. 203). One year later, the MFA had to close its embassy in Abidjan, owing to security concerns, but could expand its network within the EU; Austrian embassies were opened in Nicosia and in Valletta (BMAA, 2005, p. 216). In 2006, the Austrian embassy in Guatemala and the Bonn outpost of the Austrian embassy in Berlin were closed, while a new embassy was opened in Podgorica (BMEIA, 2006, p. 215). In 2007, a cultural forum in New Delhi as well as an embassy in Astana had been opened (BMEIA, 2007, p. 222). Upon Austria's recognition of Kosovo, Pristina, thus far an outpost of Austria's representation in Belgrade, became an embassy (BMEIA, 2008, p. 213).

By that time, effects of the economic and financial crisis led to a difficult budgetary situation in the Austrian MFA. As a result, the network of Austrian representations had been evaluated in the year 2009, in order to identify saving opportunities. This evaluation was conducted on the basis of certain criteria, like the frequency of consular services for Austrian citizens, the intensity of political visits, the trading volume between Austria and the receiving country as well as Austrian direct investment to the receiving country. Based on the results of this evaluation, the MFA developed the initiative *minus 4, plus 2*. According to this concept, the Austrian embassy in Muscat as well as the consulates general in Rio de Janeiro, Hamburg and Cape Town were closed in the budget period of 2009/2010, while an embassy in Baku and a consulate general in Frankfurt should be opened (BMEIA, 2009, p. 247). Further closures were planned for the period between 2011 and 2013, which affected the embassies in Bogotá and Harare as well as the consulates general in Chicago, Krakow and Zurich (BMEIA, 2010, p. 269). Muscat, Harare and Zurich were closed in 2011. The embassy in Bogotá was closed in 2012 (BMEIA, 2012, p. 297), Chicago and Krakow in 2013 (BMEIA, 2013).

Another strategy pursued by the Austrian MFA to ease the difficult budgetary situation is co-location. At 15 locations Austrian embassies and Foreign Trade Centres of the Austrian Federal Economic Chamber share an office. At 7 locations offices are shared with other European countries and the EEAS. One Austrian consulate general shares its office with Switzerland (BMEIA, 2014b, p. 317).

When relating the developments outlined above to Austria's EU membership and how it influences the strategic and geographical positioning of the MFA, a complex picture emerges:

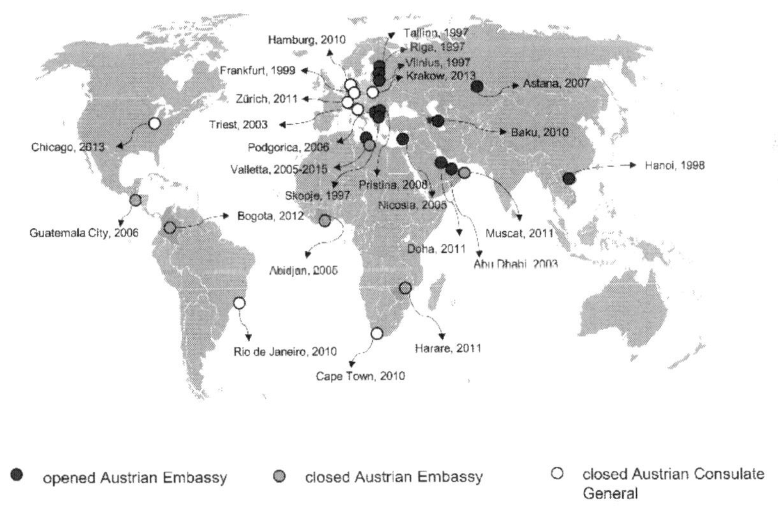

Figure 6: Geographical Display of Openings and Closures of Austrian Representations 1995-2015 (Source: Own diagram based on data from the Foreign Policy Reports 1995-2015)

First of all, it appears that there have been more openings of embassies than closures. However, so-called temporary closures, mainly caused by difficult security situations, are not considered in this display. Overall, the number of Austrian bilateral embassies remained relatively stable in the period between 1995 and 2015, as figure 5 shows. Despite the growing interconnectedness between EU member states and the emerging framework of *"Europäische Innenpolitik"*, only one embassy had been closed so far. The majority of embassies opened since Austria's EU accession are situated in new EU member states or third states, which were expected to become EU member states at the time the representation was opened. From 1995, Austria opened four embassies in Asia (Abu Dhabi, Astana, Doha, Hanoi), one between Asia and Europe (Baku) as well as eight embassies in Europe, where two countries, Cyprus and Malta, had been EU member states at the time the embassy was opened. Three countries, Estonia, Latvia and Lithuania, had applied for EU membership at the time Austrian embassies were opened and accessed the EU later on. The other three embassies were opened in Balkan countries, Macedonia, Montenegro and Kosovo, a region to which Austria is traditionally strongly committed. The embassy in Macedonia was opened in 1997, shortly after bilateral relations between Macedonia and the EU were built (EEAS, 2017a). The EU granted the status of a candidate country to Macedonia in 2005, a Stabilisation and Association Agreement entered into force in 2004 (European Commission, 2015c, p. 4). Since 2005, Macedonia has been a candidate country for EU accession. In 2006, after the declaration of independence of Montenegro, Austria opened an embassy in Podgorica. Since 2010, Montenegro is also a candidate country for EU accession; accession negotiations were opened in 2012 (European Commission, 2015b, p. 4). In 2010, after Austria recognized the independence of Kosovo, the Austrian representation in Pristina, until then, an outpost of the Austrian embassy in Belgrade, became an embassy as well. To the EU, Kosovo is a potential accession candidate and by the year 2015, the EU had signed a Stabilisation and Association Agreement with Kosovo (European Commission, 2015a, p. 4).

As mentioned before, several missions have simultaneously been closed due to the difficult budgetary situation. An efficiency evaluation, based on certain criteria of success, has been a determining factor for the decision which Austrian representations are about to be closed. These criteria had a political, an economical and a service dimension. The service dimension involved the frequency of consular services for Austrian citizens in the respective representation. Hence, the number of Austrian citizens living abroad as well as the number of Austrian citizens travelling to the respective receiving country were fundamental for the decision. The economical dimension involved the trading volume with the receiving country as well as Austrian direct investments to the receiving country. The political dimension encompassed the intensity of political visits in the receiving country (BMEIA, 2009, p. 247). Based on this evaluation, three embassies, one in Africa (Harare), one in Asia (Muscat) and one in Latin America (Bogotá), have been closed. Abidjan and Guatemala City had already been closed before the evaluation process. In the course of this evaluation process, no embassies in the EU or Europe have been closed. However, the embassy in Valletta, which was opened in 2005, had been closed in 2015 due to low utilization.

In contrast to the number of embassies, the number of consulates general significantly sank in the investigated period, from 18 to 8. In the EU, three consulates general in Western European neighbouring countries (Frankfurt, Hamburg, Trieste) and one in Eastern Europe (Krakow) have been closed. In third countries, one consulate general in Europe (Zurich), two in America (Chicago, Rio de Janeiro) and one in Africa (Cape Town) have been closed. Overall, the number of Austrian representations in total decreased between 1995 and 2015 from 117 to 99 (BMAA, 1995, p. 363; BMEIA, 2015a, p. 309). When concentrating on the situation of representations in Europe, it becomes obvious that with the exception of the consulate general in Krakow, only Western European EU member states were affected by the closures of Austrian representations. At the same time, new representations were opened in Eastern European countries with EU accession ambitions. Half of the consulates general have been closed in the EU in countries with excellent political and economic relations to Austria. Germany is Austria's most important trading partner; Italy is its second most important trading partner and Poland is among Austria's 12 most important trading partners (Statistik Austria, 2015). Beyond that, 254 000 Austrian citizens are resident in Germany and 8 200 Austrian citizens live in Italy (Statistik Austria, 2016). This indicates that the EU offers an interaction framework in which the intensity and quality of relations between countries is not bound to the number of representations in the respective country. However, the fast development of e-government has to be acknowledged in this context. Modern forms of public administration reduce the necessity for permanent representation. Austria is still, however, represented with its last two remaining consulates general (Milan and Munich) in the EU in these two countries.

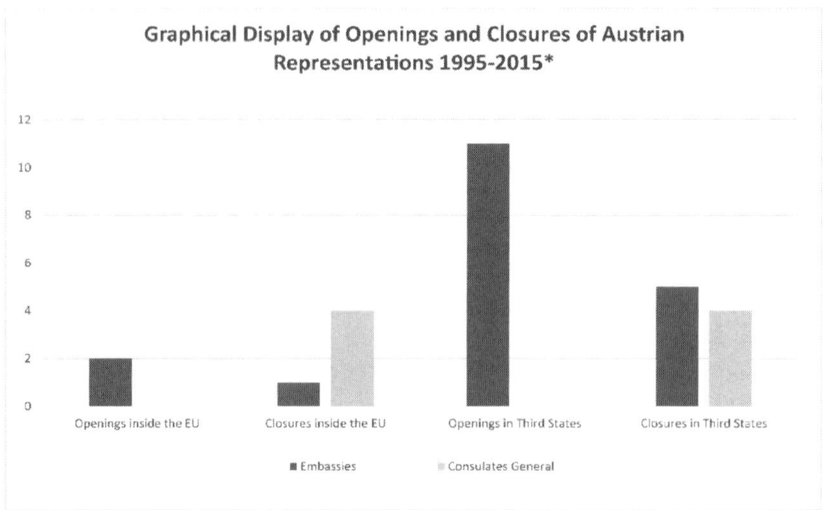

*temporarily closed representations are not counted in this display
Figure 7: Graphical Display of Openings and Closures of Austrian Representations 1995-2015 (Source: Own diagram based on data from the Foreign Policy Reports 1995-2015)

Until the year 2015, Austria was one of few EU members which are represented with an embassy in all other 27 member states (Rechnungshof, 2014, p. 185). The absence of closures of Austrian embassies in the EU for 20 years, despite the difficult budgetary situation, and the opening of embassies in the EU neighbourhood, on the one hand points at the European policy focus of the Austrian MFA, and on the other hand indicates a remaining symbolic power of embassies (Nowotny, 2011, pp. 45-46). The Austrian MFA so far stayed away from alternative organizational forms of diplomacy in the EU, like *hub embassies* or *roving ambassad*ors. It even endeavoured to be represented with an embassy in smaller EU countries. As outlined before, Austrian embassies were opened in Nicosia and Valletta shortly after Malta and Cyprus accessed the EU. Beyond that, embassies were opened in Pristina, Podgorica and Skopje; in every case shortly after the respective country, each with EU accession ambition, had declared its independence. It has to be emphasized that Austria's traditionally strong commitment to the Balkan region and its economic, political and cultural interests are a driving force behind the intent of being represented in these countries. Using the symbolic power of embassies as a sign of recognition in new emerged nation states thereby assists the implementation of Austrian foreign policy strategies (Sonnleitner, 2015, pp. 12-13).

Despite the growing interconnectedness of EU member states, the Austrian MFA so far followed a Euro-centric strategy in the development of its network of representations. This came at the expenses of non-European third countries. 26 of Austria's 79 embassies are located in the EU and further ones are located in EU neighbouring countries like in Albania, Bosnia-Herzegovina, Macedonia, Montenegro, Serbia, Turkey and Ukraine (BMEIA, 2017e). Therefore, nearly half of Austria's embassies are in Europe. As a result, many Austrian embassies in third states outside Europe are accredited in more than one country and some are responsible for large geographical areas. This circumstance complicates the achievement of the objective to be available for Austrian citizens around the globe. The Austrian MFA operates under the slogan *"Worldwide at your service"*. However, the relatively small size of the Austrian diplomatic network and a decreasing number of representations means that Austrian citizens working, living or travelling abroad probably have to cover long distances if they need to get in touch with an Austrian representative. The Austrian MFA counteracts this circumstance with an immense expansion of its network of honorary consulates. Honorary consuls are persons with a strong connection to Austria, who work voluntarily and hold sufficient assets and the necessary infrastructure in order to manage consular duties. They are able to support Austrian citizens in situations of emergency, especially if the next embassy or the next consulate general is not within easy reach. Moreover, as with other Austrian representations, honorary consulates foster the economic and cultural relation between Austria and the receiving state (BMEIA, 2012, p. 297). Within the period between 1995 and 2015, the number of honorary consulates has risen by nearly one third, from around 200 to around 300. In 2015 alone, eight new honorary consulates were opened (BMEIA, 2015a, p. 309). Thereby, selecting persons for the posts of honorary consuls is part of the responsibilities of the embassy accredited in the respective country. Here too, the EU focus of the Austrian network of diplomatic representations becomes obvious. Around 100 of the 300 Austrian honorary consulates are located in EU member states (BMEIA, 2017e). Interviews with diplomatic representatives working in Austrian embassies at the time of investigation underlined the significant role of honorary consulates in the Austrian diplomatic service. They are an important instrument of Austrian bilateral diplomacy to support Austrian citizens and Austrian companies in regions that are not in proximity to the capital city and thus, the embassy. Honorary consuls assist Austrian citizens in cases of emergency, for example by issuing emergency passports. They also strengthen political and economic relations to the receiving state by officially representing Austria at events and through their networking activities. Expanding the network of honorary consulates is an ongoing trend in Austrian bilateral diplomacy, because on the one hand, supervising a country with a single embassy located in the capital city is more difficult in large countries and countries with a less established transportation infrastructure. On the other hand, delegating tasks to other bodies is a necessity in the Austrian foreign service, due to the need to economize. Furthermore, especially outside Europe, many embassies are responsible for more than one country. Hence, honorary consulates in some cases are the only Austrian body in the receiving state.

The following graphs illustrate the budget development of the Austrian MFA between 1995 and 2015 as well as the percentage of the MFA's share of the federal budget between 1999 and 2015.

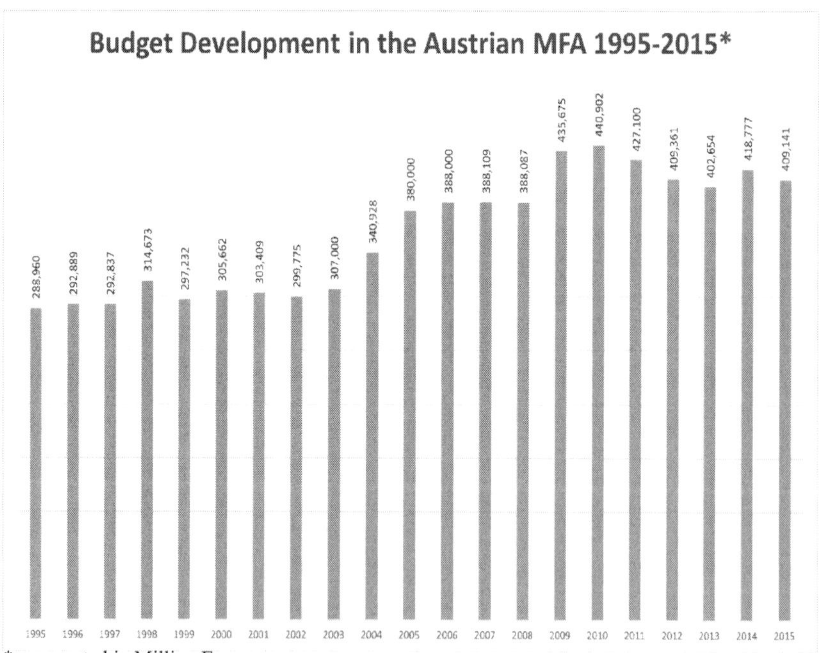

*represented in Million Euro

Figure 8: Budget Development in the Austrian MFA 1995-2015
(Source: Own diagram based on data from the Foreign Policy Reports 1995-2015)

In total numbers the budget of the MFA fluctuated between 1995 and 2003, while it followed an upward trend between 2004 and 2010, started to decrease in 2011 and increased again in 2014. Significant changes were mainly related to special expenditures. Austria held the EU presidency in 1998 and 2006. In 2004 and 2005 contributions to international organizations and development aid expenditures increased (BMAA, 2004, 2005). By 2013, a division of the Ministry of Interior was transferred to the MFA, which increased the MFA's budget in total numbers in the following year. Hence, increasing numbers do not imply growth in the operational budget. Inflation is not considered here.

The MFA's share in the federal budget follows a downward trend since 2011, after it fluctuated in the preceding years. The increase by 2014 is related to the transfer of a division from the Ministry of the Interior to the MFA as well.

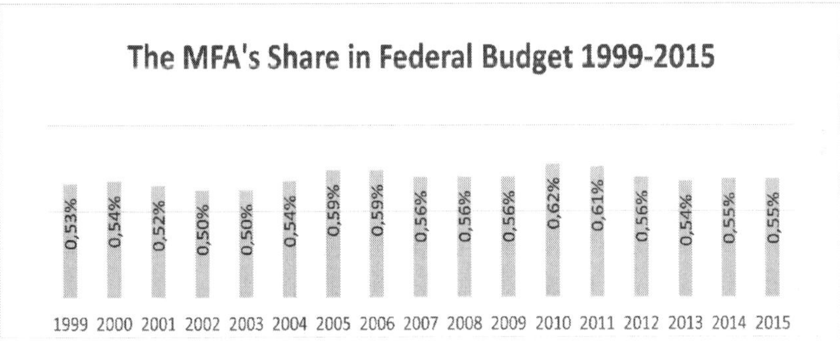

Figure 9: The MFA's Share of the Federal Budget 1999-2015
(Source: Own diagram based on data from the Foreign Policy Reports 1999-2015)

Cost saving measures not only caused a decrease in the number of Austrian representations, which had been reduced from 117 to 99 in the period between 1995 and 2015, but also affected the management of the existing infrastructure. The mission budget had been reduced by 30% and several repair and maintenance works on the MFA's estate portfolio could not be conducted (BMEIA, 2010, p. 264).

The trend to economize started to influence the MFA's organizational set-up long before the economic and financial crisis had an effect on national budgets. The number of staff has been continuously reduced since the year 2000. In 1995 the Austrian MFA employed 1616 persons, divided as follows:

Position	Total
Diplomatic Staff	477
Consular Administrative Staff	282
Technical Staff	399
Qualified Support and Office Staff	343
Auxiliary Service Staff	86
Other	29
Total	1616

(BMAA, 1995, p. 365)

By 2015, the number of employees had been reduced by 467 persons. Diplomatic staff lost 53 positions since Austria's EU accession in 1995.

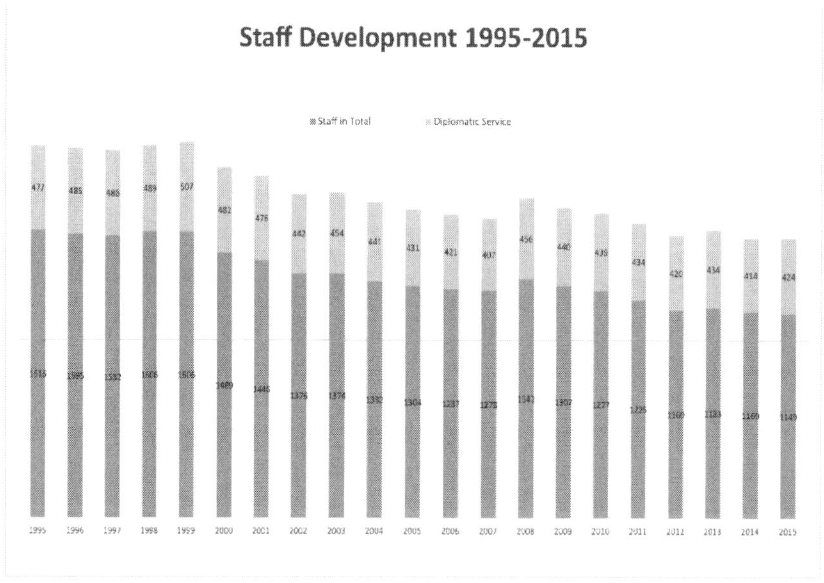

Figure 10: Staff Development 1995-2015
(Source: Own diagram based on data from the Foreign Policy Reports 1995-2015)

Concerning staff reduction, there was no trend visible towards a preference of consular service at the expense of high diplomacy in the investigated period of time. To the contrary, the number of diplomatic staff decreased by 11% between 1995 and 2015, while staff in ranks mainly entrusted with consular service and administrative work decreased by 36% in the same period. This can also be ascribed to a trend towards hiring local staff in the respective receiving state. One MFA representative mentioned that these numbers are about to rise, whereby Austria still operates with an average number of local employees, compared to other diplomatic services. This is because the MFA's visa issuing system requires the attendance of at least three diplomatic representatives from Austria at an Austrian diplomatic mission. Currently 723 people working for the Austrian MFA are employed locally (BMEIA, 2015a, p. 304), compared to 699 local employees in 2014 (BMEIA, 2014b, p. 313). However, according to a MFA representative, increasing the number of local staff is not a strategy initiated by the MFA to cover the decreasing number of personnel. Embassies are involved in this process and decide whether a certain post shall be occupied by local staff, often because continuity, local knowledge or special language skills are needed[1].

The reduction of MFA staff is accompanied by a diversification in the staff composition in the Austrian diplomatic service. Considering diplomatic posts in Austrian representations, which are not staffed by the Austrian MFA, but by other ministries and institutions, a clear shift is visible concerning the variety of topics covered in the work of Austrian representations. While until the beginning of the 1990s most so-called special attachés were posted by the Ministry of Defence and the Federal Economic Chamber, the collapse of the Soviet Union and Austria's EU accession brought a significant expansion to the Austrian diplomatic service, not only in terms of geographical extension, but also considering its staff diversity. Now also the Ministry of the Interior, the Ministry of Education, the Ministry for Social Affairs and the Austrian Development Agency (ADA) as well as the Austrian Police send representatives to Austrian diplomatic missions. Few special attachés also come from the National Bank as well as the Austrian Chamber of Labour. Latest figures on this topic date back to 2008. In this year, the Federal Economic Chamber employed around 590 persons abroad, around 125 were Austrian trade commissioners. The ADA employed about 80 persons outside Austria, about 20 of these employees were special attachés. Ministries other than the MFA posted around 280 employees abroad, around 155 as special attachés. In total, beside 243 diplomats and 149 persons from consular and administrative staff posted by the MFA, around 320 special attachés of other Austrian ministries and institutions were posted at Austrian diplomatic representations (BMEIA, 2008, pp. 208, 214-215). Thus, nearly half of the positions in the Austrian diplomatic ser-

1 Interview 16

vice abroad are staffed with employees from other institutions than the Austrian MFA. Brussels is naturally a location where many of these representatives from other institutions work. Nevertheless, special knowledge also seems to become more important in the work of bilateral missions. The question rises how this development influences the occupational image of diplomats in the Austrian MFA.

Further savings concerning infrastructure and personnel are likely especially within the EU. The Austrian Court of Audit has already criticised the MFA for its oversized network of representations in the EU. Thereby, the Court of Audit pleaded for alternative models of organizing diplomacy, like *roving ambassadors* or *hub embassies* (Rechnungshof, 2014). So far, the Austrian MFA rather stays with traditional concepts of representation. According to an MFA representative, who had been interviewed in March 2015, the MFA still sees a special need to be represented on-site in order to be able to evaluate sentiments in the receiving state, build and maintain contacts, promote Austrian interests and support Austrian citizens abroad. The MFA tends to operate with small representations than with none[2]. By June 2015, however, this strategy changed and the MFA announced to close its embassies in Estonia, Latvia and Lithuania by 2018; the embassy in Malta had already been closed by the end of the year 2015. Tasks concerning these countries will then be carried out by the Viennese headquarters or surrounding embassies. Instead, Austrian embassies were opened in other destinations. The focus thereby lied on regions with the expectation of high growth in Eastern Europe and beyond, what indicates further economization of diplomacy. In 2016 and 2017, Austrian embassies were opened in Belarus, Georgia, and Moldova as well as in Singapore. Beyond that, the MFA opened a diplomatic representation in Silicon Valley in the United States as well as a further consulate general in China (Salzburger Nachrichten, 2015; BMEIA, 2017e).

With the closures of representations inside the EU, the MFA follows recommendations of the Austrian Court of Audit. The Court of Audit also recommended to implement cultural fora to embassies in order to reduce costs. The MFA plans to do so in Budapest, London, Rome and Warsaw (Salzburger Nachrichten, 2015). Further cost reduction strategies are the expansion of the network of honorary consulates[3], co-location with other Austrian or European partners as well as the renegotiation of rental contracts (BMEIA, 2012, p. 287).

2 Interview 16
3 Interview 4

These adaptations all are made on the basis of the existing framework for diplomatic interaction. One interviewee in this investigation, however, suggested also scrutinizing the necessity of the maintenance of this framework in inner-EU bilateral diplomacy, including diplomatic immunity, extraterritoriality as well as tax exemption for diplomatic representations. The interviewee is of the opinion that all Austrian representations in a receiving country in the EU could be located in a single office, which then commonly represents Austrian interests. Such an approach would probably reduce the number of personnel needed, and newly defined slim forms of representation and a light form of diplomacy would further reduce costs[4].

Generally, many changes in the MFA's network of representations of the last 20 years have to rather be ascribed to tight budgets than to strategic foreign policy planning. Although it could be presumed that bilateral diplomacy is about to lose its significance inside the EU, due to closer interconnectedness between member states on several levels, the Austrian MFA followed a Euro-centric approach in constituting its network of representations for a long time and did not close embassies inside the EU until 2015 (Salzburger Nachrichten, 2015; BMEIA, 2017e). The following chapter illustrates the work of Austrian embassies inside the EU and explains in which areas bilateral diplomacy keeps its significance and what kind of new tasks arise in the EU framework. Beforehand, the development of the MFA's organizational set-up is depicted.

The MFA's organizational set-up remained relatively stable since Austria's accession to the EU in 1995. The impact of European integration for long only showed a visible effect in a single division of the MFA. Division III already adapted to the changing circumstances caused by EU membership before Austria's accession to the EU and then gradually adapted to the needs for interaction with the EU. One interviewee in this investigation jokingly stated that the reason for continuity in the MFA's structure could either be the far forward thinking strategy of the creators of the organizational set-up, which had been built to endure centuries, or a certain neglect to adapt to changing circumstances[5]. Half a year after this interview had been conducted, the MFA announced the implementation of an adaptation process in the form of a modernization strategy (BMEIA, 2015c). The aim of this strategy is to visualize the focus of the MFA's work and to highlight its service orientation. Services for Austrian citizens as well as for Austrian companies are in the centre of this approach. The MFA renamed its Division

4 Interview 6

5 Interview 22, see also (Sonnleitner 2015, p. 11)

on Legal and Consular Affairs and added the MFA's services for Austrian enterprises to this division. The new Service Division shall better represent the MFA's motto *"Worldwide at your service"*. This division now encompasses all departments dealing with issues concerning Austrian citizens and Austrian enterprises. Services for Austrian enterprises had so far been covered by a sub-department of division III on EU-coordination and global economic governance. Establishing such a Service Division increases the value ascribed to these services.

In the context of European integration, another step implemented by the MFA is significantly interesting. In the course of the modernization strategy, division III further developed and became the European Division, which now pools all EU competences. Until then, division III dealt with multilateral EU issues as well as economic relations, while division II on policy issues was responsible for bilateral relations. As a consequence, political and economic relations to the same country were handled in two different divisions[6]. So here, the MFA clearly adapted to the needs created by the EU framework, in which the political and economic system intertwine.

Among the remaining steps mentioned in the modernization strategy, such as establishing a special task force for situations of crisis and the opening of the selection process for the diplomatic service to graduates from all academic backgrounds, one further point is interesting in the context of this investigation. The MFA's modernization strategy includes pooling West Balkan issues, EU enlargement and twinning projects within one department in the European Division. The Balkan region is a main focus of Austria's foreign policy. The country has a well-established network of representations in this area and supports EU accession efforts of states in this region. Austria is also ascribed to have certain expertise in this field. However, in the context of shrinking budgets and staff reduction, it is increasingly difficult to maintain a high standard of expertise. The planned pooling of all areas in the MFA dealing with West Balkan issues - policy, economy and enlargement - promises to maintain this expert knowledge (Sonnleitner, 2015, p. 20). However, the coalition talks that followed the general election of 2017 brought a major disadvantage for the MFA in Austria's public administration framework. Foreign Minister Sebastian Kurz won the election with his People's Party and quit the grand coalition in favour of a coalition with the right-wing Freedom Party. Contrary to the People's Party, which posted most of Austria's foreign ministers in the Second Republic, the Freedom Party for long followed an EU-sceptical approach. Still, the coalition

6 Interview 22, 23, see also (Sonnleitner 2015, p. 20)

talks resulted in a Freedom Party-aligned foreign minister, but Sebastian Kurz will take major EU issues with him to the Federal Chancellery (Prior & Ultsch, 2017). It remains to be seen whether this is a temporary adaptation that resulted from the special circumstances of the coalition building process between a pro-EU and an EU-sceptical party, or if this will be a final shift of EU competences away from the MFA.

Austrian Bilateral Diplomacy inside the EU

There is no general answer to questions concerning the remaining relevance of bilateral diplomacy in the EU. It becomes obvious that bilateral diplomacy in the EU is about to develop a two-dimensional nature, whereby one side represents a traditional form of bilateral diplomacy focused on the relation between two states, while the other side is related to the EU framework and shaped by its demands. The latter one is what Paschke (2001) as well as Bátora and Hocking (2009) call *"European Diplomacy"*. These two sides are not mutually exclusive, they rather represent two sides of one phenomenon, of bilateral diplomacy within the EU. Several aspects influence the level of dominance of one or the other side in a specific bilateral relation. Two of these aspects can be classified as significant for the distribution of relevance between the two sides: the quality of the relation between Austria and the receiving state concerning cultural, historical and/or neighbourhood ties, as well as the level of integration in the respective receiving state. Embassies investigated in this study have been chosen according to their exemplary character concerning geography, size of the receiving state, duration of EU membership of the receiving state and the relation between Austria and the receiving state in historical and cultural terms.

Interviews conducted for this part of the investigation have shown that a dividing line between more and less traditional forms of bilateral diplomacy might be drawn alongside historical and geographical lines. Representatives of Austrian embassies in Western European old member states for example outlined that there is little traditional bilateral work to be done, because relations are excellent, economies and public administrations are closely interrelated and legal standards are similar, which diminishes the relevance of supportive or interventionist acts of diplomatic representatives[7]. This circumstance is accompanied by a declining number of ministerial visits on

7 Interview 1, 2, see also (Sonnleitner 2015, p. 14)

the bilateral level[8]. So here, where the process of integration is at an advanced stage, certain aspects of traditional bilateral diplomacy become less important, what supports the thesis of a developing system of *"Europäische Innenpolitik"*, in which interstate relations are conducted in a sort of domestic policy mode, thereby reducing the relevance of traditional bilateral diplomacy.

In some new Eastern European member states, however, an opposite trend is visible. Here, fostering bilateral diplomatic relations seems to be an important task within the Austrian diplomatic service. In these areas, the institutionalization of bilateral contact talks between embassies and MFAs is of high priority. In different countries, dialogue formats were designed in order to bring together representatives of MFAs and representatives of embassies on a bilateral level in order to discuss bilateral topics[9]. These forms of interaction are mainly embedded in neighbourhood policy contexts or extended neighbourhood policy contexts. One of these forms of interaction is a trilateral cooperation between Austria, Croatia and Slovenia, another one planned is a cooperation between Austria and the Visegrád Group[10]. Beyond that, Austria recently established closer ties to two of the Visegrád countries, the Czech Republic and Slovakia, by implementing the so-called *Nord Trilaterale*. This dialogue forum shall support communication between the heads of state with special focus on topics like energy, traffic, youth unemployment and European issues (BKA, 2015). The aim of these forms of cooperation is to facilitate a case-by-case collaboration concerning certain topics in neighbourhood or extended neighbourhood contexts[11]. Thus, in this area the number of diplomatic visits rather is about to rise than to decline, what is strongly supported by the Austrian MFA. These regular meetings intensify traditional bilateral relations between states, as they serve as a platform for bilateral concerns of both sides, with the effect that several issues, which would not be discussed in other kinds of meetings, are discussed in these settings. The regularity of these meetings offers the possibility to strategically follow defined development paths.

Neighbourhood ties and sharing a common border creates special circumstances and provides a precondition for close cooperation, especially concerning geographically determined issues, like transport, energy or la-

8 Interview 1
9 Interview 3, 4
10 Interview 4
11 Interview 4

bour market. Austria's focus on its Eastern neighbours and extended Eastern neighbourhood area in conducting traditional forms of bilateral interaction is further influenced by different levels of integration and different cultures of interaction. As mentioned before, Austrian diplomatic representatives in old Western European member states outlined that due to a progressing harmonization of economic, political and socio-cultural systems in the course of the European integration process, supportive or interventionist acts of Austrian representatives concerning Austrian foreign or economic policy issues become less important[12]. Austrian representatives in new Eastern European member states instead, for example, mentioned that supporting Austrian economy in the receiving state remains to be an important part of their work[13]. These different circumstances cannot merely be ascribed to different levels in economic and political integration, but also to differences in social and cultural structures in receiving states. In countries that are shaped by strong hierarchical structures, the title ambassador still functions as *"door-opener"* and allows access to governmental levels other representatives of the state or the Austrian economy would not be able to get[14]. However, a dividing line regarding strong and loose hierarchical structures in receiving states shall not only be drawn alongside an East-West division in the EU; this phenomenon might also have a kind of North-South-dimension.

One interviewee summarised that the role of Austrian diplomats becomes more differentiated and diversified in the context of the country's EU membership, because these circumstances further vary the set of tasks that are important for the work of a specific Austrian embassy at a certain location[15].

So Austrian bilateral diplomacy in the EU on the one hand becomes more diversified due to different levels of integration, combined with different cultures of interaction in the receiving states. On the other hand, it also takes on a new dimension in the form of *"European Diplomacy"*, where traditional forms of bilateral diplomacy lose their significance due to a high level of integration.

12 Interview 1, 2, 6
13 Interview 4, 5
14 Interview 4, 6, 9, 19, 20
15 Interview 6

Bilateral Diplomacy as Supporter of Multilateral Cooperation

In 2001, Paschke described the development of a new form of *"European Diplomacy"* alongside bilateral and multilateral diplomacy in his investigation of German embassies in the EU. Hereby, bilateral diplomacy assumes a supportive function for multilateral cooperation in the EU framework. This gives rise to the question of the relevance and importance of bilateral relations for multilateral cooperation on the EU-level.

When following Bátora and Hynek's (2014) conceptualization of diplomacy as the intermeshing of environments, actors and structures, it becomes obvious that the circumstances under which bilateral diplomacy is conducted determine its relevance. Inside the EU, especially the dynamic under which coalition building takes place on the multilateral level is evident for the relevance and importance of bilateral diplomacy.

Naurin and Wallace (2010, p. 5) point out that literature on coalition building on the Brussels-level traditionally followed the assumption that there are no *"'fixed' alignments"* that member states follow in the negotiation process. According to this, coalition building on the EU-level is issue-based and changes from topic to topic. This perspective indicates that coalition building is not predominantly determined by conflict lines found in nation state politics, like left-wing and right-wing political orientations or pro- and anti-EU orientations. It also indicates that geographical closeness does not play a significant role.

With growing access to Council protocols and voting records, and with new data collected in the form of interviews with representatives in Brussels, the possibilities to investigate these circumstances has grown and brought new insights along with it. For the period before the Eastern enlargement for example, a North-South division in coalition building became evident and according to Mattila (2010, p. 34), this trend continued to be a relevant aspect in coalition building also after the Eastern enlargement. Hagemann (2010, p. 54) however is of the opinion that no strict North-South or North-South-East division is visible. Mattila as well as Hagemann work with so-called multidimensional scaling maps of Council voting in their outlines (Hagemann, 2010, p. 54; Mattila, 2010, p. 33). These maps represent closeness and distance in the voting behaviour of member states. Austria in both illustrations is among the Southern group. Both researches investigated the post-enlargement period of 2004-2006, but the sources Hagemann and Mattila used for their investigation slightly differ and therefore the outcome also differs. In Hagemann's illustration Cyprus, Malta, France and the Czech Republic are closest to Austria, while in Mattila's illustration Malta, France, Spain and Slovakia are the closest four states to Austria.

Panke (2010, p. 802) argues that small member states have the possibility to strengthen their bargaining power through regional cooperation or alliance with bigger member states. Indeed, with the exception of Cyprus and Malta, Austria's most regular coalition partners are neighbouring countries or bigger member states. However, for investigating the relevance of bilateral diplomacy for building these coalitions, it must be considered that voting is a last step in the process of decision making. This last step is preceded by processes of communication and negotiation. In order to answer the question concerning the relevance of bilateral diplomacy for multilateral cooperation, it is necessary to examine the underlying conditions of the process of decision making and coalition building.

Lewis (2010, p. 182) argues that

> *"participation in the Council's institutional environment guides behaviour and informs interests differently than if they were based on instrumental, calculative reasoning alone."*

Kaeding and Selck (2005, pp. 273-276) share this opinion and describe four different sources of coalition building, which are based on different foundations: power-based coalition building, interest-based coalition building, ideology-based coalition building and culture-based coalition building. The first two sources - power-based and interest-based coalition building - are an expression of rationalist traditions and the last two sources - ideology-based and culture-based coalition building - are derived from constructivist ideas. Therefore, if the driving forces for coalition building on the multilateral level are power or interest, the quality of the underlying bilateral relations is less important. Coalition building that is based on ideological or cultural patterns instead goes beyond issues of contemporary discussions. Alliances which are ideologically informed can be grounded upon general political or EU-related policy orientations. Alliances that are culturally informed might be grounded upon similarities in language, history and general cultural characteristics (Kaeding & Selck, 2005, p. 275).

So how does coalition building look like from the perspective of Austrian diplomacy? Some of the diplomats interviewed for this investigation stated that coalitions on the Brussels-level become more variable and subject-related than they had been in the past[16]. One interviewee pointed out that having a big member state partner is a necessary precondition for the successful promotion of individual concerns. Coalitions of small states are seen as less fruitful, because coordinating several small member states and bundling their interests is more difficult to conduct[17]. Building these coalitions mainly takes place in Brussels, and MFAs or other institutions in the home country only get involved if the process of coalition building reaches a difficult point and higher authorities are summoned to get on with the process. One interviewee however mentioned that the MFA is not entirely satisfied with this process of independent coalition building on the Brussels-level, as it tends to develop a *"life of its own"*[18].

Solid bilateral relations are not an essential precondition for cooperation on the multilateral level, but good bilateral relations do facilitate the initiation of cooperation[19]. One interviewee, who worked in EU affairs as well as in bilateral diplomacy, stated that basic knowledge of one another and a certain kind of familiarity with the negotiating partner is essential for cooperation. Alliances are built on the multilateral level, but the multilateral environment is also influenced by the work undertaken in bilateral relations. Hence, it remains a part of bilateral diplomacy to provide information on the sending state to politicians, civil servants and diplomats in the receiving state in order to enhance knowledge and familiarity[20].Thus, bilateral diplomacy is still of relevance in the EU and developed a new dimension that is focused on working in the EU framework.

The respective culture in the receiving state thereby determines how bilateral diplomacy is conducted and in which way relations are organized. In some countries the necessity for personal contact is higher than in others. One interviewee mentioned that in some EU member states it is sufficient to send emails in order to raise a matter, explain a position or keep in contact. Conversely, in other EU member states personal contact is a necessity because other forms of communication are less accepted or even perhaps ignored. Based on this outline, the interviewee takes the idea of conducting

---

16 Interview 2, 4, 10, 19
17 Interview 10
18 Interview 10
19 Interview 2, 3, 4, 6
20 Interview 6

foreign and European policy via the internet into question, as despite ongoing globalization, working cultures in EU member states at the moment still function differently. In such cases bilateral presence and an Austrian contact person in the respective capital city is an essential factor for the quality of relations between states[21]. This statement came from an Austrian diplomat working in an Eastern European EU member state at the time the interview had been conducted. Another interviewee, working in a Western European country at the time of investigation, mentioned not to be convinced that the situation on the multilateral level in Brussels would change, if no bilateral representative would be in this country. At least not in a short term, but probably in the middle or long term because the frequency of contacts and the knowledge of one another would decrease[22].

So when taking into account that coalitions on the multilateral level are not only based on the foundation of interest or power, but also on similarities in culture and ideology, as Kaeding and Selck (2005) point out, bilateral diplomacy becomes a supportive act for multilateral cooperation on the EU-level, concerning the maintenance or further rapprochement of closeness - but not only on the EU-level. One interviewee drew attention to the fact that the quality of bilateral relations is also important in other forms of multilateral cooperation, like the UN. In particular, if states have no special interest in a certain topic that is discussed on the multilateral level, it is more likely that they support the efforts of another country if their bilateral relation is based on a solid ground[23].

Although coalitions in Brussels become more fluid and are often interest-based, reliable long-term partnerships are of lasting importance because they can be a decisive factor when lobbying for own interests. However, Austrian efforts so far have not been as successful as those of other states. One example for long term relations that build a basis for coalition building on the Brussels-level for example is the Visegrád Group, whose members regularly meet before the meetings of specialized Ministerial Councils in order to define a common standpoint. Baltic as well as Scandinavian member states follow a similar approach[24]. These examples illustrate the importance of regional forms of cooperation in multilateral contexts. Here, cultural points of contact are most likely. As mentioned before, Austria in-

21 Interview 4
22 Interview 6
23 Interview 1
24 Interview 4

itiated several efforts to closer cooperate with some of its Eastern neighbours or extended neighbours. However, the country has so far not been able to form or be part of a regional cooperation group that functions like Visegrád, the Baltic or the Scandinavian states.

When returning from the multilateral to the bilateral level, the question as to how these changed conditions transform the day-to-day work in Austrian bilateral missions is highlighted. It has already been mentioned that the work of Austrian embassies becomes more differentiated and diversified. While traditional forms of bilateral work still are of importance in some member states, especially in new Eastern European countries, other areas are dominated by a new form of inner-EU bilateral diplomacy. As in Paschke's (2001) report on changes in the work of German embassies in the EU, promoting EU positions in the receiving state also became an important task in the work of Austrian bilateral missions[25]. One of the Austrian diplomats interviewed for this investigation argued that no traditional foreign policy is made in the EU anymore. The majority of the topics worked on are related to an EU context and the interviewee perceives a clear development towards "*Europäische Innenpolitik*"[26]. Lobbying hereby has an inner-EU as well as a foreign policy dimension.

Concerning the inner-EU-level, one particular topic had been mentioned quite often as example for lobbying for Austrian interests during the period of investigation. The Austrian government has always expressed its rejection of the admission of the so-called Gigaliners in the EU, trucks with a maximum length of 25 meters and a maximum weight of 60 tonnes. In cases like this, it is the task of embassies to explain the Austrian position to for example the Ministry of Transport in the receiving state. It also is the task of embassies to search for partners with similar interests and convince those who have no strong opinion on a certain topic. In this regard, one interviewee highlighted the crucial importance of timing for this case. Promoting a certain position at an early stage in the decision making process gives the opportunity to find allies, compared with promoting it at a later stage[27]. So lobbying for internal EU matters is one aspect related to the new role of bilateral embassies in the EU.

The second aspect, and an especially important one in the context of foreign policy, is lobbying for Austrian CFSP interests in receiving EU member states. A special focus thereby lies on Austria's Balkan and West Balkan

25 Interview 1, 2, 3, 4, 5, 6, 15

26 Interview 6

27 Interview 4

policy, an area that has recently even been revalued in the course of the MFA's modernization strategy. The Austrian MFA now pools its expertise in this field in a West Balkan department, being part of the European Division in the MFA's organizational set-up (BMEIA, 2015c). Interviewees emphasized the importance of bilateral missions in promoting Austrian CFSP interests, because foreign policy positions are still confirmed in the respective capital cities where Austria has its diplomatic representatives at the embassies. Actively promoting CFSP positions and searching for potential partners is one side of the foreign policy oriented work in Austrian bilateral missions inside the EU. Another aspect of their work is explaining Austrian foreign policy positions to EU partners in situations where opinions differ from each other. One embassy representative pointed at the fact that from time to time Austrian foreign policy has to be explained in the respective receiving state. The interviewee referred to Vladimir Putin's visit to Vienna in June 2014, so at a time when the dispute between the EU and Russia over Crimea had already reached a critical status[28]. Due to its close relation to Russia, Austria refused to cancel the invitation, which caused displeasure among some EU partners.

Austrian bilateral diplomacy in the EU gained several new dimensions focused on supporting Austrian policies in the EU framework. Thereby, the forms of interaction with the receiving state changed. Besides promoting Austrian EU positions in governmental institutions, other interaction partners became increasingly important in the context of lobbying for own positions. Especially in the EU, where civil societies of several countries are confronted with similar problems, governments are no longer the sole target to convince. The society of the receiving state, interest groups and social movements as well are target groups in the course of lobbying for Austrian interests. In countries with a well-developed civil society, influencing public opinion can serve as an indirect instrument to influence governmental positions. Thus, interaction with others apart from governmental representatives and public diplomacy become increasingly important[29].

The growing importance of public diplomacy in diplomatic work has already been discussed for several years in relevant literature. However, many aspects labelled as public diplomacy today already existed in earlier forms of diplomacy as well (Melissen, 2005). Definitions of public diplomacy are off a broad variety and encompass perspectives that go beyond the assumption of diplomats being the only performers of public diplomacy. Public

28 Interview 6
29 Interview 2, 5

diplomacy might also be perceived as *"all activities by state and non-state actors that contribute to the maintenance and promotion of a country's soft power"* (Bátora, 2005b, p. 4). Such an approach offers multiple perspectives on this phenomenon. However, when concentrating on the work of the Austrian MFA and its representations in the EU, a narrowed underlying concept seems to be more appropriate. Sharp (2005, p. 106) describes public diplomacy as *"the process by which relations are pursued with a country's people to advance the interests and extend the values of those being represented"*. Melissen (2005, p. 23) argues in this context that *"for diplomats the host countries' civil society matters in a way that was inconceivable only a generation ago"*. This argument is especially true in the EU framework, where decisions of other governments, which regard public sentiments in the respective civil society, might influence the decision making process on the EU-level. Today, civil societies and interest groups within a state have better opportunities to inform and organize themselves, and also beyond nation state borders. Despite the ongoing challenges concerning the establishment of a European society and a common European identity, specific issues do have supporters in every member state. The task of diplomats in the context of public diplomacy is to identify these supporters, which can be especially beneficial if these supporters are well organized, for example in the form of an interest group or NGO. One representative of an inner-EU Austrian embassy gave a concrete example concerning environmental issues. This representative pointed out that he would support the environmental lobby in the respective receiving country if an environmental problem has to be solved at the EU-level, because this lobby follows a European, transnational and multilateral approach[30]. Austria currently holds rank 18 in the Environmental Performance Index, a country ranking that evaluates environmental health issues as well as the vitality of the ecosystem in countries around the world (Yale University, 2016). Ergo, Austria is among those countries that has already achieved high environmental standards and wants to encourage other EU members to catch up.

However, the success of public diplomacy efforts not only depends on the capacity and ability of the sending country's embassy - a circumstance that is about to change in the context of a shrinking number of personnel in the Austrian MFA - but also on the preconditions in the receiving country. Here, the different levels of integration come into effect again. The strength of civil societies varies among EU member states. Particularly in post-com-

30 Interview 5

munist countries, the long-term suppression of civil society activities continues to have an effect, although these effects vary from country to country. The same interviewee, who previously gave the example of working with environmental lobbies for supporting environmental policy and who worked in a new Eastern European member state during the time of investigation, argued that this form of public diplomacy has a double effect. It supports the specific issue Austria is lobbying for. Moreover, he assumes that on a meta-level, supporting movements like NGOs or other organizations has a strengthening effect on the civil society[31]. Hence, in inner-EU bilateral diplomacy, a democratization effect is ascribed to certain activities in the receiving state. Whether there really is an effect of this kind or not is questionable. Several scholars have recently examined this topic and Hahn-Fuhr and Worschech (2014), for example, argue that external support for NGOs in weakly developed civil societies rather leads to a division between these NGOs and the society. Beichelt and Merkel (2014) illustrate that the current conditions in Eastern Europe hamper positive effects of external influences concerning the development of consolidated democracies. Ishkanian (2014) perceives a way out of this dilemma by concentrating on the potential capability of small local NGOs in developing societies. Schimmelfennig (2014) however, who refers to these and other works, concludes that it is doubtful whether such initiatives indeed have a high potential to strengthen democracy. Thus, it cannot be assumed that such efforts of public diplomacy directly influence the development of civil societies in a positive way.

Another aspect depicted by this interviewee in the context of public diplomacy is related to the EU's efforts concerning institution-building. Twinning for example is an initiative of the EU Commission that supports the cooperation between EU member states and candidate countries or potential candidate countries as well as countries that are in the focus of the EU's neighbourhood policy. Cooperation of this kind can be situated on the administrative or judicial level. Austrian institutions were project partners in around 360 twinning projects between 1998 and 2015; around 250 in countries that have accessed the EU meanwhile. In this context, Austrian institutions have been most active in Croatia (43 projects), in Bulgaria (35 projects), in Rumania (34 projects), in Slovakia (28 projects), in Slovenia (26 projects) and in Hungary (24 projects) (BMEIA, 2015b). The interviewee pointed out the positive effect of twinning projects for Austria's image in countries where these projects and other efforts to pass on knowledge

31 Interview 5

and best practice examples have been implemented by Austrian project partners[32]. As mentioned before, the EU's neighbourhood policy is an illustrative example for the EU's ability to interfere in domestic policies via soft power, enabled by the prospect for the applying country to participate in the EU's prosperity. These soft power initiatives encompass national elements, as in twinning projects mostly nation state institutions or project partners which operate within a certain member state are related to the outcome of the twinning project in the accession candidate country. Positively accomplished projects do have the potential to support the country's positive reputation in the receiving state, where the project had been implemented. When returning to Bátora's (2005b, p. 4) definition of public diplomacy, which encompasses all activities by state and non-state actors that maintain or promote a country's soft power, it becomes obvious that the EU framework offers the possibility to build new or strengthen existing bilateral relations by means of soft power already during the accession process. The diplomatic service thereby administratively supports the implementation of these projects and therefore gets more strongly anchored to the society of the receiving country. In such cases, connections and relations were built in a pre-accession stadium, what might support cooperation in EU contexts. This assumption however still must be proven by empirical data.

New Actors in the Diplomatic Framework

The above remarks are in agreement with the assumption of the EU creating a different environment for bilateral diplomacy than the Westphalian system of states (Bátora, 2005a, pp. 53-54). As a consequence, not only tasks and the way how bilateral diplomacy is conducted in the diplomatic system changes, but also actors in this framework are about to change. The composition of actors becomes more diversified, which affects each individual actor in it. When concentrating on how the nature or self-conception of the Austrian MFA developed in the context of European integration, it is worthwhile to consider the description of former Austrian diplomat Eva Nowotny (2006, p. 33), who depicted the Austrian diplomatic service in the pre-accession period as *"captive to its own mechanisms, fascinated by its own internal power plays, absorbed by its own internal administration"*. According to Nowotny (2006, p. 33), this approach changed with the country's

32 Interview 5

accession to the EU, when the MFA had to recognize that other actors entered the field of foreign relations. The loss of the monopoly on foreign relations of MFAs not only shows its effects on the Brussels-level, where the importance of other ministries and nation-state institutions and the frequency of their interaction is about to grow. The composition of the Austrian diplomatic corps in receiving EU member states is changing as well because other Austrian ministries than the MFA have foreign policy competence. This encompasses the Ministry of Economy, the Ministry of Domestic Affairs, the Ministry of Defence as well as the Ministry of Infrastructure[33]. In situations where an Austrian ministry is especially concerned with developments in a certain region, it often sends a liaison officer to that location. Similar to the staff members of the Foreign Trade Service of the Austrian Federal Economic Chamber, these liaison officers are accredited diplomats at the Austrian embassy, but do have their own offices and do individually report to their sending ministry. Generally, like with the offices of the Federal Economic Chamber, information is shared between these liaison officers and the representatives of the embassy[34]. Thus, a second sort of diplomats developed within the Austrian national diplomatic corps, who operate under different preconditions than diplomats sent by the MFA. Working cultures differ from ministry to ministry and non-MFA representatives, for example, are not subject to the rotating system. Hence, different actors with different underlying educational and socialization backgrounds as well as actors used to different forms of organization now interact within the Austrian diplomatic corps. This leads to a process of negotiation of roles and hierarchies within the national diplomatic system that, according to interviewees, can have a conflictual dimension[35]. Long-established traditional forms of diplomacy, shaped by the conduct of MFAs, including diplomatic protocol, a rotating system and special selection procedures, compete with new forms, which are not part of this system.

The changing dynamics in the national diplomatic corps, caused by the growing importance of actors other than MFA representatives, not only leads to a more diversified composition of the national diplomatic corps, but also intensifies the interaction between embassy representatives and other ministries[36]. In general, inquiries from other ministries to embassies are rare. Cooperation between embassies and other Austrian institutions are

33 Interview 5
34 Interview 5, 16
35 Interview 5, 16
36 Interview 5

often project-based or related to a certain topic on the EU agenda. As mentioned before, the discussion about the use of so-called Gigaliners is one topic that had been on the agenda of several representatives interviewed at Austrian embassies in the period of investigation. Embassies involved in this issue therefore regularly interacted with the Austrian Ministry of Infrastructure[37]. These new arising circumstances also affect traditional diplomatic tasks usually performed by bilateral missions. In the field of political reporting from Austrian representations in the EU for example, classical comprehensive reports on certain areas of relevance from the receiving country are more and more displaced by a kind of reporting that shall support the work of other areas than foreign policy. Often political reporting is not an individual act anymore, but provides information from the respective receiving state concerning topics currently discussed in an EU context and hence follows the EU agenda[38]. Background information on the position of the receiving country on a certain EU issue is central in order to support EU processes of decision making[39]. To this end, this process has to orient itself towards the EU timetable. If a Commission report is about to be launched concerning an issue of relevance for a certain embassy, the respective Austrian representation will provide the colleagues in Brussels with the relevant information. Hence, direct contact between the representatives in Brussels and the respective embassy is common. In such cases the MFA plays a minor role. The MFA of course also receives reports, but these reports often are also directly sent to Brussels, as the two representatives interact with one another[40].

Nevertheless, traditional diplomatic reporting concerning bilateral issues remains part of the work of embassies inside the EU[41], especially in areas where Austria has an interest in further developing bilateral relations. The foremost addressee for reports still is the MFA, although other ministries are involved, if special issues are addressed[42]. The President's Office for example is an addressee for reports on bilateral topics, especially in the context of election reporting or the preparation and follow-up of state visits[43]. With the exception of particular requests by the MFA, Austrian embassies

37 Interview 3, 4, 5, 6
38 Interview 2, 3, 4, 6
39 Interview 6
40 Interview 5
41 Interview 4
42 Interview 2, 5
43 Interview 5

autonomously decide on what to report and decide which issues might be of relevance for the MFA or other Austrian institutions. This low level of supervision by the MFA in the context of political reporting also is related to the fact that MFA divisions and departments dealing with specific countries and regions are affected by staff shortage[44], which reduces the possibilities to supervise and coordinate the work of Austrian embassies. However, although Austrian embassies pass on reports autonomously to other ministries and institutions, the MFA still has a coordinating function and further spreads reports from embassies to other institutions. The practice of passing on reports autonomously conducted by embassy representatives often is based on the foundation of personal contacts and networks[45]. So besides the MFA's official information distribution channels, non-official distribution is common among Austrian civil servants in the context of established professional relations, which go beyond the MFA's staff pool.

One of the most obvious shifts concerning political reporting in the context of European integration is that the Federal Chancellery also became an important addressee of embassy reports that focus on significant topics on the EU agenda[46]. This is because meanwhile all important topics are discussed in the European Council. Consequently, the Federal Chancellery gained importance in Austria's EU policy framework[47], which further weakens the role of the MFA in this framework.

Impacts on the Diplomatic Corps

In the EU, new actors establish themselves in the national diplomatic corps, while the role of the existing actors is about to change. When concentrating on the diplomatic corps in the context of European integration, transformation processes are of a two-dimensional kind. Shifts of importance within the national diplomatic corps are one dimension. A second dimension concerns the transnational scope of the diplomatic corps.

The diplomatic corps exists in every capital city of the EU in a specific formation and traditionally is focused on bilateral exchange. Today an essential part of transnational cooperation, coordination and communication

44 Interview 5
45 Interview 5, 14
46 Interview 5, 6
47 Interview 6

is done within the framework of the EU-28 partners as well as in subgroups of this framework[48]. Hence, within the transnational part of the diplomatic corps inside the EU, different gradations become visible. EU member states build a specific group within the group of member state representatives in the respective receiving country (Sonnleitner, 2015, p. 15). This group meets more often than other members of the diplomatic corps, which strengthens personal relationships among representatives of EU member states. They furthermore also work on similar topics[49], as they often are related to the EU agenda. So representatives of EU member states in other EU countries are no longer simply bilateral representatives in the respective receiving state, but they are part of a group of partners, who interact in a different way and on a different basis than other bilateral representatives within the diplomatic corps in the receiving state do. Close interaction and regular meetings foster the relation between representatives of EU member states in receiving countries. Especially with those who are interested in and working on similar topics. In these circles information is commonly shared. One interviewee mentioned that also contents of talks with governmental representatives are shared with close partners from EU member states. This is a process of continual giving and taking[50]. So in such group constellations within the diplomatic corps, rather unusual forms of diplomatic interaction develop, which are shaped by trust, transparency and the willingness to share information with other diplomatic representatives.

When perceiving the diplomatic corps in a capital city as a transnationally informed social environment, it becomes obvious that the dynamic within this social environment is about to change due to the framework the EU imposed on it. Increased interaction between representatives of EU member states and a rising level of information distribution and trust creates the side-effect that the interaction with representatives of third states becomes less[51]. Consequently, the diplomatic corps within EU member states becomes more differentiated[52], which influences the professional life of bilateral diplomats in the European Union. This includes both groups, representatives of EU members as well as representatives of non-EU member

48 Interview 2, 4, 5, 6
49 Interview 6
50 Interview 6
51 Interview 2, 6, see also (Sonnleitner 2015, p. 15)
52 Interview 3, 6, see also (Sonnleitner 2015, p. 15)

states. Within the in-group of EU representatives further gradations are visible, as the EU framework creates different interest groups (e.g. Eurogroup)[53]. Several states work together close in small groups, if they have common interests concerning the receiving country[54].

Beyond that, new institutionalized forms of interaction bring a second level to the issue-related and interest-related types of group building. Friendship and interpersonal reliance or mutual trust between representatives of EU member states are strengthened through these forms of regular interaction. The out-group of non-EU member states is not only affected by not having access to these types of interaction, but also by a further important aspect considering the environment in which diplomacy is conducted - namely through the value the receiving state accredits to specific bilateral relations. Some receiving EU countries treat diplomats of EU member states differently than those of third countries. One interviewee, for example, pointed out that certain ministries of the receiving state regularly provide briefings and information to representatives of EU member states on EU issues[55]. Another interviewee describes a visible difference in the handling of representatives of EU members and representatives of third countries in the respective receiving state. According to that, the receiving country follows a more open-minded, transparent and partner-like approach when interacting with EU member states than with non-EU members[56]. Consequently, actors within the diplomatic corps in the EU are not primarily classified by different qualities concerning the bilateral relation between the sending and the receiving state anymore. They are primarily classified as EU-members and non-EU members. This separating line will become more significant as the process of integration moves on. However, this form of separation is not a phenomenon that evolved recently. A former representative of the Austrian MFA interviewed for this investigation hint at the fact that close cooperation between EC members in the diplomatic corps in a receiving state had already been common when Austria still was in the out-group[57]. Today's dynamics in the EU however are different than they were 20 years ago (Sonnleitner, 2015, p. 15) and further studies explicitly focussing on third state embassies in the EU and developments in the diplomatic corps could provide better insights to changes European integration

53 Interview 5, 19, see also (Sonnleitner 2015, p. 15)
54 Interview 5, 6
55 Interview 4
56 Interview 6
57 Interview 19

brings to this field. Here again, Great Britain, which will depart from the in-group in the course of BREXIT, would be an interesting example for further investigating such dynamics.

The following chapter illustrates how the second dimension of Austrian bilateral diplomacy is influenced by developments emerging in the context of Austria's EU membership: Austrian bilateral diplomacy in third states.

Austrian Bilateral Diplomacy in Third States

Investigating how Austrian bilateral diplomacy in third states is affected by the country's EU membership beforehand requires a consideration as to how the EU's foreign policy, conducted by the EEAS, influences bilateral diplomacy and the work of the diplomatic corps in third states.

Bátora and Hynek (2014, p. 153) argue that in this setting, traditional diplomatic cultures meet with new forms of organization. Like in inner-EU bilateral diplomacy, where the EU adds a new dimension to bilateral diplomacy by creating a rule-based legal environment (Bátora, 2005a, p. 54), the EU also adds another dimension to bilateral diplomacy in third states. Bilateral diplomacy is not only influenced by the quality of the relation between Austria and the receiving state, but also the quality between the EU and the receiving state is an influential factor for how Austrian bilateral diplomacy is conducted in the respective receiving state. So a sort of triangular relation developed which shapes the work of Austrian embassies in third countries (Sonnleitner, 2015, p. 17).

Some third states perceive the EU as the most important or one of the most important actors in the diplomatic corps, especially when it provides financial aid[58]. The EU together with its member states is the biggest donor of development aid worldwide. By 2013 for instance, 56,5 billion euros of development aid were provided, 52% of the worldwide development aid budget that year. Thereby, the biggest beneficiaries were developing countries in sub-Saharan Africa (33%) and developing countries in Europe (18%) (European Commission, 2014, pp. 3, 12). Elsewhere, different relation patterns are significant. Some third states still have close ties and maintain good relations to their former colonial powers, which leads to a special position given to representatives of these former powers in the diplomatic

58 Interview 14

corps in the receiving state[59]. In some areas the EU is not yet perceived as a political actor in third state relations, but rather as an economic area, as described by some interviewees[60]. These statements are related to a certain geographical positioning, and were made by interviewees, who work in destinations at a considerable distance from the EU, or by interviewees, who referred to such destinations in their statements. So the political clout in these areas still rather is ascribed to the member states, especially to bigger ones and their diplomatic representatives. This is different in areas with neighbourhood policy connections to the EU and especially in relations to accession or potential future accession candidates. Here, the influence of the EU gives a special position to the head of delegation in the diplomatic corps[61].

Regardless of whether the EU is perceived as political or economic power in third states, being part of it holds benefits for small member states like Austria in terms of diplomatic work. According to one interviewee, being part of the EU provides more political clout to a small state than the state could gain when operating on its own. The practice of close and regular interaction among EU representatives and member state representatives in third countries is noticed by receiving states. For them, it guarantees that information offered to Austria is passed on to the EU and other EU members. Small member states are often preferred partners to the receiving state for passing on information or giving statements to the EU. Hence, Austria in such situations is perceived as a port of access to the EU[62].

In other third states, the EU and its delegation in principal are in a difficult situation due to a strained relationship between the receiving country and the EU[63]. In such a constellation, nation state embassies can be in a more favourable position and do have easier access to governmental information and governmental institutions than EU representatives[64]. This might be interrelated to a certain behaviour of member states that seemed to develop within this triangular relation. Interviewees state that in receiving countries where the EU promotes its own values and criticises governments for example due to democratic deficits or the violation of human rights, Austria and other member states rather leave these soft power initiatives

59 Interview 14
60 Interview 9, 10, 12, 20
61 Interview 10
62 Interview 9
63 Interview 11, 14
64 Interview 14

and the promotion of specific values up to the EU[65], especially when own economic interests are involved[66]. Similar findings were provided by Terpan (2013, p. 133) in investigating the French foreign service.

A New Framework for Cooperation

Thus, the environment in which bilateral diplomacy is conducted is not only changing inside the EU, but changes in third states as well. The new dimension brought to bilateral diplomacy by the EU in third countries is represented by the triangular relation to which embassies are about to adjust their role. Beyond that, working with the EEAS also brings a sort of rule-based legal environment to the bilateral diplomatic work done by member states in third countries, as it changes the form of interaction among member state representatives. Interviewees describe a close form of cooperation with EU delegations in the respective receiving states, which is based on regular meetings; not only on the level of heads of missions, but also on the level of political counsellors, administrative staff, economic attachés and even in the field of press and culture, although the EU has no competence in these areas[67]. These meetings provide the opportunity for the exchange of views between the member states as well as the member states and the EU delegation and shall also be used to define a common guideline[68]. This close form of cooperation leads to a working mode with divided responsibilities and it is mentioned that within this cooperation in third states, the question of competences can be an area of conflict between the EU delegation and the member states[69]. Other interviewees however were amazed by the fast acceptance of the leadership role of the head of delegation[70].

A new order within the member states' part of the diplomatic corps is about to develop in the course of a process of conflict and adjustment, whereby the head of delegation is a central figure in this process. In the work constellation of EEAS representatives and representatives of member states, different working cultures and mind-sets do collide. A similar phenomenon is visible within the framework of the EEAS, where Commission

65 Interview 11, see also (Sonnleitner 2015, p. 17)
66 Interview 14
67 Interview 7, 8, 9, 11, 12
68 Interview 7, 12
69 Interview 8
70 Interview 10, 11

staff members, members of the General Secretariat of the Council and national diplomats interact. This phenomenon has already been discussed in academic contexts (Duke, 2012; Spence, 2012). In interviews conducted for this investigation, some Austrian diplomats mentioned that not all of the former Commission members do already fit into their new role in the EEAS[71]. One interviewee referred to the difficulties experienced by some former Commission members, who were used to primarily dealing with technical programmes and development aid issues, if they now need to make political statements concerning misconducts of the receiving state[72]. Others mentioned that before the establishment of the EEAS, delegations also were staffed with individuals who came from work areas, where they had never been working with member state representatives before and rather did not perceive them as colleagues and partners, but as *"the others"*. This might occur less frequently today, but illustrates that not only issue-related, but also culture-related sources of conflict appear in this work constellation.

Hence, a dividing line between the working culture of national diplomats and the working culture of Commission and Secretary members is not only a challenging element within the EEAS, but also in the cooperation between the EEAS and the member states (Sonnleitner, 2015, p. 16). When answering the question concerning the quality of the relation between the Austrian embassy and the EU delegation, comments ranged from average to very good. Thereby, some of the interviewees had the chance to compare different ways of how to manage an EU delegation and different forms of cooperation with the member states. Due to Austria's Euro-centric network of representations, many Austrian embassies in third countries are accredited in more than one receiving state. The EEAS is represented with about 140 delegations. So several Austrian embassies work with more than one delegation in their area of responsibility. The respective head of delegation is, therefore, a key figure for the quality of the relation between the EU delegation and the embassy[73]. One interviewee, who works with several EU delegations in the respective area of responsibility, especially mentioned one head of delegation in a positive way, who was able to create a close and well working mode of operation between the EU delegation and the member states. Here, the EU delegation apparently was able to, at least from the

71 Interview 9, 11, 14, 15, see also (Sonnleitner, 2015, p. 16)
72 Interview 14
73 Interview 7, 8, 9, 11, see also (Sonnleitner 2015, p. 16)

Austrian perspective, create a beneficial work relation, where communication and the distribution of information are central. Of interest in this context is the reasoning given by this interviewee. The interviewee explained that the head of delegation in this country is a former bilateral diplomat from a small member state, who appreciates the importance of sharing information[74]. This example cannot be generalized for describing the relation between representatives of big and small member states in the work constellation between EU delegations and national embassies. It does still provide an example of how diversified working cultures are in this constellation.

Differences in working cultures not only become visible when Commission members and national diplomats meet in EEAS contexts, but also when embassy representatives meet former national diplomats in the EEAS. The size of states represents just one aspect that defines differences and similarities in the organizational cultures of MFAs and therefore in the working cultures that diplomats are socialized in (Sonnleitner, 2015, pp. 16-17).

The head of delegation not only plays a significant role in the interaction process between the member states and the EU delegation, but he or she also is a central figure in the relation between the EU delegation and the receiving state. In this context, one interviewee mentioned a certain dissatisfaction with the choice of heads of delegation the EEAS made in some countries in the past. The concrete example was Latin America, where for a long time, it was mainly individuals originally coming from Portugal or Spain who became head of delegation. Individuals from certain countries bring specific expertise to the EEAS, not only concerning languages, but also concerning cultural and historical ties. The interviewee referred to a similar development in the Balkan region, where people socialized within the Austrian MFA have some advantages when applying for a head of delegation position due to Austria's special focus on this area. Nevertheless, when considering Europe's colonial past, certain constellations might give rise to resentments. However, this is the description of a past experience, meanwhile greater balance is about to develop[75].

Thus, the head of delegation is a significant factor for how cooperation between the EU delegation and the receiving state is conducted, as well as for how cooperation between the EU delegation and the member states and also between the member states in the receiving country is conducted. As a

74 Interview 9, see also (Sonnleitner 2015, p. 16)
75 Interview 11

consequence of the enhanced role of the EU delegation, the role of the EU presidency in third states, which had formerly been similar to the delegation's role today, nearly became invisible[76]. One interviewee mentioned that the presidencies after 2010 tried to secure their position within the diplomatic corps, but were unable to do so[77]. Nowadays, some countries focus on areas during their term of presidency where the EU has no competence, for example, promoting culture. Beyond that, their function is reduced to activities related to ceremony and protocol[78]. Whereby the mixed competences of the EU, the member states and the presidency lead to further adaptation processes in diplomacy, because EU delegation representatives now have to be taken into account by the diplomatic protocol as well. The shift of competences from the changing EU presidency to the permanent representation by the EEAS is generally perceived positively and as beneficial for EU foreign policy making by interviewees. Changing presidencies resulted in changing qualities of organization. Before the EEAS was established, each presidency had a different mode of operation and the time of familiarization with the tasks of an EU presidency and the handover period reduced the presidency's time of full operating capability. Now the mode of organization is streamlined[79] and the foreign policy making system has an institutional memory[80]. This new established continuity provides better preconditions for organization, coordination as well as for long-term projects. However, this continuity also leads to less variability. One interviewee confirmed that during the time of changing EU presidencies, certain concerns have rather been presented to the one presidency than the other, in order to bring it through[81].

Nevertheless, the new mode of operation provides several benefits to the Austrian diplomatic service, similar to those described in the context of cooperation between member states in inner-EU bilateral diplomacy. A small country like Austria benefits considerably from the distribution of information between the EU delegation and the member states as well as between the member states[82]. Not only inside the EU, but also in third states, the framework the EU implemented to the member states' part of the diplomatic corps leads to a rising level of trust and rising distribution of information.

---

76 Interview 7, 10, 11
77 Interview 10
78 Interview 11
79 Interview 7
80 Interview 24
81 Interview 24
82 Interview 9, 10, 11, 12, 15

Due to the fact that Austria has a rather small network of diplomatic representations and many embassies in third countries are accredited in more than one state, information from EU delegations is of special importance for these so-called *cluster embassies*. Some EU delegations are even located in countries where no other member state is represented. Receiving information from these EU delegations is of huge benefit for member state embassies, especially for those with a small network of representations. Depending on the intensity of cooperation in the respective third country between the EU delegation, the Austrian representation and representations of other member states, the intensity of this information flow may further rise. One of the interviewees, who worked at a *cluster embassy* at the time of investigation, and was responsible for several states in the respective area, described the form of cooperation between the EU delegations and the member states as well as among the member states as an open-minded pooling and sharing of information in both directions. Not just political reports are shared, but also information from talks and meetings with representatives of the receiving state is passed on. In this context, the interviewee spoke of an explosion of information, because the ties between the EU delegations and the member state embassies, as well as between the embassies of the member states are tight and many follow the principle of sharing information within this group of EU members. This does not only occur in using the instrument of traditional diplomatic reporting, but also in using more informal ways of communication. Consequently, the information load heavily increased and the exchange of information happens on a daily basis. This is not only a consequence of the closer cooperation within the community of EU members in third states, but also of the increasing use of new information technologies[83]. The interviewee who provided this example further stated that with the establishment of regularity in group meetings, the exchange of information between EU member states, which had to be initiated on a bilateral level before these forms of cooperation were institutionalized, now happens in a kind of *"natural manner"*[84]. However, the interviewee also mentioned that the emergence of such a *"natural manner"* of cooperation depends on the individual willingness to share information of the persons who work in this constellation[85]. Two other interviewees highlighted that a pro-active attitude of diplomats still is necessary to get

83 Interview 9

84 Interview 9

85 Interview 9

information, also within this framework and especially for small member states[86].

It can thus be said that the EU did not establish a hierarchically shaped mode of interaction in the member states' part of the diplomatic corps in third countries. Sharing non-official information with EU partners is a voluntary act, guided by the assumption that mutual giving and taking holds benefits for all partners. The same interviewee, who spoke of a *"natural manner",* further spoke of a kind of communitarization of information because the EU and the group of member state representatives have an interest to share the same level of information[87], what can be especially beneficial in difficult working environments. Another interviewee, who was exposed to such a situation at the time the interviews had been conducted, due to a restricted information policy of the receiving state, pointed out that this minimum form of access to information is multiplied through the continuous exchange of information among member state representatives as well as between member state and EU representatives. This opportunity is not available to representatives of non-EU states. They have to use the *"arduous traditional diplomatic path"* of searching for friends and establishing networks, as the interviewee called it[88]. So especially in difficult environments, a strong network between the representatives of the EU and its member states facilitates diplomatic work. This could indicate that in surroundings where diplomatic work is done under difficult conditions, ties between the EU delegation and its member states as well as among the member states within the EU framework become more intense or intensify faster than in less difficult situations. In any case, this example shows that the differentiation in the diplomatic corps between in-group and out-group, EU members and non-EU members, is also visible in third states and will probably intensify with growing interconnectedness between the member states through the coordinating function of the EU delegation. However, this is not a phenomenon that evolved recently. A retired Austrian diplomat interviewed for this investigation argued that close cooperation between EC members in the diplomatic corps in a receiving state had already been common in the 1980s, when Austria still was in the out-group. The interviewee, who represented a European non-EC member state that time, perceived this circumstance as

86 Interview 11, 13

87 Interview 9

88 Interview 11

a disadvantage for Austria and had been particularly irked by the EC members' attitude to represent Europe and to hold European meetings, although Austria was part of Europe as well[89]. This might indicate how representatives of non-EU member states, who relate themselves to Europe, might feel today, especially because the EEAS intensifies the dynamics in the in-group. In this context, it would be interesting to investigate the perception of non-EU member state representatives in the diplomatic corps in third states as well, concerning the growing interconnectedness between EU members.

Such intensified forms of sharing and multiplying information among and between member state representatives as well as between the EU delegation and the member states is a sort of interaction that is highly dependent on the environment in which diplomacy is conducted as well as on the willingness of the actors involved. The distribution of information is therefore situated on two levels: a formal and a more informal kind of information sharing. The more informal kind of information sharing is based on mutual confidence and driven by individual initiative, as well as the idea to create more beneficial conditions for conducting diplomacy through cooperation. The formal kind of information sharing is offered by reports the EEAS provides. Through this, the amount of information the Austrian diplomatic service has to handle, became a lot higher. Through the EEAS, the Austrian diplomatic service now also receives reports from regions, in which it cannot be represented and benefits from reports concerning special issues that cover topics on which the Austrian diplomatic service usually would not elaborate[90]. This is the result of the combination of two working cultures in the EEAS; the one of national diplomats and that of members of the European Commission. Knowledge of Commission specialists in certain areas of relevance now is available to diplomats. In particular, small diplomatic services, such as the Austrian one benefit from expert knowledge, as the size of the Austrian service only allows to build special expertise to a limited extent. So the information coming from the EEAS widens and broadens the knowledge within the Austrian diplomatic service.

By considering these information flows and new forms of interaction – informal as well as formal – certain Europeanization effects on Austrian bilateral missions in third countries become obvious. First of all, behavioural patterns are adapted to the new common system of interaction and

89 Interview 19, see also (Sonnleitner 2015, p. 15)
90 Interview 9, 13, 14, 22

cooperation. Information is not only shared with preferred partners anymore, but becomes a shared good within the member states' part of the diplomatic corps, in order to commonly achieve better circumstances for diplomatic work in the respective receiving state. This is supported by the introduction of technical systems to facilitate information sharing[91]. Different development levels in the diplomatic services and MFAs of the member states, however, still complicate the establishment of a unified information system[92]. Secondly, the information transmitted by these missions to the MFA or other national institutions carries Europeanized elements itself, as it develops in a Europeanized environment. Both, new technologies that facilitate the distribution of information and the active exchange with European partners in the receiving state, lead to an information explosion, as one interviewee termed it[93]. Hence, the task of embassies shifted from collecting information to assessing information. In the case of a small country like Austria, which only has few personnel resources for conducting its own research, it is likely that a major part of the information handed on to national institutions emerged in the context of interaction with other European partners.

In the light of the comprehensive information policy of the EEAS and the current easy access to information from third countries via the internet, the question arises as to whether political reporting from Austrian embassies in third countries still provides an added value to the work of the Austrian MFA or the Permanent Representation in Brussels. According to an EU-based representative, the material coming from the EEAS is a great source and provides especially detailed reports of a kind the Austrian diplomatic service would never be able to provide. However, the interviewee also pointed out that the real essence of diplomatic reporting is missing in EEAS reports. These reports provide factual knowledge and the interviewee described reading them as similar to reading newspaper articles. They are not subject to secrecy and essential non-official information that might influence foreign or economic policy decisions is missing. EEAS reports, which cover sensitive issues are not passed on to the Austrian diplomatic service. National diplomatic services instead also provide information on a speculative level. The interviewee called it the *"juicy parts"*, which can

91 Interview 11, 15
92 Interview 15
93 Interview 9

serve as basis for policy or economic policy decision making.[94]. MFA representatives have a similar view on the importance of reporting from Austrian embassies. Reports and estimations from embassy representatives still serve as a basis for accountable and reliable decision making in the Austrian MFA.

However, the added value of political reporting for the MFA is dependent upon the quality of bilateral relations as well as the access opportunities of Austrian diplomatic representatives in the receiving state, in order to get special information. This leads one back to the issue of hierarchies within the diplomatic corps. In the Balkan region for example, Austrian representatives often play an important role within the diplomatic corps, have close connections to government representatives and are therefore able to provide sufficient information on developments in this region[95].

Like in inner-EU bilateral diplomacy, the primary receiver of reports from Austrian representations in third states is the MFA. But embassies also autonomously address reports to other offices if the information is relevant to them. Reports with an economic background are also addressed to the Federal Economic Chamber via their Foreign Economic Service. Other Austrian ministries are involved if reports cover issues in their area of competence. Further receivers might be the Austrian Parliament as well as the Federal Chancellery, the President's Office and the Permanent Representation in Brussels as well as other embassies in the respective region. In the field of neighbourhood policy, governments of Austrian Federal States may additionally become involved in the process of information sharing. Thereby, there is no regulation existing that defines to which offices embassies have to report to, with the exception of the MFA. Embassies are, however, able to independently decide on where to send their information. The MFA primarily takes the role of a distributor and sends reports to those offices which are concerned[96].

So although the EEAS became a big provider and distributor of information, political reporting from embassies in third countries remains to be a relevant basis for the work of the Austrian MFA as well as other Austrian institutions. Beyond that, establishing and expanding networks in the receiving country still is a significant task of Austrian representatives on-site, in order to be able to provide specific information. However, the manner in which this information is gathered changed due to the framework the EEAS

94 Interview 14, see also (Sonnleitner 2015, p. 15-16)
95 Interview 10, 22
96 Interview 7, 8, 9, 10

established for the cooperation with the member states in the receiving countries. Changing effects thereby are not limited to the work in third countries.

Effects on the Austrian Ministry of Foreign Affairs

In Brussels, an interesting turn is perceived concerning the cooperation between the member states and the EEAS. One interviewee, who experienced the initial period of the EEAS in Brussels, outlined that at the beginning, the EEAS had been quite dependent on the member states as it still had to develop its personnel structure and physical presence. Nevertheless, from the beginning the EEAS was keen to gain independence from the member states and according to this EU-based interviewee, it had been able to do so in the last years. The growing independence and strength of the EEAS initiated changing processes in the relation between the member states and the EEAS. The interviewee described the rise of a sense of common foreign policy making among EU member states in the period before the EEAS had been established[97]. Now roles in the EU's foreign policy making system are about to be renegotiated, because the member states have to accept the growing importance of the EEAS and at the same time need to find their position within this framework. In this sensitive period, the relation has to be stabilized between the effort of the EEAS to make EU foreign policy independently and to become a strong foreign policy actor, and the effort of the member states to co-create the EU's foreign policy and also play a monitoring role in formulating EU foreign policy goals. From the interviewee's perspective as a nation state representative, there is a danger of the emergence of a *"mini commission"* because EEAS staff members originally come from the Commission and, according to this interviewee, carry the basic thought that member states are potential *"treaty violators"* and have to be mistrusted. The interviewee further mentioned that there is a gap between the mind-set of the representatives of the member states and the mind-set of EEAS representatives. Hence, the EEAS and the member states are currently in an area of tension between mistrust and team play[98]. However, also within the EEAS a clear positioning towards the member states remains to be found. According to this interviewee, the different mind-sets within the EEAS give rise to a *"tug-of-war"* between those who advocate

97 Interview 14
98 Interview 14, see also (Sonnleitner 2015, p. 23)

for an independent EEAS and those who see a need to further integrate the member states. The interviewee perceives the danger that if member states are kept at distance and are not motivated to participate in common European foreign policy making, they will start to go on with their own and independent foreign policy, which consequently will restrict the EEAS' ability to act[99].

The introduction of a new actor to the diplomatic system by the EU in the form of the EEAS has the consequence that on several levels, processes of role negotiation are currently conducted. In third states, as in the EU, dynamics within the diplomatic corps are about to change due to the enforced interaction between the member states as well as between the EU delegation and the member states. Group-building has probably always been a common phenomenon within the diplomatic corps. Cultural similarities, geographical proximity, regional cooperation and/or overlapping interests, but also sympathy define closeness in the diplomatic corps. The EEAS however established an institutionalized form of interaction that consciously strengthens European integration within the diplomatic corps in third states and therefore fosters the in-group/out-group situation. In the in-group, hierarchies are not only defined by the interaction between the member states and the EU delegation, but also by the importance the receiving state accredits to each of these actors. In Brussels, the general direction concerning the EEAS' formation and role is currently negotiated between pro-intergovernmental and pro-supranational elements. This negotiation process is proceeded between the member states and the EEAS as well as inside the EEAS. Within this process of role negotiation, the Austrian example shows that a transfer of competences from Vienna to Brussels is observable. One EU-based interviewee perceives the emergence of a new foreign policy centre in Brussels. At the very beginning of the establishment of the EEAS, instructions on foreign policy issues still came from the EU's capital cities and had been represented in Brussels by the member state representatives. Here, the ongoing development of the EEAS brought a beginning turnaround of circumstances. Now, as the EEAS is the one to initiate and lead foreign policy meetings and the one who initiates preliminary talks, much more foreign policy action takes place in Brussels. The interviewee outlined that this situation led to a shift in competence concerning the formulation of foreign policy positions. Previously, it had been common to get an instruction from the capital city to be promoted in Brussels. With growing

99 Interview 14

foreign policy interaction in Brussels, the process of defining a certain foreign policy position started to change. The interviewee pointed out that now in many cases the representative in Brussels does not take the instruction from the capital city concerning a certain topic, but contacts the capital with the information he or she gained through talks and meetings in Brussels, explains the situation and the standpoints of the EEAS and other member states to the headquarters in his or her capital and proposes a national foreign policy position the capital probably accepts[100]. Hence, various different aspects and numerous different actors influence the development of Austrian foreign policy positions today. The direction of decision making in formulating foreign policy positions changed.

From the Austrian perspective, a new foreign policy centre is about to develop in Brussels. The EU-based interviewee stated that this is a much discussed topic among national diplomats in Brussels who work in foreign policy contexts. Here size seems to matter. According to Comelli and Matarazzo (2011, p. 5), smaller states are more willing to transfer competences to the EEAS than bigger member states, due to their limited resources. Such a tendency is also visible in the formation of foreign policy positions. The interviewee outlined that bigger member states, especially the biggest member states still influence EU foreign policy through guidelines developed in their capital cities and not like in Austria, developed in the context of interaction processes in Brussels. Here, the example of France was mentioned as one of those states, where the MFA is the driving force behind all foreign policy statements made in Brussels, while MFAs of smaller member states rather rely on their EU-based representatives[101]. When perceiving this development against the backdrop of an unfavourable budgetary situation, which causes staff reduction in the Austrian MFA, the growing foreign policy community in Brussels can serve as a source of information and as vital exchange platform that might is able to compensate the MFA's reduced ability to act in some areas. One example brought up by the EU-based interviewee was that the MFA uses information from its representatives in Brussels to prepare bilateral state visits, in order to be aware of the current EU position concerning the country to be visited. To this interviewee, this is an evidence that a shift of importance from Vienna to Brussels has already taken place[102].

100 Interview 14
101 Interview 14
102 Interview 14

The establishment of the EEAS also caused changes in the mode of operation within the Austrian MFA. The EEAS works more routinized than most presidencies did, has more staff and produces more information and more papers. The deadlines to react to this papers are short and now define the time tables in those departments of the MFA, which are involved in EEAS-related decision making processes. A fast and unconventional mode of operation developed in the context of EU decision making, where even traditional work hierarchies are softened[103]. Hence, EU-related areas in the MFA are clearly affected by a sort of Europeanization that transforms the MFA's organizational culture and influences essential elements, like long-established hierarchies. Beyond that, the workload became higher, because Council Working Groups also deal with areas the Austrian MFA would not work on from its national perspective. The MFA and its representatives need to be up-to-date in these areas as well nowadays[104].

In these contexts, the role of the Austrian MFA is about to change, because strategies and decisions are not solely prepared in the MFA and transmitted to other levels anymore. Dynamics induced by the Brussels-level change the mode of operation in the MFA and even absorb tasks and processes, which had been located in the MFA before. On the one hand, this might facilitate the work of MFAs in times of less personnel and financial resources, as interaction processes in Brussels offer a pool of information and contacts that can easily be accessed by Austrian representatives working in Brussels. On the other hand, this Brussels-centric focus implies that the Viennese headquarters is not the only head of the organization anymore, but has to accept another one, represented by the Permanent Representation in Brussels. When considering that several Austrian organizations beside the MFA operate and cooperate in Brussels, the Permanent Representation might be able to not only function as a second head of the MFA's organization, but also as a multi-linked head that coordinates information of several organizations, in order to formulate Austrian policy positions, by accommodating the needs of all parties involved.

The question remains as to how these heads of the double-headed organization are going to develop in the context of foreign policy making. A paradigm shift is about to occur, as Austrian foreign policy positions are less and less formulated sovereignly, but more and more result from a process of interaction of several foreign policy actors on the EU-level. Hence, EU membership, at least in the example of Austria, does intensively influence

103 Interview 15
104 Interview 22

the country's foreign policy character. When referring to Europeanization in this context, it could be assumed that any member state operates with partly Europeanized foreign policy positions, which were created through interaction processes in EU contexts. In the Austrian example, the MFA's orientation towards Brussels rather indicates a top-down than a bottom-up process in foreign policy making. This observation cannot be generalized for small member states acting in the context of the EEAS, but case studies on other small state MFAs might be able to reveal such a tendency. The work of Balfour and Raik from 2013 does not really consider this aspect.

When observing how the conduct of big member states is perceived by Austrian representatives, a different tendency is visible. The three biggest member states: Germany, Great Britain and France play a significant role in EU foreign policy making, as their size allows them to invest time, personnel and money to this field. An EU-based interviewee also perceives a greater foreign policy ambition among these countries[105]. In the case of Great Britain and France, their colonial past creates certain obligations and with the heritage of being a former global power, the willingness to step back, in order to give opportunities to the EEAS to distinguish itself, is limited. The interviewee hints at the fact that the EEAS still has to cooperate, because big operations, especially in the field of defence and security policy, are not feasible without the political, financial and military power of the big member states[106]. This assessment underlines the interviewee's previous statement concerning the *"tug-of-war"* in the EEAS between those who advocate for an independent EEAS and those who see a need to further integrate the member states. Losing the participation of the big member states would restrict the EEAS' ability to act.

One example from the Balkan region, brought up by an Austrian representative, illustrates the current importance of the big member states in EU foreign policy making. This representative spoke of coordination meetings of the ambassadors of Germany, France and the US, together with the head of the EU delegation in this area. The interviewee labelled this form of cooperation as *"great power policy"* and mentioned that the frequency of these meetings is about to rise[107]. This brings up the question as to the importance of small member states in terms of EU foreign policy making and

105 Interview 14
106 Interview 14
107 Interview 10

which opportunities they have for participation. According to this interviewee, a strategy for small states to be involved in EU foreign policy making in such situations is to be well-informed, to know about these meetings and to be in touch with people who attend these meetings, in order get information and to be able to promote own positions[108].

Austrian Diplomats in the EEAS

Generally, small member states have the possibility to establish an own foreign policy profile within the EU's foreign policy making system. The Austrian diplomatic service has a considerable interest to co-create the work of the EEAS by influencing it on two levels: with its special expertise and in the field of human resources. Member states have the possibility to send a certain number of diplomats to the EEAS, whereby the number is regulated according to the country's size. One representative of the Austrian MFA, however, stated that no concrete numbers are announced by the EEAS. In 2015, 9 Austrian diplomats had been part of the EEAS, the maximum number so far was 11[109]. The Austrian MFA supports efforts of Austrian diplomats to join the EEAS[110]. Successful Austrians in the EEAS often are presented as figureheads of the Austrian diplomatic service. Two examples regularly mentioned in this context are Hans Dietmar Schweisgut, who was head of the EU delegation in Japan from 2011 to 2014 and became head of the EU delegation in China in 2014, as well as Thomas Mayr-Harting, who was head of the EU delegation to the UN in New York from 2011 to 2015.

Occupying prestigious posts and occupying a high number of positions in the EEAS is an aspired goal of the Austrian MFA. The underlying aim of this approach is to benefit from the network Austrian diplomats generate during their term at the EEAS as well as to benefit from the knowledge of returnees. The MFA thereby is most interested in national diplomats, who decide to complete a term in the EEAS in the middle or at the beginning of their career, and return after the maximum period of two terms. This way, returnees are able to contribute their knowledge to the Austrian diplomatic

108 Interview 10
109 Interview 16
110 Interview 14, 16, 24

service and are able to use their EEAS contacts for their work in the Austrian diplomatic service[111]. One interviewee hinted at the fact that national diplomats in the EEAS are not only working in EU delegations, but also in the EEAS system in Brussels[112]. Returnees from such posts bring significant internal knowledge concerning processes in the EEAS headquarters to the Austrian diplomatic service. In practice, however, the size and capacity of the Austrian MFA does not always allow to position returnees at posts where they can properly apply the knowledge gained in the EEAS. First returnees have already started to work in the MFA again and there is an attempt to find positions where this experience can be used, but the limited number of posts does not always offer respective feasibilities[113].

At this early stage of staff exchange between the MFA and the EEAS, the sort of long-term effects returnees will have cannot be simply anticipated. Interviewees however state that the Austrian diplomatic service benefits from national diplomats in the EEAS already during their term in the European diplomatic service. Although national diplomats do not represent Austrian foreign policy during their term in the EEAS, they are usually somehow still connected to their home diplomatic service and can serve as contact person within the EEAS. Austria was among those member states, which advocated the possibility of sending national diplomats to the EEAS[114]. The MFA is able to benefit not only through getting information from the EEAS through Austrian networks, but also by promoting its own positions through Austrian representatives in the EEAS. One interviewee explained that asking an Austrian EEAS representative to act in a certain way is a common form of taking influence[115].

Working for the EEAS is often perceived as an interesting opportunity by Austrian diplomats because it offers the possibility to represent the EU and to work in receiving countries, areas and fields that are not covered by the Austrian diplomatic service[116]. Financial incentives might play a role as well however[117]. The interest among Austrian diplomats to join the EEAS was high in the period shortly after the establishment of the service but since then, the initial enthusiasm has waned. First of all because fewer positions

111 Interview 7, 8, 13, 16, 24, see also (Sonnleitner 2015, p. 23)
112 Interview 8
113 Interview 16
114 Interview 13
115 Interview 7
116 Interview 8, 13, 14, 16
117 Interview 7, 8

are available now than was the case in the beginning, but also because interviewees perceive a tendency of the Commission to offer attractive posts to their staff members and not to diplomats from nation states[118]. Interviewees pointed out that member states' diplomatic services are in a difficult situation, because they are not treated well and ranked lower and lower in the competition for posts in the EEAS. Some member states complain about only having few and insignificant posts as well as about not being involved in EEAS processes. Here, the *"tug of war"*[119] in the EEAS between establishing an independent service and further integrating the member states, as mentioned by another interviewee, becomes apparent again. Beyond that, the EEAS is still in a process of development and job descriptions are not absolutely clear so far and work conditions differ in some cases. Therefore, some Austrian returnees were dissatisfied by perceiving a gap between their expectations and the actual situation[120]. According to one interviewee, the general orientation of the EEAS currently vacillates between a *"team-player organization"* and a *"mini-Commission"*[121]. The direction this general orientation will take is decisive for how interesting EEAS positions will be in the future for Austrian diplomats.

Austrian Expertise in the EEAS

The Austrian MFA generally follows an integration-friendly effort, supports a strong EEAS and wants to participate in common European foreign policy making[122]. Besides human resources, a second area in which the Austrian diplomatic service wants to contribute to the EEAS is its special expertise in certain areas. According to Austrian representatives interviewed for this investigation, Austria is acknowledged for expertise in the fields of human rights[123], human trafficking[124], disarmament[125], international law[126],

---

118 Interview 15, 16, 24, see also (Sonnleitner 2015, p. 23)
119 Interview 14
120 Interview 14, 16
121 Interview 14
122 Interview 14, 16
123 Interview 7, 9, 14
124 Interview 7
125 Interview 7, 14
126 Interview 9

freedom of the media[127], experience as UN location[128] as well as local experience in the Middle East[129], Central and Southeast Europe and especially in the Balkan region[130]. Austria has a dense network of representations in the Balkan area and invested considerable attention to the development of this region. Therefore, Austria is in a leading position to provide information concerning the Balkans to the EU, to other member states as well as to the EEAS[131]. With its modernization strategy announced in 2015, the MFA explicitly wants to maintain and strengthen this expertise (BMEIA, 2015c).

The pro-EEAS attitude of the Austrian MFA raises the question of how Austria benefits or wants to benefit from a strong EEAS and its participation in it. A desired effect named by MFA representatives in Brussels and Vienna is the multiplying factor of the EEAS. If Austrian representatives are able to successfully promote Austrian foreign policy concerns on the EU-level, these concerns may become European foreign policy concerns and are promoted by the EEAS, what increases their importance[132]. Such a process also happens on a small scale in interaction with the EU delegation and other member states in third countries[133]. From the viewpoint of the MFA, Austria is able, to a high degree, to implement its interests to the EEAS and therefore to promote them via the EU, especially in the fields of disarmament, human rights, EU enlargement and Balkan policy.

Indeed, the annual *European Foreign Policy Scorecard*, issued by the pan-European think-tank European Council on Foreign Relations (ECFR), which categorizes member states as either *leaders* or *slackers* in specific EU foreign policy contexts, ascribes a leading role to Austria in some of these areas. By 2012, the ECFR (2012, pp. 135-140) labelled Austria as a *leader* in Kosovo issues, but as a *slacker* in the area of development aid and global health. It is also noteworthy that Austria has only been mentioned in 2 of the 29 categories the ECFR developed for the *European Foreign Policy Scorecard 2012*. The 29 categories are summed under the general topics China, Russia, United States, Wider Europe, Middle East and North Africa as well as Multilateral Issues and Crisis Management. Finland and Sweden, which accessed the EU at the same time as Austria and are also comparable

127 Interview 14
128 Interview 8
129 Interview 8
130 Interview 7, 8, 14
131 Interview 14, see also (Sonnleitner 2015, p. 20)
132 Interview 14, 15
133 Interview 7, 8, 12

in size, are mentioned in 5 as well as 12 categories, whereby Finland is labelled as a *leader* in all 5 categories, while Sweden is labelled as a *leader* 11 times and as a *slacker* once. Categories changed a little in the *European Foreign Policy Scorecard 2013*, but still oriented towards the general topics. Austria here is mentioned in 5 categories, in 2 categories as a *slacker* and in 3 categories as a *leader*. According to this, Austria plays a leading role in encouraging Serbia to normalize its relations with the Kosovo. It is a *leader* in facilitating the consolidation of a European seat at the International Monetary Fund (IMF) and it also is categorized as a *leader* in contributing to CSDP missions in the field of crisis management. At the same time Austria is categorized as a *slacker* concerning its contribution to joint defence projects within the NATO or CSDP and Austria still is categorized as a *slacker* concerning the increase of development aid in order to reach agreed targets (ECFR, 2013, pp. 134-139). Austria changed its approach in this field by 2014 and is categorized as a *leader* by the ECFR (2014, pp. 118-123) in increasing development aid as well as humanitarian aid and was also ascribed a leading role in assisting Syrian refugees in 2014. Again Austria is labelled as a *leader* in supporting the negotiations between Serbia and Kosovo, but as a *slacker* in relations with Russia on energy issues because Austria, together with other member states, signed a bilateral agreement with Russia on the South Stream pipeline project (ECFR, 2014, p. 47). Consequently, Austria was also labelled in 2015 as a *slacker* in the field of diversifying gas supplies away from Russia and was labelled as a *slacker* again in development aid and humanitarian aid. But Austria is categorized as a *leader* in two new categories: pushing for European policy on privacy and intelligence as well as fighting climate change. Again, Austria was categorized as a *leader* in Balkan-related issues, this time concerning the development of a strong European position on the crisis in Bosnia (ECFR, 2015, pp. 114-119). In 2016, Austria was labelled as a *leader* in strengthening EU enlargement in the Western Balkans as well as in supporting TTIP negotiations (ECFR, 2016, pp. 148-149).

The *Foreign Policy Scorecard* might be a rather superficial outline of member state activities in the context of European foreign policy, but it enables to compare member state foreign policy initiatives in a European context and allows to observe certain prioritizations within the categories defined for the *Scorecard*. So as described by MFA representatives, Austria is in a leading position concerning Balkan issues in EU foreign policy making. However, in the field of human rights, another area mentioned by MFA representatives as a field where Austria to a high degree is able to implement its interests on the EU-level, the country is not listed among the *leaders* in the *Foreign Policy Scorecards*. Other fields mentioned by Austrian diplomats as areas of expertise are not or not explicitly mentioned in the *Scorecards*, or none of the member states are identified as either *leaders* or *slackers* in a certain EU foreign policy field.

When focusing on a country's special foreign policy expertise, it should be regarded that the EU framework creates a different environment than the international state system does. A EU-based interviewee stated that in contrast to international organizations like the UN, where small states have the opportunity to distinguish themselves on the basis of personal involvement, with personalities and the establishment of norms, states in the EU are much more bound to their real political power and need to invest money and human resources in order to co-create EU foreign policy guidelines[134]. Even though Austria might be a successful promoter of human rights, disarmament or the freedom of the media in international organizations, this does not necessarily apply to the situation in the EU.

Consequently, Austria will only be able to benefit from a multiplying effect of the EEAS, if it establishes a specific foreign policy profile and is able to take a leading role in certain policy areas. Such a tendency is visible in issues concerning the Balkan region, especially when regarding the focus of the MFA's modernization strategy. Nevertheless, shrinking budgets and a constantly decreasing number of personnel will impede the development of further and new expertise and maybe even hamper the maintenance of existing expertise in the future.

Furthermore, Austrian diplomats are, as a rule, not developing specified expertise during their career, but rather are generalists, who need to be able to become acquainted to, and to work in different areas[135]. Specialization only happens occasionally, most commonly in the fields of international law or culture. Regional expertise might be developed if diplomats spend several time in receiving countries in the same region[136]. Beyond that, staff members, who regularly work in EU contexts, are able to gain special expertise on mechanisms in this area[137]. In general, however, the Austrian diplomatic service rarely specializes experts, whose knowledge is of special interest for the EEAS. So the question remains how Austria might success-

134 Interview 14
135 Interview 19, 22, 24, 29
136 Interview 22, 24
137 Interview 19, 22

fully participate in EU foreign policy making, despite diminishing resources. A possible option could be to concentrate resources in certain areas of diplomacy, probably by transferring resources from the field of bilateral-oriented diplomacy to the field of multilateral-oriented diplomacy. Therefore, it would be necessary to evaluate two aspects: the remaining necessity of certain aspects of traditional bilateral diplomacy in third states as well as the possible future and success of the EEAS. In order to do so, it is of interest to consider the statements of Austrian diplomats concerning the nature and development of the EEAS, because these assumptions will influence the future orientation of the MFA.

None of the diplomatic representatives interviewed for this investigation described the EEAS as a conventional diplomatic service, but rather as a kind of *sui-generis* system[138]. This system still is about to develop and has to find its mode of function[139]. Moreover, opinions in the Austrian diplomatic service on the character and the role of the EEAS differ. One interviewee pointed out that the uniqueness of the EEAS spreads from the approach to intermingle several working cultures. Nation state diplomats meet staff members of the European Commission and the Council Secretariat, who are rather used to the working culture of international organizations than the working culture of diplomatic services[140]. Another one described the competition between these different groups as a source of success for the EEAS, because the best people from all three areas meet here[141] and will probably enrich each other. From this point of view, the EEAS will remain to be of a hybrid character, situated between political player and international organization, whereby some interviewees are of the opinion that it might rather develop in the direction of a bilateral service than in that of an international organization[142]. Others, however, are convinced that the EEAS will not be able to establish itself as a bilateral player with essential competences in the field of bilateral diplomacy[143]. This is particularly the case because EU delegations are not able to fully provide significant diplomatic services, like consular duties, the promotion of language, culture and national images as well as the support of national economies[144]. These insights from a practical perspective go in line with Bátora's (2013) explanation of

138 Interview 8, 14
139 Interview 8, 9, 14
140 Interview 14
141 Interview 21
142 Interview 7, 14
143 Interview 8, 9, 12
144 Interview 9

the EEAS as an organization operating in interstices, as outlined in the chapter on the EEAS as diplomatic actor.

The following chapters will concentrate on certain aspects of traditional bilateral diplomacy, like consular work as well as promoting Austrian culture and economy, in third states as well as inside the EU, in order to assess how other dimensions of Austrian diplomacy than the political one are influenced by developments in the context of European integration.

Cultural Heritage in Austrian Bilateral Diplomacy

As depicted in the last chapter, the Austrian MFA follows a pro-European attitude and wants to actively participate in common EU foreign policy making. Austria is willing to get behind the EEAS in the field of foreign policy making because it expects to benefit from the greater political leverage of the EU. However, in areas where the EEAS has no competence, the MFA and its representations try to enforce a specific Austrian profile that stands out from the EU and the other member states. Promoting Austrian culture is one of these areas. Interviewees ascribed a very high potential to Austrian national culture concerning the promotion of the nation's brand. This assumption seems to be built on what Rathkolb (2011, p. 37) calls the *"Austrianization"* of the cultural heydays of the Habsburg monarchy. The term *"Austrianization"* describes a process in which the most attractive elements of the cultural life in the Habsburg Empire were transformed to the history and culture of the Second Republic of Austria. Therein, the territorial size and cultural diversity of the environment in which these achievements developed, had not been considered.

Interviewees spoke of Austria as a *"cultural nation"*[145], where especially particular types of music are associated with Austria around the world. One interviewee mentioned that even in remote parts of Africa, people are aware of the *The Sound of Music*[146]; a Broadway Musical that tells the story of the Austrian musical family Trapp. In the 1960s, *The Sound of Music* became a film which beautifully depicted Austrian sights and landscapes, and strongly shaped the Austrian image in foreign countries. According to this interviewee, Mozart is also very much identified with Austria and Vienna, even in countries that do not have close relations to Austria. Therefore, the country's global image seems to go in line with its self-definition and self-

145 Interview 3, 5
146 Interview 9

perception as a *"small nation with a great culture"* (Gärtner et al., 2005, p. 12). To Höll's (2002, p. 372) opinion, this image is outdated and should be reconsidered in the context of Austria's EU membership. Resources therefore should be focused on contributing to common European policy making.

Austrian diplomats, however, outlined that using these well-known and accepted clichés and stereotypes for their work is beneficial for certain fields of bilateral diplomacy they are operating in[147]. One interviewee was of the opinion that Austria's special cultural image should be used to support the promotion of Austrian interests. The diplomatic service thereby should not be deterred from benefiting from classical Austrian clichés, like operettas, Vienna's New Year's Concert or Austrian wine. Events that promote these images are mostly very welcomed and clearly valuable for the embassy as networking possibility with representatives of the government, the economy and culture of the receiving state[148]. The success of events related to classical Austrian images are confirmed by diplomatic representatives in third states as well as inside the EU[149]. So using Austria's well-established traditional cultural image and the country's nation brand remains to be an essential part of Austrian bilateral diplomacy, because its prominence can serve as a link to networks and decision makers in the receiving state.

Promoting different and modern images of Austria and Austrian culture is certainly part of the work of Austrian embassies and cultural fora. However, this area is also affected by savings. One interviewee stated that in the promotion of Austrian culture, hardly any distinct and substantial points can be set. Austria is able to partly appear in the cultural scene of the receiving states, but not as an influencing factor[150]. Each embassy and each cultural forum of course has its own approach on promoting Austrian culture. Nevertheless, the success of existing traditional images and their beneficial use in receiving states by Austrian diplomacy as well as budget limitations for promoting different images of Austria will probably preserve the country's outdated image, as Höll (2002, p. 372) called it.

147 Interview 4, 5
148 Interview 4
149 Interview 1, 2
150 Interview 7

Consular Services in Austrian Bilateral Diplomacy

In the field of consular work, the Austrian MFA follows its principle of service orientation and even strengthened this approach in the context of its modernization strategy by 2015 (BMEIA, 2015c).

The MFA operates under the slogan *"Worldwide at your service"* and especially now, when the necessity of bilateral diplomacy is brought into question, due to the close interconnectedness between EU member states on several levels and the outside representation of the EU by the EEAS, the MFA is under particular pressure to justify the maintenance of its network of representations. Indeed, inside the EU travel freedom reduced the necessity of one major aspect of consular work, the task of issuing visas. However, travel freedom also enhanced the mobility of Austrian citizens, which causes more cases of emergency in which Austrian citizens need to be supported by the Austrian embassy in the respective country[151]. In the context of growing legitimation pressure, consular services offer a clear answer to the question as to what Austrian bilateral missions actually do[152]. The support of Austrian citizens in situations of crisis as well as crisis management attract more media attention than the MFA's actions in other fields of operation do[153]. Consequently, the MFA strongly promotes its service-oriented approach.

In using new technologies, it provides a comprehensive support system for Austrian citizens travelling abroad. The so-called *Foreign Service App* (BMEIA, 2017a) combines certain information on travel destinations with special attention to the services of Austrian representations in the respective destination. Moreover, another tool, the so-called *Travel Registration* (BMEIA, 2017d) had been launched. This platform offers the possibility to register at the MFA's website before starting a journey. The aim is to give embassies the opportunity to contact Austrian citizens, who are travelling in a certain country if the security situation changes. It also helps them to be better prepared if an Austrian citizen contacts the embassy in the case of emergency.

However, following the guiding principle *"Worldwide at your service"* becomes increasingly difficult with a shrinking network of representations

151 Interview 1, 2, 3, 4, 5, 6
152 Interview 5, see also (Sonnleitner 2015, p. 19)
153 Interview 5, 19, see also (Sonnleitner 2015, p. 19)

which is concentrated on Europe. The MFA wants to compensate this reduction in the number of embassies and consulates general with an enormous expansion of the network of honorary consulates. As illustrated in the chapter on structural developments, the number of honorary consulates has risen by nearly one third, from around 200 to around 300 (BMAA, 1995; BMEIA, 2015a) and shall be further expanded[154]. Beyond that, in the course of consular cooperation, Austrian citizens also have the opportunity to ask embassies of other EU members for help if no Austrian representation is available[155]. Furthermore, the MFA from the beginning was convinced by the opportunity for cost reduction by cooperating with the EEAS (BMEIA, 2010, p. 264) and has an interest in transferring certain consular competences to the EEAS, especially in the area of crisis management. This approach shall provide better service for Austrian citizens in countries where Austria has no representation[156].

Hence, Austria as a small member state with limited resources is willing to give further competences to the EEAS in fields, where the management of these competences becomes increasingly difficult. At the same time the MFA highlights its special service orientation in areas, where it is able to provide comprehensive services, in order to face the growing legitimation pressure.

Economy in Austrian Bilateral Diplomacy

Supporting Austrian economy is one of the major tasks of Austrian bilateral diplomacy and continues to gain importance in the context of the MFA's modernization strategy. The influence of European integration thereby generally brings more diversification to this field of activity.

Inside the EU, the level of integration of the receiving state determines the extent to which support of Austrian economy by diplomatic representatives is necessary. In receiving states with a similar level of integration and similar standards, supportive acts of embassies are less necessary than in countries with different standards. One interviewee stated that in Western Europe major supportive acts of diplomatic representatives are rare, be-

---

154 Interview 4, 16, see also (Sonnleitner 2015, p. 19)

155 Interview 9

156 Interview 7, 13, see also (Sonnleitner 2015, p. 23)

cause the political and legal preconditions for companies are similar. Consulting activities concerning economic contractual relationships are necessary from time to time, but significantly less than in other world regions[157]. A MFA representative, who works in the field of economic relations, pointed out that there is a gap between different development standards concerning the rule of law[158]. Hence, in some areas of the EU, especially in some new member states, where legal certainty for instance is not sufficiently given, Austrian bilateral representations are concerned. In such a case not only the Foreign Trade Service of the Federal Economic Chamber is involved in supporting and advising Austrian companies, but also MFA representatives of the respective embassy might take action. Especially if stiff hierarchical structures play a significant role in the receiving state, because individuals in the rank of an ambassador are more likely to achieve goals than representatives of the Federal Economic Chamber's Foreign Trade Service. Particularly in situations where an economic issue takes on a political or legal dimension, ambassadors still are able to function as *"door-openers"* to ministries and governmental institutions[159]. In situations where Austrian companies need support, Austrian representatives often take the role of mediators between the Austrian Economic Ministry and the Economic Ministry of the receiving state[160]. A growing level of integration inside the EU, including further harmonization of economic, legal and political systems and standards, will probably diminish the importance of this function.

In third states, promoting Austrian economy is one of the most important or even the most important task of Austrian bilateral diplomacy[161]. Especially in growing economies, the economic focus is of outstanding importance. Although member states' foreign policy activities in third countries are integrated to the common EU foreign policy framework, member states or companies from member states are in competition with each other in the field of economy; for example when major contracts are awarded and companies from different EU countries do apply. Supporting efforts of Austrian companies more and more becomes a major aspect in Austrian diplomacy[162], which is also visible when looking at the MFA's modernization

157 Interview 1, see also (Sonnleitner 2015, p. 14)
158 Interview 17
159 Interview 4, 5, 9, 10, 11, 13, 19, see also (Sonnleitner 2015, p. 19)
160 Interview 4
161 Interview 7, 9, 19
162 Interview 8, 10, 13

strategy (BMEIA, 2015c). The MFA now intensively promotes its services for Austrian enterprises.

This is an interesting development in the Austrian public administration structure, because with the Foreign Trade Service of the Federal Economic Chamber, Austrian companies actually are already supported by an Austrian organization abroad. Austria works with a dual system of foreign services. The Foreign Trade Service of the Federal Economic Chamber and the representations of the Austrian MFA operate within two separated organizational networks, although according to international law, the foreign offices of the Federal Economic Chamber are part of the Austrian diplomatic service. This means that these offices are perceived as a part of the embassy in receiving states and delegates of the foreign service of the Federal Economic Chamber are accredited as Austrian diplomats in the receiving country. Still, these are two separated organizational forms, in most cases even with separated offices. Hence, these two organizations operate independently from each other, but in many cases they work together in close cooperation. The means of this cooperation differs from country to country. Most ideally, they hold strategic meetings together and conduct a division of labour, for example concerning the representation of Austria in events, the support of economic delegations or political and economic reporting[163]. According to an internal regulation between the Austrian MFA and the Federal Economic Chamber, representatives of the Federal Economic Chamber in third states are also able to attend the head of missions meetings on economic topics with the EEAS and other EU member states[164]. Foreign Trade Centres are primarily responsible for Austrian companies and supporting them in their internationalization and export efforts. Thus, Foreign Trade Centres are the first points of contact for Austrian enterprises abroad[165]. The question arises as to how the strengthened focus of the MFA on supporting Austrian companies fits into this division of labour. One MFA representative, who is concerned with economic issues, stated that the MFA does not want to enter into competition with the Federal Economic Chamber. It instead wants to highlight its ability to support Austrian enterprises, which have trouble with the institutional setting of the receiving country, for ex-

163 Interview 8
164 Interview 7
165 Interview 11

ample in legal or political terms. The interviewee also referred to the enhanced opportunities the rank of an ambassador offers when trying to get in touch with governmental representatives[166].

Thus, strengthening the support for Austrian companies in the course of the MFA's modernization strategy does not give a new function to Austrian bilateral diplomacy. This step is rather supposed to highlight the MFA's possibilities in this field of operation and to strengthen its legitimacy in times where the outcome of bilateral diplomacy becomes less visible (Sonnleitner, 2015, p. 20).

Impacts on the Profession of Diplomacy

The preceding chapters gave insights on how Austrian bilateral diplomacy changes both inside and outside the EU in the context of the country's EU membership. Tasks become more diversified and the field of operation widens. This gives rise to the question if and how these developments affect the occupational image and professional identity of Austrian diplomats.

Interviews conducted with representatives of three generations of Austrian diplomats for this investigation illustrate that there are significant differences between the professional life of diplomats today and the professional life of diplomats who started their career decades ago. EU accession thereby only is one of several aspects that influence and change the occupational image. Therefore, this chapter not only focuses on the impact of Austria's EU membership on the development of the occupational image, but will also outline other aspects that had been mentioned by interviewees as significant drivers of change in their professional life, in order to provide a comprehensive picture.

From Neutrality to European Identity

Interviewees selected from three generations of diplomats for this investigation experienced different stages of the process of European integration. Most of them started their career before Austria's accession to the EU and therefore also have pre-accession experience. 25 or 30 years ago, when many members of the diplomatic service, who are now in the rank of ambassadors, started their career, Austria's position between East and West

166 Interview 17

constituted the framework for Austrian diplomacy. A senior diplomat, who joined the MFA in 1988, pointed out that Austria's status as a neutral country still shaped the professional identity of Austrian diplomats in this period of time. The occupational image was a traditional one[167]. Thus, it is of no surprise that interviewees perceive a turnaround in the diplomatic service by 1995. One of the already retired interviewees spoke of a new diplomatic service that emerged in the context of EU accession[168]. A junior diplomat described the difference by the example of different operating principles conducted by diplomats, who were socialized in different periods of time. According to this interviewee, younger diplomats, who grew into the mode of operation conducted between the MFA and the EU, simultaneously consider processes and events in Vienna as well as in Brussels for decision making in their work. The older generation instead does not consider processes in Brussels as much, but still rather tend to orient themselves towards bilateral issues[169]. This statement is differentiated by others, who illustrate that preferences concerning a rather bilateral or a rather multilateral orientation do exist among older as well as among younger diplomats[170]. A further interviewee stated that parts of the older generation missed developments the EU has taken since Austria accessed in 1995 and are therefore unable to understand the system. Other parts of this generation, especially those who supported Austria's EU accession and participated in the accession process, became part of the system, were socialized into it and were able to become successful in it. The interviewee undermined this statement by adding that those, who faced up with the EU early, bet on the right horse[171].

These are indeed personal views that cannot simply be generalized. However, they illustrate the kind of transition the profession experienced with Austria's accession to the EU. As outlined in the preceding chapters, representing an EU member state changes the mode of how bilateral diplomacy is conducted. Outside the EU, Austria does not represent its individual foreign policy position anymore, but a compromise, which has to be found in the context of common European foreign policy making[172]. Finding this

167 Interview 6
168 Interview 19
169 Interview 26
170 Interview 26, 27
171 Interview 10
172 Interview 19, 22, 23, 26

compromise can be an exhausting and time-consuming task, including discussions focussing on single words in a statement[173]. Giving up foreign policy sovereignty in order to participate in a common European project with common European goals, leads to modified preconditions under which Austrian diplomats conduct their profession.

Different Preconditions for Conducting Diplomacy

These modified preconditions induce gradations concerning the profession inside and outside the EU. The tasks and duties of Austrian diplomats in bilateral relations become more diversified. Hence, diplomacy and the profession of Austrian diplomats obtain new dimensions.

Inside the EU, the respective receiving state gained importance. The receiving country is no longer just a state to have a certain quality of bilateral relation with, but it also might be a potential partner or potential opponent when promoting interests on the EU-level. So taking into account the EU policy focus of the receiving country became an important task of Austrian diplomats working inside the EU. It even became the most important task in areas where traditional bilateral diplomacy lost its significance, due to an advanced level of integration. Consequently, the new form of *"European Diplomacy"*, described by Paschke (2001) as well as Bátora and Hocking (2009), creates new requirements for diplomats working in the field of bilateral diplomacy. However, the rule-based legal environment for bilateral diplomacy induced by the EU (Bátora, 2005a, pp. 53-54) and the slim form of multilateral cooperation within the EU called "*Europäische Innenpolitik*" (Höll, 2002, p. 370) are so far unthreatening to the role of bilateral diplomats working in this field; they become part of it. As outlined in the preceding chapters, ongoing integration reduces the necessity for traditional tasks in bilateral diplomacy. Consequently, the occupational image of diplomats working in bilateral missions inside the EU will continue to transform. This will lead to a new role definition for diplomats in inner-EU bilateral diplomacy. They indeed are about to primarily become supporters of multilateral diplomacy. A turn that had already been suggested by Nowotny (2011, p. 273) with regard to a shift in importance from bilateral to multilateral diplomacy.

Outside the EU, in third states, a more traditional form of bilateral diplomacy is still conducted. However, operating within the triangular relation

173 Interview 22

between the receiving state, Austria and the EU in third countries, based on the quality of the bilateral relation between Austria and the receiving state as well as the EU and the receiving state, can lead to situations where Austrian diplomats have to mediate between Austria's pre-EU foreign policy orientation and a new one emerging in the context of the country's EU membership. The Austrian government generally follows a pro-European orientation, as does the Austrian MFA and so do contemporary Austrian diplomats. In specific areas, Austria's foreign policy position, however, differs from the EU-mainstream. Austria for example traditionally has close relations with Russia, which originate from the foundation of the Second Republic. The ties between the two countries are especially close in the field of economy. By 2011, Austria and Russia started a modernization partnership that should create new investment opportunities and increase exports (BMWFW, 2011). By 2013, the Austrian Ministry of Economy estimated the investment volume of this modernization partnership at 500 million euros (BMWFW, 2013). According to the Austrian Institute of Economic Research, economic consequences of the EU's sanctions against Russia and the following sanctions of Russia against the EU are rather low for Austria, because the goods affected by the sanctions only represent a small part of Austria's export volume. Nevertheless, the Institute of Economic Research perceives negative effects caused by a deterioration of trade relations that arose in the context of the diplomatic dispute on Crimea (Christen, Fritz, Huber, & Streicher, 2014, p. 1). Austria therefore counteracted the EU's strategy of isolating Russia by accepting a visit of Vladimir Putin in June 2014, at a time when the conflict between Russia and Ukraine had already escalated. The story behind this visit is that Austrian President Heinz Fischer visited Russia in May 2011 and responded with a return invitation. This return visit had to be postponed several times and Austria did not cancel the invitation in the context of the Crimea crisis. So at the end of June 2014, Vladimir Putin made an official working visit to Austria, spent a day in Vienna and met President Heinz Fischer, Chancellor Werner Faymann and held a speech at the Austrian Federal Economic Chamber. Most notably, the United States expressed their displeasure with Austria's behaviour in this situation. In the EU, Austria was reproached to support Putin's purpose to divide the EU. Sweden's Foreign Minister Carl Bildt criticised Austria's solo effort. In defending Austria's approach, Foreign Minister Kurz referred to the country's status of neutrality and pointed out that it is important to keep the channels of discussion open and a neutral country like Austria is able to offer these channels. He further saw a need to point out that Austria always followed a straight path concerning the conflict between

Russia and Ukraine, with the primary goal to offer a place for dialogue (Kramar, 2014). This defence strategy has an economic policy, a domestic policy as well as a foreign policy dimension. As outlined in the chapter on Austria's neutrality, the status of neutrality is well-accepted by the Austrian population and its normative and identity-promoting power in Austria's national identity construction remains relatively stable, even after 20 years of EU membership. So from a domestic policy perspective, reverting to Austria's neutrality is a useful instrument to explain Austria's conduct in this matter to its population. Neutrality is similarly used to justify Austria's approach to maintain its well-established foreign policy and economic relations to Russia. The country's handling of this situation illustrates the challenging moments, which can develop in the context of national foreign policy identity and EU membership. This approach had even been strengthened by 2017, after Sebastian Kurz took over the People's Party and won the general election. He then quit the tradition of grand coalitions and formed a coalition with the right-wing Freedom Party. Concerning EU issues, the two parties followed different approaches in the past. While the People's Party is pro-EU oriented, the Freedom Party had so far been sceptical towards the EU. In the course of coalition talks, the People's Party was able to transfer its approach to the government program, where it is mentioned that Austria is an integral part of the EU. However, Austria's neutrality is referred to as important identity-building factor, which has to be considered in the conclusion of international agreements. Beyond that, the government program indeed further refers to Austria's past as a neutral state between East and West and pursuing a policy of détente between Russia and the West is defined as a central goal for Austria's foreign policy (ÖVP/FPÖ, 2017, p. 22). Hence, more challenging moments in the area of tension between Austria's national foreign policy identity and its EU membership are expectable.

A further example for a field of tensions between good bilateral relations to the receiving country and diffident relations between the receiving state and the EU in which Austria operates is Switzerland. Austrian bilateral missions also represent the country's EU membership, but in the case of Switzerland, long lasting excellent bilateral relations between the two countries dominate the interaction. One interviewee outlined that Switzerland brings certain expectations to Austria in terms of understanding for Switzerland's difficult situation in its interaction with the EU and also concerning support and assistance by Austria in this situation[174]. In such a constellation, norms and values linked to different relations and based on different foundations

174 Interview 8

do collide. Foreign policy, the diplomatic service and the respective representatives have to sensitively manoeuvre between long-established bilateral ties and Austria's commitment to a common European foreign policy (Sonnleitner, 2015, p. 17).

Austrian neutrality is not a significant factor for the conduct of bilateral diplomacy in most third countries, but in some it can be. According to two interviewees, Austria's status of neutrality often is misinterpreted, but often in a positive way for Austria[175]. In such cases, certain norms are ascribed to Austrian neutrality that rather have no connection to its legal status. It can be an advantage not to be predominantly identified with the EU, but as a neutral state, especially if the relation between the EU and the receiving state is tense. In situations like this, Austrian embassies are in a more favourable position and do have easier access to governmental information and governmental institutions[176]. However, also in a broader multilateral context these norms ascribed to Austria's neutrality can play a role. One interviewee for example stated that Austria is perceived as an *"honest broker"* in negotiation contexts and as neutral in the sense of a mediating actor, who does not primarily pursue self-interests in every situation[177]. Another however pointed out that Austria's status of neutrality is rather harmful in the EU, because it is perceived as a lack of solidarity by some member states[178]. However, even in the EU certain actors exist who would like to see Austria in an active foreign policy position again, similar to during the era Kreisky, for example in the field of Middle East policy. One interviewee brought up an example where an EU member state representative positively mentioned Austria's past foreign policy initiatives in this field and expressed the wish that Austria should become more active in this issue again[179]. An already retired diplomat mentioned similar concerns raised by representatives of Middle Eastern countries during his period in office, who referred to the Kreisky era and Austria's active approach on neutrality that time[180].

Whether implementing a new form of active neutrality is feasible remains to be questionable when taking Austria's budget expenditures in the field of foreign and security policy into account. However, the EU frame-

175 Interview 6, 11
176 Interview 11, 14
177 Interview 22, see also (Sonnleitner 2015, p. 18)
178 Interview 6
179 Interview 26
180 Interview 19, see also (Sonnleitner 2015, p. 18)

work offers the opportunity to conduct a similar form of soft power diplomacy in a broader, more powerful framework, if a country is able to upload its ideas to the EU foreign policy level (Sonnleitner, 2015, pp. 18-19). Austria had already been able to do so in the case of Balkan countries, where it took a supportive role. Austria supported Croatia in its accession efforts and also supports Albania in its rapprochement to the EU. Although Austria is a small actor in this framework, it is a major player for countries that benefit from its support. This kind of engagement raises Austria's visibility on the multilateral level and further strengthens bilateral ties between Austria and these countries. Being perceived as a supporter enhances the status the receiving state accredits to Austrian members in the diplomatic corps, what facilitates the access to political leaders and information[181].

New Professional Roles in Bilateral Diplomacy

The preceding assumptions illustrated that Austrian diplomats currently work in a highly complex and diversified field, where not only roles between different actors are negotiated and renegotiated, but where the diplomatic service is about to redefine its role as well. Thereby, the MFA's modernization strategy sets the direction for this redefinition. Austria's expertise on Balkan issues shall be maintained and further enhanced. Beyond that, all EU competences - bilateral and multilateral - are now bundled in one division (BMEIA, 2015c). Pooling these knowledge resources can be seen as a reaction to the necessity for small member states to occupy expertise niches, in order play a role in decision making processes in European foreign policy.

So after 20 years of EU membership, an adaptation process was initiated by the Austrian MFA that reflects the necessities created by European integration. The visibility of traditional forms of diplomacy is about to decrease. Inside the EU for instance by the decline of bilateral diplomatic visits. Outside the EU by the representation of common positions by the EEAS. Such developments increase the pressure on the profession of diplomacy to legitimate itself (Sonnleitner, 2015, p. 20). Representing the state as a diplomat, for many citizens is still primarily linked to elegant buildings, cars, lifestyles as well as parking privileges[182]. Former Austrian diplomat Eva

181 Interview 10
182 Interview 5, 6, 18, 19, 22, 24, 25, 26, 27, 28, see also (Sonnleitner 2015, p. 19)

Nowotny (2006, p. 35) describes the public image of diplomats as one of *"neatly dressed, overprivileged and underemployed champagne drinkers"*. Assessing the added value created by the work done by diplomats is rather difficult[183], and the added value of the work done by the MFA is a lot harder to quantify than in the case of other ministries[184]. There is no clear job description for diplomats and also no visible outcome produced by diplomats. The growing demand for transparency in democratic societies creates the pressure to prove, if embassies provide a kind of added value to the Austrian society. Beyond that, interviewees speak of growing envy in the Austrian society, or generally in Western societies concerning the privileges ascribed to members of the diplomatic service[185]. The economic crisis and tight national budgets strengthen this tendency. One interviewee outlined that diplomats now need to show a certain restraint, in order to avoid creating resentments against the profession[186]. The maximum size of residences, the homes and representational buildings of ambassadors, for instance had been reduced to 400m^2; some buildings however still are bigger[187]. But many embassy buildings and residences are owned by Austria for already quite a while. Thus, buying or renting other and more modest facilities would not necessarily be cheaper for taxpayers. Beyond that, several interviewees, both younger and older, stated that to their opinion a certain standard of representation has to be maintained, in order to properly conduct diplomacy[188]. Representational acts, events and invitations are still perceived as essential elements for establishing networks and matchmaking in politics, economy and culture in the receiving state[189]. Thereby, especially interpersonal communication is classified as an important factor[190]. Budgets for representation are about to decrease, but the diplomatic corps still has certain codes that determine how representation is conducted. This circumstance might lead to tense situations. One representative of the oldest generation

183 Interview 5, 6, 18, 27, see also (Sonnleitner 2015, p. 19)
184 Interview 22, see also (Sonnleitner 2015, p. 19)
185 Interview 6, 21
186 Interview 6
187 Interview 5, 6
188 Interview 5, 22, 24, 27, 28
189 Interview 4, 5, 9, 20, 27
190 Interview 4, 9, 20, 26

pointed out that due to the lower representation budgets available to diplomats now, some see the need to privately contribute, in order to not be ashamed of being stingy[191].

Younger diplomats are well aware of the changing circumstances and perceive their future occupational image as very different from that of the last generations. The youngest generation of diplomats is socialized into a different working culture, shaped by decreasing budgets and the pressure to legitimate themselves. Therefore, this generation is about to follow different attitudes. One interviewee from the youngest generation stated that the profession is about to normalize and diplomats must come down to earth because privileges do not matter anymore[192]. Another interviewee pointed out that the decreasing number of employees leads to new models of how to conduct diplomacy. Regarding future prospects, this interviewee expects to live the life of a so-called *laptop ambassador* or *roving ambassador*. In this occupational image, not only representational elements are missing, but also a broad variety of tasks have to be covered by the respective diplomat, even concerning administrative issues[193]. A third interviewee from the youngest generation described the difference between former generations of Austrian diplomats and new ones by different understandings of the profession. Formerly, the understanding of the profession had been focused on the aspects of policy and representation. Now, more flexible and service-oriented approaches are about to develop[194].

This goes in line with the MFA's reaction to growing legitimation pressure on the profession, caused by tight budgets and decreasing visibility of the outcome of diplomacy in the context of European integration. The Austrian MFA responds by emphasizing certain services that cannot be provided by the EU. The EEAS so far does not offer consular services for EU citizens and does not support individual economic actors of member states (Sonnleitner, 2015, p. 20). Services for Austrian citizens as well as for Austrian enterprises are especially highlighted in the MFA's modernization strategy (BMEIA, 2015c). Diplomats from the older and middle generation however stated that providing support for Austrian citizens abroad had always been an important issue in the Second Republic's diplomatic service

191 Interview 21
192 Interview 26
193 Interview 28
194 Interview 29

and has a long tradition[195]. One of the interviewees, who spent most of his career in the Austrian diplomatic service before Austria's accession to the EU, pointed out that already at the beginning of his career, Foreign Minister Kirchschläger insistently reminded diplomats to never mistreat Austrian citizens[196]. Nevertheless, the growing legitimation pressure further enforces the importance of consular duties; also as supporting Austrian citizens in crisis situations promises positive news coverage for the Austrian MFA[197]. Therefore, this generates a visible outcome of the work of Austrian diplomats. As mentioned in the chapter on consular services, the MFA has improved its support for Austrian citizens abroad by developing online services that facilitate the communication between Austrians abroad and the respective embassy or the MFA. Most interviewees highlighted the importance of these developments for the MFA's legitimacy and the legitimacy of the diplomatic service in Austria's public administration framework. Nevertheless, one interviewee criticized these developments, as with this service approach, more work has to be done with less personnel resources. In the past, embassies had been closed on weekends and in the evening and had not been accessible to Austrian citizens during this time. The advancement of communication technologies enabled the MFA to establish a 24-hour-on-call-service and embassy employees now have to share stand-by service hours at nights, weekends and bank holidays, where they carry an emergency mobile telephone. At any time, one of the embassy employees can be contacted by telephone. The respective employee must be able to come to the embassy within a short time window and support Austrian citizens in cases of emergency, for example if a temporary passport is needed. Due to the fact that personnel resources are about to decrease, individual employees become affected more often by on-call-service duties[198]. Furthermore, in the MFA an on-call-service had likewise been established. The interviewee explained that in earlier times, usually only real cases of emergency were reported to this service. With easier access to communication technologies, for example by the MFA's *Foreign Service App*, the calls of Austrian citizens multiplied and therefore also more non-emergency cases, like unsatisfactory hotel rooms, are reported to the MFA[199].

195 Interview 5, 18
196 Interview 18
197 Interview 19
198 Interview 25
199 Interview 25

Efforts to strengthen the MFA's service orientation not only become obvious in the field of consular services, but also in the field of economy, as outlined before in the chapter on this topic. The growing importance of economic issues and economic policy issues in Austrian diplomacy is challenging for some members of the Austrian diplomatic service because they have no economic education or economic background[200]. So far applying for the MFA's diplomatic service had been possible for graduates from studies of law, economy and political sciences, as well as for graduates from diplomatic academies (BMEIA, 2017b). In the context of the MFA's modernization strategy, the admission requirements for the diplomatic service had been loosened and the selection procedure now is open for graduates from all disciplines in order to broaden the professional expertise in the Austrian diplomatic service (BMEIA, 2015c). There are no statistics available on the educational backgrounds of Austrian diplomats currently working in the MFA, but according to an MFA representative, who works in the field of staff development, at present, one third of Austrian diplomats holds a degree in law[201]. One interviewee coming from this educational background hinted at the fact that with the exception of the youngest generation, Austrian diplomats are insufficiently educated in the field of economy. Thereby, the interviewee especially mentioned missing knowledge on Austria's SME landscape and the economic interests of Austrian companies[202]. The MFA reacts to this issue by strengthening the ties between the younger generation of Austrian diplomats and employees in the foreign service of the Federal Economic Chamber. Future representatives of both services shall get to know each other at an early stage of their career and shall build networks[203]. So the interconnectedness between the two services will further increase in the future and probably further enrich each other, as representatives of the Federal Economic Chamber do have specific economic knowledge and MFA representatives, especially ambassadors, still benefit from the remaining power of the status of diplomacy in many world regions.

The MFA is generally interested in connecting its young generation with individuals from other Austrian organizations working in international contexts. Young diplomats get the chance to take part in a cross mentoring pro-

200 Interview 6, 17
201 Interview 16
202 Interview 6
203 Interview 16

gramme of the Austrian Republic as well as in the EU's European Diplomatic Programme[204]. The last programme mentioned had been developed to create networks among diplomats in the EU, in order to strengthen the European dimension in nation state diplomacy. Participants are diplomats from the member states, the EEAS, the European Commission as well as the Council Secretariat (EEAS, 2016).

Beyond that, the European dimension of diplomacy also shall be further considered in the MFA's selection procedure. In the course of the MFA's modernization strategy, the diplomatic service had not only been opened to graduates from all disciplines, but it had also been decided that selection committees shall be supported by external experts from the EEAS (BMEIA, 2015c). As early as the selection procedure, the MFA is interested in selecting staff members who fulfil the necessary conditions to succeed in Europeanized forms of diplomacy, or even succeed as national diplomats in the EEAS.

Consulting external assessors might also be a reaction to continuing criticism concerning the MFA's selection procedure. This criticism is based on the assumption of easier accessibility of diplomatic posts for persons with a certain family or political background. By 2015, Austrian journalist Moritz Moser wrote two articles dealing with family and other affiliations in the Austrian MFA, where he collected statements from diplomats, graduates of the Austrian Diplomatic Academy as well as former trainees in the MFA on this issue. According to an anonymous source, 20% to 30% of the posts available are occupied due to family relationships (Moser, 2015a). The articles contain a variety of statements reaching from the classification of the selection procedure as outrageous, to statements classifying the procedure as fair and transparent, or at least more fair and transparent than in other Austrian ministries (Moser, 2015a, 2015b). Occasionally also diplomats who were interviewed for this investigation mentioned external influences on the selection of Austrian diplomats, while especially the necessity of a certain party affiliation was highlighted[205].

Using external expertise for selecting suitable candidates might weaken this criticism. If Austrian national diplomats who are temporarily working in the EEAS are going to take part in the selection procedures, they will be able to select suitable candidates for the demands of the MFA as well as for the demands of *"European Diplomacy"*, but it will not necessarily change the reputation of the MFA's selection procedure. Beyond that, one of the

204 Interview 16
205 Interview 18, 26

interviewees, who spoke about the selection procedure, mentioned that although only very few people are selected for the diplomatic service, there are repeatedly selected candidates who do not fulfil the full range of necessary competences, especially in the field of social and communication skills[206]. Here, the MFA wants to counteract. According to the modernization strategy, selection procedures shall pay more attention to social competences, communication skills as well as IT knowledge (BMEIA, 2015c).

Hence, the MFA adapts to other changing circumstances than those caused by European integration as well. Excellent communication skills, especially in intercultural and transcultural contexts, have always been an important element of the profession of diplomacy. However, the target groups of these communication efforts become more diversified. Due to Austria's strong service orientation, political and governmental representatives are not the only individuals anymore with whom diplomats are in contact. Representatives of the Austrian economy and Austrian enterprises are going to be contact partners more often in the future as the MFA started to promote its strengthened economy focus among Austrian companies. At the Ambassadors Conference in Vienna in September 2014, public events were held for the first time and representatives of the Austrian economy were also invited (BMEIA, 2014a). Moreover, in April 2015 representatives of the platform *Leitbetriebe Austria*, which encompasses leading Austrian companies, were invited to the MFA (Leitbetriebe Austria, 2015). By 2016, the MFA, the Federal Economic Chamber and the Federation of Austrian Industry launched the so-called *Austrian Leadership Programs*. In the course of this visitors programme, young international leaders from countries of interest for Austria in political and economic terms are invited, in order to grow a network and strengthen relationships (BMEIA, 2016).

Due to a strong service orientation in the field of consular duties, diplomats also must be able to communicate with people from different social backgrounds and with different personalities, especially in situations of crisis. One interviewee brought up the example of homeless Austrians stranded in neighbouring countries, who have to get the same attention as high-ranking politicians[207]. Actors have also become more diversified on the political level. The necessity to promote own interests not only enhances the need for public diplomacy among political representatives in the receiving state, but also among representatives of the civil society. Therefore, the

206 Interview 26

207 Interview 22

necessity of communication skills in the profession of diplomacy is not limited anymore to negotiation contexts, interpersonal communication or speaking in front of an audience. Today diplomats also have to be able to distribute their messages and statements via media channels. This happens via traditional channels like newspapers or TV, but increasingly also via the easier more accessible modern channels, like social networks and new media. Hence, diplomats have to know how to present information and how to present themselves in different kinds of media. Therefore, the MFA not only will consider communication skills of candidates in future selection procedures, but also their IT skills.

Such skills are also of relevance for diplomats in service and are taught in courses and continuing education programs. Interviewees however still argued in favour of a reinforced focus on social networking and new media[208]. Thereby, a generation gap is perceived between junior and senior diplomats. One of the younger interviewees mentioned that many of those, who are not digital natives, obviously do have problems with this new form of communication[209]. This is confirmed by a senior diplomat, who points out that less familiarity with new and social media is not the only reason for not using these facilities. The interviewee hints at the fact that in the generation of senior diplomats the question is discussed as to whether this form of communication is compatible with diplomatic work, especially concerning the issue of secrecy and the issue of respectful interaction with the receiving state. This discussion includes questions such as if information given in a confidential setting might be commented upon in social media channels, or if diplomats can give public statements on the country they currently are stationed in without causing negative effects for their diplomatic work. Topics like this are currently discussed in the MFA and are considered in education measures[210]. Sensitizing representatives for how to speak on behalf of the MFA in social media channels becomes a main issue in the MFA's media training efforts[211].

Generally, the current information revolution is perceived as one of the most influential driving forces, or even the most influential driving force behind change in the profession of diplomacy[212]. Individuals are challenged

208 Interview 2, 6, 16, 29
209 Interview 27
210 Interview 6
211 Interview 16
212 Interview 3, 7, 9, 14, 18, 19, 20, 22, 25, 27, 28

by new demands of how to conduct diplomacy. Beyond that, the occupational image itself as well as processes in the MFA do change. However, this is not a new phenomenon. Adaptation processes in MFAs and the profession of diplomacy, caused by new information technologies or easier ways to travel, had for example already been visible during the industrial revolution (Jones, 1983, pp. 116-120). Bátora (2008, p. 50) states that this transformation could be described as

> *"a gradual change of the role of the ambassador from an independent and influential figure with a great leeway to conduct foreign policy towards a 'self-effacing, subordinate and anonymous' (Jones, 1983, p. 116) official ready to execute the policy of the foreign minister."*

Statements made by the oldest generation of diplomats interviewed for his investigation illustrate that this development continued in the 20th century. One interviewee, who started his career in the 1960s and often worked in long-distance destinations from Austria, explained that a telegram took three days that time and getting a connection to make a telephone call took hours. Today permanent interaction is common. The interviewee described the current situation like being next door. He further stated that new technologies are not the only reason for intensified communication. Physical communication possibilities between the MFA and its representatives abroad increased as well, because travelling became much easier and more frequent[213]. The interviewee assessed this development during his career in a similar way as Jones (1983, p. 116) and Bátora (2008, p. 50) describe the change in the occupational image of ambassadors caused by new communication and travel possibilities during the industrial revolution. He pointed out that the independence of diplomats changed, as in earlier times large distances and limited communication possibilities enhanced the need to make decisions independently from the MFA. According to the interviewee, this could have turned out all right. If not, the MFA in Vienna may did not even notice. Furthermore, he added his perception of today's totally different situation, where secretaries type every tone spoken by diplomats in negotiations into their notebooks in order to check and recheck positions with the MFA[214].

New information technologies not only change the role of diplomats, but they also influence the balance between the MFA and its embassies

213 Interview 20
214 Interview 20

(Nowotny, 2006, pp. 31-32). One of the representatives of the oldest generation stated that when he entered the diplomatic service, a tally was kept of the reports received by the MFA from its embassies. The ambassador got a reminder if no report had been received for a long period of time. These reports were regularly written in literary style and particularly well written and funny ones were passed on to the minister[215]. A similar picture is drawn by former Austrian diplomat Eva Nowotny in a book chapter describing the transformation of the Austrian foreign service:

> *"In matters of relating to official business, communication other than via the official hierarchic channels was not only frowned upon, but it was also punished. Truly relevant were only things that happened within the confines of this monastic entity. Other state bureaucracies were automatically assumed to be of a lesser kind of negligible relevance. The role model was the elegant, slightly cynical ambassador writing, every two months or so, witty, highly readable, and quotable reports based on periodic encounters with the political director of the Foreign Ministry of his receiving state."* (Nowotny, 2006, p. 27)

Nowotny (2006, p. 33) further states that this form of reporting had rather been a proof of the author's writing skills than an information base to act upon. This form of reporting meanwhile made way for an issue-related approach on diplomatic reporting in the Austrian MFA that shall provide guiding principles. However, interviewees state that today's fast and worldwide accessibility of information, produced by media, diminishes the relevance of this information service by embassies, as it can be easily done by the MFA itself. Small missions with few personnel resources, which many Austrian embassies are, cannot keep up with the research capacities of media companies. Hence, embassies lost their monopoly on information from the receiving states[216].

Nowotny (2006, pp. 31-32) points out that the relationship between the Austrian MFA and its embassies generally changed. In the past, diplomatic posts abroad at embassies had been regarded as more desirable for diplomats, not only due to extended privileges and supplementary income, but also because *"working abroad was considered to be the true core of diplomacy"*. Now this dividing line blurred. The mobility among diplomats working in the MFA is about to rise. According to Nowotny (2006, p. 32), each week 20% of Austrian diplomats, working in the MFA, are on business

215 Interview 18
216 Interview 4, 7, 9, 18, 19, 22, 27

trips and missions. Beyond that, privileges of diplomats working abroad became less, because tight budgets restrict the opportunities and due to closer interaction with the MFA embassies lost some of their independence. Ambassadors at embassies now, for example, are advised to prepare working concepts in order to present concrete initiatives to the MFA[217]. Although the MFA seems to be less dependent on the work of bilateral missions in certain fields, this work does not necessarily lose its significance. The chapters on bilateral diplomacy inside and outside the EU illustrated that new tasks are arising in the EU framework. In particular, the promotion of Austrian interests and public diplomacy gained importance.

Growing legitimation pressure also requires the MFA and its embassies to present their work to the Austrian population. Social media channels are an easy and accessible way to do so. Hence, diplomats have to deal with a broader range of target groups as well as with the need to learn adequate forms of communication for each target group. For this new form of diplomacy, different skills and different approaches are required, which leads to the development of a new kind of diplomat in the Austrian diplomatic service.

Reflecting these developments steers the focus towards the perception of the persons who are affected, and their opinions on necessary skills to conduct diplomacy. When Austrian diplomats in this investigation were asked to describe what diplomacy is to them, traditional ascriptions, like negotiation, finding compromise as well as having tact and instinct, were named by representatives of all three generations[218]. One representative of the oldest generation especially highlighted aspects that can be related to the Second Republic's foreign policy effort before Austria's EU accession, when the country followed a different role concept than it does today. This interviewee named peace keeping and improving international relations as well as international understanding as central functions of diplomacy, and further stated that diplomacy is also a task of fixing errors made by politicians and military representatives in international relations[219]. These statements represent a globally oriented approach on diplomacy, which goes in line with Austria's past diplomatic identity as a mediator in international relations. Several other interviewees highlighted interpersonal communication

217 Interview 5
218 Interview 19, 22, 24, 29
219 Interview 19

as well as networking and matchmaking as essential elements of diplomacy[220]. Some however follow a rather rationalist approach and named promoting own interests as central task of diplomacy[221]. All of the aspects described so far are rather traditional components of the profession of diplomacy and are covered by the educational system in the field of diplomacy.

New elements described by interviewees are, for example, the need to familiarize oneself with different and new forms of communication or the ability to conduct management skills[222]. Today, management approaches from the private business sector become popular in the field of public administration as well, but they are still underrepresented in the education and further education system of the MFA. One of the interviewees from the youngest generation mentioned that Austrian diplomats are not sufficiently prepared for the leadership responsibilities that the profession involves. The interviewee compared leading an embassy with leading a business, a task for which profound knowledge on the circumstances in the receiving state is not a sufficient enough basis. Certain skills, like staff management and leadership competences would be especially needed, but are neglected in education and training in the Austrian MFA, but not only in the MFA, also in the EEAS, as shown by a study of Duke (2015, p. 412). This, according to the interviewee, is a topic of discussion among younger diplomats[223]. It is of interest in this context that also those divisions of the MFA that handle management and administrative issues as well as human resources, are occupied with diplomats who are subject to the rotating system and were selected due to certain criteria of relevance, specifically defined for the MFA's selection procedure. The selection procedure still mainly focuses on traditional elements of diplomacy and does not develop towards the areas just mentioned. Hence, there is few expertise available on these topics in the MFA. The possibility to generate special knowledge in one of these fields is limited, because the persons in charge do change every four years. The interviewee suggested to have one or two experts for human resources in the MFA, who do not rotate, but stay in Vienna and are able to further develop this field. In saying this, the interviewee advocated for better career guidance and more feedback, also because the culture of communication among diplomats in the Austrian MFA rather is of a distant nature[224].

220 Interview 4, 5, 9, 20, 26
221 Interview 5, 8, 24, 28
222 Interview 5, 16, 22, 24, 26
223 Interview 26
224 Interview 26

A similar picture as drawn by this interviewee had already been shown in an evaluation of the organization of Austrian foreign policy from 1983, conducted by Kneucker (1983, p. 54). He stated that organizational goals and formal structures are overestimated, while little attention is given to the importance of other aspects that shape an organization, like certain styles and traditions in staff development, leadership, training, informal relations and well-practiced behaviour.

This interviewee therefore generally raised the question as to whether the rotating system is practicable in all areas of the MFA's organizational set-up. Introducing non-diplomats to certain fields of the organizational set-up could have lasting impact on the profession, as exclusivity and seclusion in the diplomatic service could suffer and the associated working culture would probably change on a large scale if experts from certain management fields start to shape the MFA's organization and staff constitution. However, when considering that this suggestion was brought up by a young diplomat, who mentioned that it is topic of discussion in this generation, it becomes evident that changes like this might be implemented in the future. Opening up the diplomatic service to this kind of expertise would change the MFA's organizational culture, because having one or more non-rotating divisions in the organizational set-up, with persons from specific educational backgrounds, would create different dynamics. Furthermore, the professional identity could also be influenced, as the rather closed sphere of the diplomatic service would further open up and accept influences from different disciplines. The upcoming years will show whether the MFA will initiate a further modernization strategy, which encompasses such steps.

Beyond the aspect of management and leadership, the field of crisis management had similarly been mentioned in the context of new challenges for the profession of diplomacy. Due to growing instability in international relations and a growing number of receiving states that are in a situation of crisis or potentially are in danger to get in a situation of crisis, a certain flexibility and resistance is required when working in these countries. Interviewees stated that this is an aspect diplomats must be prepared for[225]. A MFA representative working in the context of human resources stated that the MFA still is at the very beginning in implementing crisis management techniques to its training programme. An obstacle are the costs of external expertise in this field which can hardly be afforded by the MFA[226].

225 Interview 16, 24
226 Interview 16

A further changing aspect mentioned by interviewees which influences the profession of diplomacy is the rising number of women in the diplomatic service. The MFA is willing to further increase the number of female diplomats in its organization and now commissions in the MFA's selection procedures shall consist of 50% female commission members (BMEIA, 2015c). Supporting career paths of women in the public sector is not a particularly new phenomenon, as the public sector in Austria has rather been a forerunner in this field, compared to many areas of the private sector. By 2015, women were represented with 48,3% in the MFA's staff composition. The rate is still lower in the diplomatic service, 35,6% of Austria's diplomatic staff are women (BMEIA, 2015a, p. 304). A growing number of women in the diplomatic service is a further promoter of change in the occupational image because until not very long ago, gender role definitions in diplomacy had been clearly defined. If one regards traditional images of the profession of diplomacy, male diplomats, accompanied by their spouses and probably their children, had been the most common constellation within the diplomatic corps. Thereby, spouses had and often still have a special role and representational function in the diplomatic service[227]. One interviewee jokingly stated that the ambassador's wife was administering the ambassador's residence like a board and lodging business[228]. This traditional picture is in the process of changing, as according to interviewees, husbands or partners of female diplomats are rather not willing to overtake this role or even to follow to the receiving country[229], which challenges the occupational image on two dimensions. On the one hand, diplomatic representation is about to transform, because partner and family contexts in representation fade into the background. On the other hand, the social environment provided by the family, probably constituting some continuity and facilitating the familiarization with continuously changing work environments, partly disappears. One interviewee pointed out that female diplomats today take a high risk of staying alone against their will[230]. However, this is not an exclusive problem of female diplomats. Especially in the younger generation, well-educated partners of female and male diplomats often do not want to sacrifice their career in order to follow their partner and change their home and job every four years. Such situations cause conflicts in partnerships and

227 Interview 20, 22, 23
228 Interview 22
229 Interview 19, 22, 24
230 Interview 22

the divorce rate in the Austrian diplomatic service is above the average in Austria[231]. The MFA has to face up to these new challenges, especially in terms of employee satisfaction. Interviewees stated that the human resources department tries to consider personal life situations if this is possible[232]. Nonetheless, the staff committee sees a need to more suitably considering these changing conditions and tries to enforce the discussion on reconciling work and family life in the diplomatic service[233].

This chapter illustrated that several different aspects currently challenge and change the occupational image of Austrian diplomats. Influences of European integration thereby only represent one of several areas, in which certain developments affect the profession. The information revolution, economization, legitimation pressure as well as societal change also challenge the occupational image on a large scale. Nevertheless, EU membership and the necessity to adjust the bilateral diplomatic conduct to the new circumstances triggered a substantial shift that leads to differentiation and changing dynamics in the profession. This does not only affect diplomatic representatives of member states, but the diplomatic corps itself as well.

The last chapter of this work will summarize and discuss the research results outlined in the preceding chapters and presents concluding remarks.

231 Interview 22, 26, 27
232 Interview 19, 24, 26, 27, 28
233 Interview 27

Discussion and Conclusion

This book focused on the question of how the conduct of bilateral diplomacy is influenced by the process of European integration, illustrated by the example of Austria. The first part of this work concentrated on theorizing diplomacy and its change in the context of the European Union. The investigation followed the perception of diplomacy being an institution and used elements of several theoretical approaches that argue in this sense. MFAs thereby represent the common organizational framework to support the conduct of diplomacy in the Westphalian system of states. Modern diplomacy is inseparably linked to this organizational framework, and empirical access to the institution of diplomacy is possible through investigating the organization. Thus, regarding changing processes in MFAs offers conclusions on how the institution of diplomacy is about to change in the context of contemporary developments.

This book is a step in that direction and presents adaptation processes in the organizational framework and organizational culture of the Austrian MFA. The aim was to evaluate how the role of the Austrian MFA is changing in the context of Austria's EU membership. Conducting an in-depth investigation of a single MFA, concerning changing processes in bilateral relations in the context of European integration, against the background of institutionalist and organizational approaches, can serve as a starting point for similar investigations in the future. Comparing a number of surveys of this kind offers to give insights on how MFAs in the EU generally develop in the context of European integration, which also allows a forecast on implications for the institution of diplomacy itself.

Methodologically, this work followed a case study approach. In using *"pattern matching technique"* (Yin, 2009, pp. 136-141), empirical data was compared with predicted patterns. These patterns were constructed as ideal-types, which are based on theoretical assumptions, previous studies and preliminary observations. Due to the fact that bilateral diplomacy is exposed to different influential factors inside and outside the EU, these two levels were investigated apart from each other. Thus, for each of the two levels, different development patterns had been defined, which are outlined in detail in the chapter on the case of the Austrian MFA.

The research design of this work derives from elements institutions consist of, based on the underlying theoretical approaches used. Results are based upon the investigation of three central elements: the structure of the Austrian MFA, tasks and working procedures as well as the occupational image and professional identity of Austrian diplomats. The first element, structure, is represented by the historical development and the legal framework as well as the organizational set-up, infrastructure and staff development of the Austrian MFA. Concerning the second element, tasks and working procedures, developments in significant divisions of the MFA as well as in selected missions inside and outside the EU were considered. The third level focused on attitudes of Austrian diplomats towards their occupational image as well as norms and values related to the occupational image. Documentation and qualitative interviews were used complementarily in this work. Details on the research design are outlined in the chapter on the case of the Austrian MFA.

The preceding chapters displayed the results of the investigation by first illustrating developments and changes in the Austrian MFA and adaptation processes in tasks and working procedures related to inner-EU bilateral diplomacy as well as to bilateral relations to third states. Afterwards, specific tasks of bilateral diplomacy were depicted, like consular services and promoting Austrian culture and economy. Finally, developments in the occupational image and professional identity of Austrian diplomats were outlined.

Direct and Indirect Effects on the Structural Level

The first element that was investigated, namely developments in the structure of the Austrian MFA, has shown that during the first 20 years of Austria's EU membership the internal organizational set-up in total remained to be relatively stable. Adaptations related to the EU were mainly reduced to a single division which continuously adapted to the changing needs for cooperation and interaction with the EU. A more comprehensive shift was implemented by 2015, in the course of a modernization strategy, which hints at the fact that the long lasting stability of the organizational set-up can rather be ascribed to a certain omission to adapt than a missing necessity to do so. The modernization strategy had the aim to visualize the emphases of the MFA's work in its organizational set-up, as outlined in the chapter on structural developments (BMEIA, 2015c).

With regard to the field of tasks and working procedures, it becomes obvious that processes of adaptation in the context of Austria's EU membership did occur on a larger scale on this level, but had not been implemented to the organizational set-up in an appropriate manner for long. Therefore, the current process of transition in the Austrian MFA reflects developments that have been triggered by European integration. Besides pooling all bilateral and multilateral EU-related issues in one division, the MFA focused in particular on highlighting and visualizing its service approach. It renamed its Division on Legal and Consular Affairs and added the MFA's services for Austrian enterprises to this division. The new Service Division now encompasses all departments dealing with issues concerning Austrian citizens and Austrian enterprises. Service orientation had always played a major role in the MFA's general direction, not just since the modernization strategy was implemented, but already before the organization operated under the slogan *"Worldwide at your service"*. Selecting this focus can be interpreted as a strategy to face the disappearing visibility of traditional forms of bilateral diplomacy in the context of EU membership. Inside the EU, traditional rites of the institution of diplomacy, which usually attract media and public attention, like bilateral state visits, became less important. Outside the EU, participating in common European foreign policy making represses individual Austrian foreign policy activities. These developments reduce the public visibility of the work done by the Austrian MFA.

Reduced visibility, tight budgets and growing public interest in transparency concerning the spending of taxpayers' money enhances the pressure on the MFA to legitimate itself in the Austrian public administration network (Sonnleitner, 2015, p. 20). Suchmann (1995) describes three forms of legitimacy, as outlined in the chapter on theorizing diplomacy. The MFA is not losing its pragmatic legitimacy, which is based on compliance with rules and regulations, but it loses some of its moral and cognitive legitimacy. Moral legitimacy is achieved by acting in accordance with accepted norms and values. Norms and values concerning the spending of taxpayers' money are seemingly about to change in the context of the financial and economic crisis. As outlined in the display of results in the chapter on the profession of diplomacy, diplomats are more and more confronted with resentments, caused by clichés concerning the conveniences of the diplomatic life style. Although the MFA has to cope with budget cuts and has had to adapt its mode of operation to the new circumstances, the general perception of diplomacy being a profession that provides several advantages, paid by taxpayers, will probably remain unchanged for a while. Cognitive legitimacy is based on the society's acceptance of the goals of the organization as appropriate and desirable. In this field the MFA loses legitimacy due to the above mentioned reduction of the visibility of its work.

Organizations are able to counteract a loss of legitimacy. The Austrian MFA does so by highlighting its service approach. In particular, the support of Austrian citizens travelling in receiving countries promises to bring legitimacy back to the Austrian MFA in two ways. Firstly, individual positive experiences of Austrian travellers concerning the around-the-clock service approach of Austrian embassies might be shared at home among family, friends and colleagues, which supports cognitive as well as moral legitimacy. Meeting friendly and supportive embassy staff that helps to solve problems in the receiving country probably also reduces resentments against the profession and generates better acceptance for the goals of the organization and the norms and values it follows. Secondly, interviewees mentioned that the MFA never gets better or more media coverage than when it cares for the safety of Austrian citizens abroad in a situation of crisis. These media images are able to influence public perception and probably also affect moral and cognitive legitimacy in a positive way.

The strategy of focusing on the enhancement of certain services in order to compensate the growing legitimation pressure, caused by reduced visibility of Austrian diplomacy in the EU framework, can be classified as a sort of indirect effect of Europeanization on the Austrian MFA. This development might also be seen in the context of a transition in the public sector from bureaucratic to post-bureaucratic organizations. According to Kernaghan (2000, p. 92), this transition process might take place on several levels, whereby the development from an organization-centred culture to a citizen-centred culture is central in this process.

Direct effects are visible as well. Before the implementation of the modernization strategy in 2015, bilateral and multilateral EU-related issues were treated separately in two divisions of the MFA. Now, the European Division pools multilateral as well as bilateral EU issues in the same organizational unit. This can be seen as an expression of the development of a European form of diplomacy (Paschke, 2001; Bátora & Hocking, 2009), which is depicted in the chapter on the impact of European integration on bilateral diplomacy. The term *"European Diplomacy"* describes developments in inner-EU diplomatic relations, where bilateral diplomacy is about to take a supportive role for the work done on the multilateral level. However, the MFA experienced a major setback concerning its development after the general election in 2017. The coalition talks between the pro-EU People's Party and the right-wing EU-sceptical Freedom Party resulted in a transfer of major EU competences from the MFA, which is led by a Freedom Party-aligned minister in the new government, to the Federal Chancellery, now led by former Foreign Minister Sebastian Kurz. This might be a temporary shift related to the special circumstances of the coalition building process between a pro-EU and an EU-sceptical party, but if not, this development will put further pressure on the MFA to legitimate itself in Austria's public administration framework.

Between Traditional and New Forms of Bilateral Diplomacy inside the EU

Inside the EU, the way bilateral diplomacy is conducted in the respective receiving country is influenced by different levels of integration and different cultures of interaction. As outlined in the chapter on Austrian bilateral diplomacy inside the EU, representatives in old Western European member states depicted that due to a progressing harmonization of economic, political and socio-cultural systems in the course of European integration, supportive or interventionist acts of Austrian representatives in the receiving country reduce in number. Austrian representatives in new Eastern European member states instead outlined that supporting Austrian issues, especially Austrian economy, remains to be a relevant part of their work. These different preconditions for conducting bilateral diplomacy inside the EU cannot only be ascribed to different levels in economic and political integration, but also to differences in the social and cultural structures of the receiving states. Hierarchies and the status of being a diplomat in some countries play a more significant role than in others. A dividing line concerning strong and loose hierarchical structures in receiving states however cannot be drawn alongside an East-West division within the EU. This phenomenon might also have some kind of North-South-dimension.

In countries with a high level of integration, the focus of bilateral work shifts from traditional bilateral tasks to EU-related work, concentrated on the support of promoting Austrian interests and coalition building on the EU-level. Thereby, the sources upon which coalitions are built determine whether the quality of bilateral relations do indeed play a significant role in this process. Kaeding and Selck (2005, pp. 273-276) describe four different sources of coalition building: power-based, interest-based, ideology-based and culture-based coalition building. If the driving forces for coalition building on the multilateral level are power or interest, the quality of the underlying bilateral relations is less important. Coalition building that is based on ideological or cultural patterns instead goes beyond issues of contemporary discussions. Alliances that are ideologically informed can be grounded on general political or EU-related policy orientations. Alliances that are culturally informed might be grounded on similarities in language, history and general cultural characteristics. So both more technical-oriented as well as more relation-oriented coalitions are to be found on the Brussels-level. Thus, solid bilateral relations are not an essential precondition for co-operation on the multilateral level. However, according to interviewees, a certain kind of familiarity with the negotiating partner remains an important element. Being represented in the respective receiving state enhances this kind of familiarity, which might facilitate the initiation of multilateral co-operation. So although a high level of integration diminishes the need for traditional bilateral diplomacy inside the EU, bilateral diplomacy does not become redundant, but gets a new function in supporting multilateral cooperation on the EU-level.

This work focused on how bilateral diplomacy and the work of bilateral missions is changing in the context of Austria's EU membership. It therefore cannot provide insights on how influential the work of Austrian inner-EU bilateral missions really is on the multilateral level. This would be an interesting starting point for further research. However, the MFA so far clearly followed the strategy of permanent representation inside the EU. For a long time, Austria was represented with an embassy in all other member states. Embassies were opened in Cyprus and Malta after the accession of these countries. In the Baltic region as well as in the Balkan region, Austria opened embassies at times when the respective states became candidate countries or achieved significant steps in the rapprochement to the EU. Details on this are to be found in the chapter on structural developments and changes in the Austrian MFA.

These developments can be interpreted within the background of rapprochement to the new nation states, which the countries in the Balkan and the Baltic region had been at the time Austria opened its embassies. Opening an embassy in a new state not only paves the way for promoting Austria's policy and economic interests in the new country, but can also be seen as an act of recognition for the new state. Hence, opening embassies in new and potential future new member states is primarily linked to traditional forms of bilateral diplomacy and is not an expression of the new EU-oriented form of bilateral diplomacy. This is because a low level of integration requires more traditional tasks to be done. However, Austria's special affiliation to the Balkan region must also be taken into account, which gives a more important role to permanent representation in this area.

Despite growing budget pressure, the MFA has long followed the strategy of keeping all embassies inside the EU, while embassies in third states were closed. Representatives of the MFA ascribe high potential to both forms, the traditional one and the new EU-oriented form of bilateral diplomacy, for their political work done in the EU. The tenor of the interviews conducted for this investigation was that small representation in the EU is better than no representation. Nevertheless, by June 2015 the MFA announced it would close four embassies in small EU member states in the coming years, due to low utilization. The first of these, Malta, was already closed by the end of 2015. Whether this will lead to a change in the MFA's Eurocentric approach concerning its network of representations is not yet clear. The MFA opened new missions in areas with the expectation of high growth in Eastern Europe and beyond, what indicates further economization of bilateral diplomacy. Nevertheless, the MFA's future strategy for inner-EU bilateral diplomacy will mainly be influenced by the role the MFA plays in Austria's EU policy framework. This role is currently challenged in two respects. First, the Viennese headquarters has to cope with a loss in importance as the mechanisms in Brussels gain momentum. One interviewee aptly described the situation by stating that Brussels takes a *"life of its own"*. This reduces the MFA's impact on developments on this level. Secondly, other Austrian actors than the MFA became increasingly important in representing Austrian interests on the Brussels-level. The growing importance of the European Council, for example, gives more leverage to the Federal Chancellery in Austrian diplomacy. Furthermore, recent developments in Europe and beyond made other ministries, like the Ministry of Finance or the Ministry of the Interior, important actors in the EU framework. So the field of activity for the Austrian MFA in inner-EU related issues is shrinking.

When referring to the development patterns formulated for this case study in the field of inner-EU bilateral diplomacy, in order to compare empirical results with predicted ideal-types of development, it becomes obvious that in inner-EU bilateral diplomacy the Austrian MFA combines elements of both predicted patterns - of the role of a provider as well as the role of a promoter.

The provider-pattern assumes that due to growing interconnectedness on the Brussels-level, MFAs lose traditional competences, but they could instead focus on supporting the interaction processes on the Brussels-level in organizational terms and provide their outcome of political reporting to other institutions. The Austrian MFA is not currently giving organizational support to other institutions and obviously is not planning to do so in the future. It rather tries to legitimate itself by promoting its service character. The MFA indeed provides the outcome of its research activities to other organizations in the Austrian public administration framework by passing on political reporting, but also through more informal ways of communication, grounded on well-established relations between MFA representatives and representatives of other ministries. Still, the second predicted development pattern, perceiving the MFA in the role of a promoter, appropriates better to the work currently conducted by the MFA and its bilateral missions.

The promoter-pattern assumes that within the EU framework, inner-EU bilateral diplomacy gains new significance in promoting Austrian interests in other member states, which achieves a key position between multilateral and bilateral cooperation to the MFA. The newly emerged tasks of embassies inside the EU currently confirm this assumption, whereby a visible effect of the process of European integration on inner-EU bilateral diplomacy is evident, as the level of integration of the receiving state decides, whether the share of *"European Diplomacy"* or of traditional forms of bilateral diplomacy is higher. More elements of traditional bilateral diplomacy are to be found in receiving states whose political and economic systems have not yet adapted to the EU-mainstream, as well as in countries with strong hierarchical structures. However, these traditional forms are about to lose their significance in the relation between member states at a high level of integration. Here, new forms of *"European Diplomacy"* are predominantly represented and this will probably increase as the process of integration moves on. This speaks for the MFA taking the role of a promoter within the EU. The progress of this role and the opportunities it holds for the MFA however are closely linked to developments in the coalition building system in Brussels. The Austrian MFA was represented with an embassy in all member states for a period of 20 years. This approach was based on the assumption that being on-site guarantees better understanding for the sentiment in the receiving country and also guarantees closer contact to its representatives. Two main aspects will decide how important this form of representation and diplomacy will be in the future within the EU framework. First, it depends on how the growing independence of the decision-making sphere in Brussels develops. Proceeding detachment from the capital cities to the benefit of the extension of the mentioned *"life of its own"* would diminish the relevance of well-established contacts in the capital cities of the member states for multilateral cooperation, because all important decision makers would then be located in Brussels. Second, the sources upon which coalition building is based, decide to which extent bilateral relations are of relevance for multilateral coalition building. Power-based and interest-based forms of coalition building, as described by Kaeding and Selck (2005, pp. 273-276), are less dependent on solid underlying relations than ideology-based and culture-based forms of coalition building.

Role Negotiation in the European Foreign Policy Making System

As with inside the EU, where different actors enhanced their position in diplomacy, which affects the MFA's role, ongoing processes of role negotiation and renegotiation also take place in the foreign policy network concerning relations to third states. In the European foreign policy making system, member states on the one hand have to accept the growing importance of the EEAS, and on the other hand need to find their own position and role within this framework. Bátora and Hynek (2014, p. 153) argue that traditional diplomatic cultures meet with new forms of organization in this setting. This does not only apply to the modes of operation of diplomacy, but also to the general preconditions under which diplomacy is conducted. The quality of the relation between Austria and the receiving state is not the only influential factor for conducting diplomacy in third states anymore. The quality of the relation between the EU and the receiving state also influences how Austrian bilateral diplomacy is conducted in the respective receiving country. Being part of the EU brings huge benefits to the work of Austrian missions in some receiving countries, especially in places where the EU is highly respected. However, in other countries, Austrian bilateral missions are in a more difficult position, especially in states with which Austria maintains well-established good bilateral relations, but the relation between the EU and the receiving country is strained. In constellations like this, norms and values, linked to different relations and based on different foundations, do collide and diplomats have to sensitively manoeuvre between long-established bilateral ties and Austria's commitment to a common European foreign policy. Therefore, the new dimension the EU brought to bilateral diplomacy in third countries is represented by a triangular relation to which embassies are about to adjust their role. Moreover, working with the EEAS also brings a sort of rule-based legal environment to bilateral diplomatic work done by member states in third countries, because the coordination function of the EEAS transforms and reinforces the cooperation among the member states as well as between the EEAS and the member states in third countries.

In order to investigate the nature of the cooperation between the EEAS and the MFA more closely, and also to examine the development of the role of the MFA in this context, Bátora's (2011a) three foreign policy models are consulted in this case study. These three models stem from organization theory and serve as predicted development patterns for the investigation of the level of bilateral relations to third states. The three models describe a foreign policy market, a foreign policy hierarchy and a foreign policy network. Market systems are characterized by low integrative effects on actors, opportunism and cost-orientation. In a market system, the main objective of cooperation is cost efficiency and cost reduction, which keeps the level of loyalty between the partners low. Expertise is solely shared in order to improve one's own position. Hierarchies are systems with clear role definitions and lines of authority. A hierarchically structured EU foreign policy making system would provide similar conditions as usual in federal states. The EEAS would be in charge of the EU's external relations and balancing member states' foreign policies, while Austria would maintain its own external relations. Network forms of cooperation are established through recurring and long-term interaction between actors that create a form of mutual obligation. In a foreign policy network, Austria would reduce its individual foreign policy activity and instead participate in EU foreign policy activities. Mutual obligation would thereby enable Austria to upload its own foreign policy preferences to the EU-level more easily.

When referring now to the results displayed in the preceding chapters concerning the interaction between the Austrian MFA and the EEAS, there are, however, no signs of a hierarchy system developing thus far, as roles are not stabilized yet and also the division of competences remains an object of discussion and negotiation (Sonnleitner, 2015, p. 23). Nevertheless, there are some aspects in the relation between the MFA and the EEAS which indicate the development of a market system. When taking into account the aspect of cost reduction and efficiency as central driving force behind cooperation in a market system, the MFA's notion to transfer certain duties to the EEAS can be interpreted in this way. From the beginning, the Austrian MFA had been convinced of the possibility of cost reduction through cooperation with the EEAS. Austria is interested in transferring certain consular competences to the EU, especially in the field of crisis management. This would provide better support to Austrian citizens, as the MFA's network of representations outside the EU is rather small, what hampers the implementation of the MFA's service approach, represented by its slogan *"Worldwide at your service"*. Due to its limited resources, the MFA is willing to give competences to the EEAS, in order to provide more efficient consular services to Austrian citizens. A second aspect hinting at the possible development of a market system is to be found in the MFA's modernization strategy. This strategy includes the pooling of all West Balkan competences within one department. Balkan issues are a main focus of Austrian foreign policy and the country is ascribed to have special expertise in this field. Concentrating on maintaining and expanding this expertise in a specialized department could be interpreted as an indicator of a market system, where providing special expertise to the EEAS in turn promises to be able to easier implement own interests to the EU's foreign policy system. A significant characteristic of a market system, however, is not fulfilled in the relation between the Austrian MFA and the EEAS. A market system is grounded on a low level of loyalty that rather is bound to individual external actions. The interviews conducted with Austrian diplomats for this investigation were characterized by a very pro-European notion and several interviewees referred to a high pro-European attitude in the Austrian diplomatic service. The Austrian MFA had been a supporter of establishing a strong EEAS and always hoped to benefit from synergies in cooperating with it. Such synergy effects are clearly evident in the field of information distribution, in formal as well as in informal ways. The Austrian MFA and its embassies benefit from official EEAS reports as well as from increased information exchange among member states and EU representatives within the interaction framework the EEAS established in third states. The success, however, varies from country to country and is highly dependent on the respective head of delegation. Furthermore, the MFA clearly sees a chance to multiply its foreign policy interests through the EEAS and therefore is interested in participating in common European foreign policy making (Sonnleitner, 2015, p. 23). Whether this indicates the development of a network relation between the Austrian MFA and the EEAS remains to be seen, as network forms of organization develop in recurring and long-term interaction processes between actors. When considering the MFA's human resources approach with regard to the EEAS, such a development might be assumed. Austria did support the idea of integrating national diplomats to the EEAS from the very beginning. This approach is driven by the idea of benefiting from the knowledge of returnees concerning the EEAS-system and processes within this system as well as from the personal network national diplomats establish during their term in the EEAS. Furthermore, interviewees stated that the MFA benefits from Austrian diplomats in the EEAS already during their term in office, as they provide access to knowledge on current discussions in the EEAS (Sonnleitner, 2015, p. 23). These relation-building efforts indicate a form of cooperation that goes beyond the cost and efficiency-oriented approach of the market model. It rather seems to tend towards mutual obligation as foundation for cooperation, what characterizes a network form of organization.

The perspective on the Austrian MFA, however, is only one side of this cooperation. A process of role negotiation as well as negotiation of the organizational identity currently not only occurs in interaction between the EEAS and the member states, but also within the EEAS. The different mind-sets meeting in this organizational set-up create tensions concerning the positioning against the member states. From the perspective of an EU-based interviewee, the self-finding process of the EEAS currently vacillates between the development of a *"team-player organization"*, where member states are further integrated, and the development of a *"mini-Commission"* that wants to operate independently from the member states. The outcome of this conflict of mind-sets will define the future form of cooperation between member states MFAs and the EEAS (Sonnleitner, 2015, pp. 23-24).

From National to Europeanized Diplomatic Processes

Hence, on both levels, on the level of bilateral diplomacy inside as well as outside the EU, developments in the multilateral sphere in Brussels are decisive as to how the MFA will organize this field of work in the future. Inside the EU, bilateral diplomacy has not yet lost its significance, but rather has gained a new dimension, which may become the predominant form of bilateral diplomacy in the EU when the process of integration moves on. The future relevance of this form of diplomacy however is dependent on how coalition building processes in Brussels are about to develop. Outside the EU, Austria, as a small member state with few resources, benefits on several levels from the cooperation with the EEAS in conducting bilateral diplomacy. The MFA is willing to fit into and participate in common European foreign policy making. It thereby expects to be able to promote own interests via this framework. The success of such an approach is dependent on the MFA's capacity and its resources to upload these interests to the EU-level. Furthermore, it is also dependent on the willingness of the EEAS to integrate the member states to European foreign policy making. However, interviews conducted for this investigation highlighted that now, after several years of cooperation, the initial EEAS-euphoria in the Austrian MFA has already receded.

When considering these developments against the background of Hocking's (2005b) two images of diplomatic systems, with different roles for MFAs and diplomats, it becomes obvious that the Austrian example clearly confirms Hocking's assumption of MFAs in the EU turning from gatekeepers to boundary spanners.

In the gatekeeper model, the territorial state and the control of boundaries as well as communication flows are central. In this concept, the MFA is a dominant actor in the diplomatic system and coordination is structured as a hierarchical top-down process. This outline definitely does not apply to contemporary Austrian bilateral diplomacy. The increasing importance of other actors than the MFA in the diplomatic system undermine its dominance and make it lose the monopoly on foreign relations. The subtle shift of decision making competences from the Viennese headquarters to the Brussels policy making sphere challenges the role of the MFA. This is especially noticeable in common European foreign policy making, where Austrian positions increasingly emerge in Brussels and are confirmed in Vienna, rather than they emerge in Vienna and are promoted in Brussels, as outlined in the chapter on Austrian bilateral diplomacy in third states. Hence, national foreign policy positions, which formerly developed in a nationally shaped environment, now emerge in a transnationally shaped environment that is influenced by a variety of circumstances. Austrian representatives in Brussels establish information networks and search for like-minded partners by clarifying positions of other member states. The development of Austrian foreign policy positions is based on this assessment. This circumstance as well as the new form of *"European Diplomacy"* conducted inside the EU, in order to support coalition building, speak for the second image of the diplomatic system described by Hocking (2005b).

In the boundary spanner model, actors take the role of mediators or brokers, who operate within and outside their organization. Contrary to the gatekeeper image, where the objective is to control national boundaries and to isolate the state from its environment, the boundary spanner image follows the aim to mediate within and across spaces between the state and its environment through points of interface. In this context, Hocking (2005a, p. 285) assumed a transition from national to Europeanized diplomatic processes. This clearly is the case in the example of Austria.

The preceding chapters outlined that Europeanization tendencies are visible on several levels of bilateral diplomacy, inside as well as outside the EU. Inner-EU bilateral diplomacy gained a whole new focus, concentrated on the support of multilateral EU diplomacy. The mode of operation at embassies therefore had been adjusted and follows the EU agenda. Now, structural adjustments in the MFA are also implemented by pooling bilateral and multilateral EU issues within one division. In the conduct of diplomacy in bilateral relations to third states, the interaction with the EEAS generates Europeanization effects in Austrian bilateral missions as well as in the MFA in Vienna. In receiving third countries, increased interaction between the EU and the member states as well as among the member states, encouraged by the EEAS and the framework it offers, provides a comprehensive pool of information to Austrian representatives, which is evaluated and passed on by them to Vienna and Brussels. This information can be classified as Europeanized, because it occurs and multiplies in interaction processes within a network of EU partners. This network substitutes, to a certain extent, traditional forms of information gathering for political reporting in bilateral diplomacy. Hence, increased interaction between EU partners also affects the processes conducted in Austrian bilateral missions.

Adjustment of processes is also visible in the Viennese headquarters in the context of cooperation with the EEAS. The major Europeanization effect here is the shift of importance from Vienna to Brussels. Hocking (2005a, p. 285) points out that a turn from national to Europeanized diplomatic processes would render national diplomatic systems redundant. This does not necessarily mean that national diplomatic services disappear, but some traditional forms of how to conduct national diplomacy might do. Such a paradigm shift is predictable, when considering that Austrian foreign policy positions are less and less formulated sovereignly, but more and more result from a process of interaction of several foreign policy actors on the EU-level. Of further interest in this context is the socializing effect of working in EU institutions. Adler-Nissen (2009) illustrated that a high level of socialization within EU institutions gives rise to a merging of national interests and EU-interests among national representatives in Brussels. Hence, the growing importance of EU-based representatives in formulating foreign policy positions probably further Europeanizes these positions. As mentioned before, it could be assumed that any member state operates with partly Europeanized foreign policy positions as they emerged through interaction processes in EU contexts. Small member states like Austria, which support the EEAS, because they expect to benefit from this cooperation, are probably more affected by this development than member states with their own distinct foreign policy efforts.

A Third Dimension in the Professional Identity

Effects of socialization, as mentioned above, do not only occur in multilateral EU contexts, but embassy and MFA representatives as well are socialized by interacting with the EU and other member states in bilateral contexts. This case study focused on how this circumstance shapes the occupational image and professional identity of Austrian diplomats.

The profession of diplomacy is of a *"Janus-faced character"* (Bátora, 2005a, p. 45). In principle, diplomats guard and promote national interests, but they are also part of a professional group that acts in a transnational environment and shares a common culture of interaction. This duality of representing a sovereign nation state and being part of a transnational professional group creates fundamental tension in the profession, which is accommodated by a professionalization process, conducted in MFAs, in order to socialize diplomats into this dual role. This process is carried out by MFAs in their specific manner, based on the respective national identity and organizational culture (Bátora, 2005a, p. 45). Hence, Europeanization effects on the organizational culture of the MFA consequently also affect this socialization process and therefore the professional identity of diplomats.

In the Austrian example, such tendencies are visible in statements of diplomats from different generations. Austria's accession to the EU is perceived as a major turnaround because the focus on neutrality, previously being the central component of professional identities of Austrian diplomats, lost its significance. Some of the diplomats who were socialized in the traditional system immediately adapted to the EU, especially those who participated in the accession process and therefore were socialized into the EU system and became part of it. Others have failed to follow the developments taken by the EU. They did not proactively adjust to the new circumstances and rather maintained their traditional occupational image. Representatives of the youngest generation of Austrian diplomats do not have pre-accession experience and entered the Austrian diplomatic service at a stage when cooperation with the EU already worked in a routinized manner. Hence, this generation grew into a more established means of operation conducted between the MFA and the EU. They simultaneously consider processes and events in Vienna as well as in Brussels for decision making in their work. Hence, socialization effects of the EU not only are visible on the Brussels-level in EU institutions, but already also on the level of the MFA, through recurring and well-established interaction processes between the MFA and the EU.

When focusing on bilateral diplomacy in this context, the growing interconnectedness between member states through EU-coordination in receiving states creates a Europeanized working environment. This environment might have similar socialization effects on national diplomats as known from EU institutions. Bátora (2005a, pp. 54-55) speaks of a third dimension that is added to the nationally and transnationally informed work done by diplomats. Such a transformation encourages the development of an additional set of roles and identities in MFAs and therefore promotes changes in training and socialization procedures. Indeed, adaptations of this kind are obvious in the Austrian diplomatic service. Courses on EU developments became part of the MFA's training programme. Beyond that, the MFA decided to use selection commissions in its selection procedure comprising of members of the MFA as well as the EEAS, which brings the European dimension already to the first step of the career.

Roles of diplomats in bilateral diplomacy changed in the context of EU membership, because inside the EU the multilateral-oriented form of *"European Diplomacy"* brings new and different tasks to the occupation and also diversifies the field of bilateral diplomacy, as its traditional and new dimension exist side by side. Several aspects influence the level of dominance of one or the other side in a specific bilateral relation, whereby the quality of the relation between Austria and the receiving state as well as the level of integration in the respective receiving country are central components. In third states, bilateral diplomacy is still conducted in a rather traditional manner. The future development and success of the EEAS and common European foreign policy making will determine whether a sort of multilateralization of bilateral diplomacy will occur in third states as well.

Moreover, indirect effects of Europeanization on the role of Austrian diplomats occur, related to new role definitions of the MFA, emerging in the context of less visibility of its diplomatic work. Growing legitimation pressure directs the focus towards servicing Austrian citizens and companies abroad, which leads to a shift in the understanding of the profession. Traditionally the profession had been concentrated on policy and representation. At present, more flexible and service-oriented approaches are about to develop. So currently, the professional identity of Austrian diplomats is in a process of transition, where direct and indirect influences of European integration add a European dimension to its *"Janus-faced character"*.

Results related to the Institution of Diplomacy

When relating these developments to the observation of transformation processes within the institution of diplomacy, the Austrian example exhibits similar features as outlined by Bátora and Hynek (2014, pp. 54-55) in the transformation from medieval diplomacy to modern diplomacy. They perceived continuity concerning the core function of diplomacy in this process of transition, while the organizational basis changed.

Mediation, the core function of diplomacy in medieval times was conducted in an environment consisting of individual sovereigns, while the environment of modern diplomacy consists of sovereign nation states. This caused a shift in the organizational structure of the institution. MFAs were established and became the managers of foreign policy and diplomacy in the Westphalian system of states. Furthermore, the underlying concept of the professional identity of diplomats changed additionally as the rise of the nation state made national identity into a central component in the conduct of diplomacy.

With the EU currently challenging the Westphalian system of states, the environment of diplomacy is in a process of transition again. Contrary to the Westphalian system, which for long defined the framework for bilateral diplomacy, the EU framework combines sovereign and non-sovereign actors, including territorial states as well as intergovernmental und supranational institutions (Bátora & Hynek, 2014, p. 138). Bátora and Hynek (2014, pp. 150-156) describe the EU's acting in the institution of diplomacy as a combination of adjusting to established standards and stretching these standards at the same time. They perceive a shift towards a condition they term *"new heteronomy"*. Due to the fact that the EU does not fully integrate itself into the diplomatic system and therefore remains to be a systematically different actor in the Westphalian diplomatic order, the EU contributes to gradual transformation of the system and functions as a *"driver of change"*. Hence, nation states are not confronted with a new actor that simply adjusts to their form of interaction in diplomacy, but a new actor that challenges their framework of interaction. Traditional actors, mainly nation state MFAs, need to adapt to the changing circumstances, triggered by the EU.

The Europeanization tendencies determined in Austrian bilateral diplomacy display changes on the organizational level concerning structure, processes as well as the professional identity of Austrian diplomats. Hence, the Austrian example is one that exhibits comprehensive transformation.

Developments on the structural level can be divided into direct and indirect Europeanization effects. Direct effects for example are the integration of bilateral and multilateral EU-related issues to a European Division in the MFA's organizational set-up, or the effort to maintain Austria's expertise on West Balkan issues by pooling all related topics within one organizational unit. Indirect effects are strategies used to compensate a loss in legitimacy, caused by less visibility of the MFA's work, due to growing interconnectedness inside the EU and a growing presence of the EEAS in third states. The MFA strongly emphasizes its service approach in order to underline the added value it provides to the Austrian population.

Concerning processes, namely tasks and working procedures, traditional forms of conducting diplomacy exist alongside the new form of *"European Diplomacy"* inside the EU, which is aimed to support multilateral cooperation on the EU-level. In third states, a rather traditional form of bilateral diplomacy is still conducted. However, the EEAS brought a new cooperation framework to the diplomatic corps in third states, which coordinates the interaction between the member states and the EU, as well as among the member states in third countries. As a result, this cooperation framework Europeanizes the work done by Austrian embassies.

Concerning the occupational image and professional identity, a European dimension develops alongside the nationally and transnationally informed sides of diplomacy in the process of interaction between the MFA and the EU.

The example of the Austrian MFA shows that the underlying concept of diplomacy, namely the logic of appropriateness on which the conduct of interstate diplomacy in bilateral relations is based, is in a process of transition in all investigated fields, related to Austria's EU membership. Traditional forms of diplomacy exist beside new emerging ones.

However, recent developments, like the rise of nationalist populist parties and especially the British BREXIT-vote, call continuing European integration into question and disintegrating dynamics open a new field in the research on bilateral diplomacy in post-Westphalian times.

Bibliography

Adebahr, C. (2013). The 'Good Europeans': Germany and the European External Action Service. In R. Balfour & K. Raik (Eds.), *The European External Action Service and National Diplomacies* (pp. 13-21). EPC Issue Paper (73): European Policy Centre

Adler-Nissen, R. (2009). Late Sovereign Diplomacy. *The Hague Journal of Diplomacy, 4*(2), 121-141

Alecu de Flers, N. (2012). *EU Foreign Policy and the Europeanization of Neutral States: Comparing Irish and Austrian Foreign Policy*. Abingdon/New York: Routledge

Alecu de Flers, N., & Müller, P. (2012). Dimensions and Mechanisms of the Europeanization of Member State Foreign Policy: State of the Art and New Research Avenues. *Journal of European Integration, 34*(1), 19-35

Anderson, M. S. (1993). *The Rise of Modern Diplomacy: 1450-1919*. London: Longman

Angerer, T. (2014). Integrität vor Integration: Österreich und "Europa" aus französischer Sicht 1949-1960. In M. Gehler & R. Steininger (Eds.), *Österreich und die Europäische Integration seit 1945: Aspekte einer wechselvollen Entwicklung* (pp. 183-208). Wien: Böhlau

Ansell, C. K., & Weber, S. (1999). Organizing International Politics: Sovereignty and Open Systems. *International Political Science Review, 20*(1), 73-93

Balfour, R., & Raik, K. (2013). Introduction. In R. Balfour & K. Raik (Eds.), *The European External Action Service and National Diplomacies* (pp. 1-11). EPC Issue Paper (73): European Policy Centre

Balfour, R., & Raik, K. (2015). National Adaptation and Survival in a Changing European Diplomacy. In D. Spence & J. Bátora (Eds.), *The European External Action Service: European Diplomacy Post-Westphalia* (pp. 257-273). Basingstoke, New York: Palgrave Macmillan

Bátora, J. (2005a). Does the European Union Transform the Institution of Diplomacy? *Journal of European Public Policy, 12*(1), 44-66

Bátora, J. (2005b). Public Diplomacy in Small and Medium-Sized States: Norway and Canada. In D. Kelly & J. Melissen (Eds.), *Discussion Papers in Diplomacy*: Netherlands Institute of International Relations 'Clingendael'

Bátora, J. (2008). *Foreign Ministries and the Information Revolution: Going Virtual?* (Vol. 2). Leiden: Brill

Bátora, J. (2011a). Emerging System of EU Foreign Policy Making: Market, Hierarchy or Network? *EUFORPOL Working Paper Series (1)*: Institute of European Studies and International Relations, Comenius University Bratislava

Bátora, J. (2011b). European External Action Service as a Litmus Test of the Emerging Foreign Policy Making System in the EU: An Organization Theory Approach *EUFORPOL Working Paper Series (2)*: Institute of European Studies and International Relations, Comenius University Bratislava

Bátora, J. (2013). The 'Mitrailleuse Effect': The EEAS as an Interstitial Organization and the Dynamics of Innovation in Diplomacy. *Journal of Common Market Studies, 51*(4), 598-613

Bátora, J., & Hocking, B. (2009). EU-oriented Bilateralism: Evaluating the Role of Member State Embassies in the European Union. *Cambridge Review of International Affairs, 22*(1), 163-182

Bátora, J., & Hynek, N. (2014). *Fringe Players and the Diplomatic Order: The 'New' Heteronomy*. Basingstoke/New York: Palgrave Macmillan

Beichelt, T., & Merkel, W. (2014). Democracy Promotion and Civil Society: Regime Types, Transitions Modes and Effects. In T. Beichelt, I. Hahn-Fuhr, F. Schimmelfennig, & S. Worschech (Eds.), *Civil Society and Democracy Promotion. Challenges to Democracy in the 21st Century* (pp. 42-64). Basingstoke/New York: Palgrave Macmillan

Beneš, V. (2013). The Czech Republic and the European External Action Service. In R. Balfour & K. Raik (Eds.), *The European External Action Service and National Diplomacies* (pp. 149-162). EPC Issue Paper 73: European Policy Centre

Berridge, G. R. (2002). *Diplomacy: Theory and Practice*: Palgrave Macmillan

Bielka, E. (1983). Österreich und seine volksdemokratischen Nachbarn. In E. Bielka, P. Jankowitsch, & H. Thalberg (Eds.), *Die Ära Kreisky: Schwerpunkte der österreichischen Außenpolitik* (pp. 195-231). Wien/Zürich/München: Europa Verlag

Bischof, G. (1993). Die Instrumentalisierung der Moskauer Erklärung nach dem 2. Weltkrieg. *Zeitgeschichte, 20*(11-12), 345-366

BKA (1986). *Bundesgesetz über die Zahl, den Wirkungsbereich und die Einrichtung der Bundesministerien (Federal Ministries Act)*. Federal Chancellery of Austria. Retrieved from http://www.ris.bka.gv.at/GeltendeFassung.wxe?Abfrage=Bundesnormen&Gesetzesnummer=10000873&FassungVom=3456-12-31

BKA (1999). *Bundesgesetz Aufgaben und Organisation des auswärtigen Dienstes (Federal Act on the Functions and Organization of the Foreign Service)*. Federal

Chancellery of Austria. Retrieved from https://www.ris.bka.gv.at/GeltendeFassung.wxe?Abfrage=Bundesnormen&Gesetzesnummer=10001572

BKA (2015). Faymann, Sobotka und Fico: Skeptisch bezüglich Russland-Sanktionen (Press Release of the Federal Chancellery). Retrieved 2nd of May, 2017, from https://www.bka.gv.at/site/cob__58420/currentpage__1/6856/default.aspx

BMAA (1979). *Außenpolitischer Bericht (Foreign Policy Report).* Wien: Bundesministerium für Auswärtige Angelegenheiten (Federal Ministry for Foreign Affairs)

BMAA (1980). *Außenpolitischer Bericht (Foreign Policy Report).* Wien: Bundesministerium für Auswärtige Angelegenheiten (Federal Ministry for Foreign Affairs)

BMAA (1981). *Außenpolitischer Bericht (Foreign Policy Report).* Wien: Bundesministerium für Auswärtige Angelegenheiten (Federal Ministry for Foreign Affairs)

BMAA (1982). *Außenpolitischer Bericht (Foreign Policy Report).* Wien: Bundesministerium für Auswärtige Angelegenheiten (Federal Ministry for Foreign Affairs)

BMAA (1983). *Außenpolitischer Bericht (Foreign Policy Report).* Wien: Bundesministerium für Auswärtige Angelegenheiten (Federal Ministry for Foreign Affairs)

BMAA (1984). *Außenpolitischer Bericht (Foreign Policy Report)* Wien: Bundesministerium für Auswärtige Angelegenheiten (Federal Ministry for Foreign Affairs)

BMAA (1985). *Außenpolitischer Bericht (Foreign Policy Report)* Wien: Bundesministerium für Auswärtige Angelegenheiten (Federal Ministry for Foreign Affairs)

BMAA (1987). *Außenpolitischer Bericht (Foreign Policy Report).* Wien: Bundesministerium für Auswärtige Angelegenheiten (Federal Ministry for Foreign Affairs)

BMAA (1988). *Außenpolitischer Bericht (Foreign Policy Report).* Wien: Bundesministerium für Auswärtige Angelegenheiten (Federal Ministry for Foreign Affairs)

BMAA (1989). *Außenpolitischer Bericht (Foreign Policy Report).* Wien: Bundesministerium für Auswärtige Angelegenheiten (Federal Ministry for Foreign Affairs)

BMAA (1990). *Außenpolitischer Bericht (Foreign Policy Report)* Wien: Bundesministerium für Auswärtige Angelegenheiten (Federal Ministry for Foreign Affairs)

BMAA (1991). *Außenpolitischer Bericht (Foreign Policy Report)* Wien: Bundesministerium für Auswärtige Angelegenheiten (Federal Ministry for Foreign Affairs)

BMAA (1992). *Außenpolitischer Bericht (Foreign Policy Report).* Wien: Bundesministerium für Auswärtige Angelegenheiten (Federal Ministry for Foreign Affairs)

BMAA (1993). *Außenpolitischer Bericht (Foreign Policy Report).* Wien: Bundesministerium für Auswärtige Angelegenheiten (Federal Ministry for Foreign Affairs)

BMAA (1994). *Außenpolitischer Bericht (Foreign Policy Report).* Wien: Bundesministerium für Auswärtige Angelegenheiten (Federal Ministry for Foreign Affairs)

BMAA (1995). *Außenpolitischer Bericht (Foreign Policy Report).* Wien: Bundesministerium für Auswärtige Angelegenheiten (Federal Ministry for Foreign Affairs)

BMAA (1996). *Außenpolitischer Bericht (Foreign Policy Report).* Wien: Bundesministerium für Auswärtige Angelegenheiten (Federal Ministry for Foreign Affairs)

BMAA (1997). *Außenpolitischer Bericht (Foreign Policy Report).* Wien: Bundesministerium für Auswärtige Angelegenheiten (Federal Ministry for Foreign Affairs)

BMAA (1998). *Außenpolitischer Bericht (Foreign Policy Report).* Wien: Bundesministerium für Auswärtige Angelegenheiten (Federal Ministry for Foreign Affairs)

BMAA (1999). *Außenpolitischer Bericht (Foreign Policy Report).* Wien: Bundesministerium für Auswärtige Angelegenheiten (Federal Ministry for Foreign Affairs)

BMAA (2000). *Außenpolitischer Bericht (Foreign Policy Report).* Wien: Bundesministerium für Auswärtige Angelegenheiten (Federal Ministry for Foreign Affairs)

BMAA (2001). *Außenpolitischer Bericht (Foreign Policy Report).* Wien: Bundesministerium für Auswärtige Angelegenheiten (Federal Ministry for Foreign Affairs)

BMAA (2003). *Außenpolitischer Bericht (Foreign Policy Report).* Wien: Bundesministerium für Auswärtige Angelegenheiten (Federal Ministry for Foreign Affairs)

BMAA (2004). *Außenpolitischer Bericht (Foreign Policy Report)*. Wien: Bundesministerium für Auswärtige Angelegenheiten (Federal Ministry for Foreign Affairs)

BMAA (2005). *Außenpolitischer Bericht (Foreign Policy Report)*. Wien: Bundesministerium für Auswärtige Angelegenheiten (Federal Ministry for Foreign Affairs)

BMEIA (2006). *Außenpolitischer Bericht (Foreign Policy Report)*. Wien: Bundesministerium für europäische und internationale Angelegenheiten (Federal Ministry for European and International Affairs)

BMEIA (2007). *Außenpolitischer Bericht (Foreign Policy Report)*. Wien: Bundesministerium für europäische und internationale Angelegenheiten (Federal Ministry for European and International Affairs)

BMEIA (2008). *Außenpolitischer Bericht (Foreign Policy Report)*. Wien: Bundesministerium für europäische und internationale Angelegenheiten (Federal Ministry for European and International Affairs)

BMEIA (2009). *Außenpolitischer Bericht (Foreign Policy Report)*. Wien: Bundesministerium für europäische und internationale Angelegenheiten (Federal Ministry for European and International Affairs)

BMEIA (2010). *Außen- und Europapolitischer Bericht (Foreign and European Policy Report)*. Wien: Bundesministerium für europäische und internationale Angelegenheiten (Federal Ministry for European and International Affairs)

BMEIA (2012). *Außen- und Europapolitischer Bericht (Foreign and European Policy Report)*. Wien: Bundesministerium für europäische und internationale Angelegenheiten (Federal Ministry for European and International Affairs)

BMEIA (2013). *Außen- und Europapolitischer Bericht (Foreign and European Policy Report)*. Wien: Bundesministerium für Europa, Integration und Äußeres (Federal Ministry for Europe, Integration and Foreign Affairs)

BMEIA (2014a). APA: Botschafterkonferenz 2014: Erstmals auch öffentliche Termine (Press Release of the Federal Ministry for Europe, Integration and Foreign Affairs). Retrieved 2nd of May, 2017, from http://www.bmeia.gv.at/das-ministerium/presse/aussendungen/2014/09/apa-botschafterkonferenz-2014-erstmals-auch-oeffentliche-termine/

BMEIA (2014b). *Außen- und Europapolitischer Bericht (Foreign and European Policy Report)*. Wien: Bundesministerium für Europa, Integration und Äußeres (Federal Ministry for Europe, Integration and Foreign Affairs)

BMEIA (2015a). *Außen- und Europapolitischer Bericht (Foreign and European Policy Report)*. Wien: Bundesministerium für Europa, Integration und Äußeres (Federal Ministry for Europe, Integration and Foreign Affairs)

BMEIA (2015b). EU-Twinning: Projektzuschläge an Österreich (List of Austrian EU Twinning Projects). Retrieved 20th of May, 2015, from http://www.bmeia.gv.at/europa-aussenpolitik/europapolitik/eu-twinning/projektzuschlaege-an-oesterreich/

BMEIA (2015c). Modernisierung des Außenministeriums (Press Release of the Federal Ministry for Europe, Integration and Foreign Affairs). Retrieved 2nd of May, 2017, from http://www.bmeia.gv.at/das-ministerium/presse/aktuelles/modernisierung-des-aussenministeriums/

BMEIA (2016). Federal Minister Kurz: "Launching 'Austrian Leadership Programs' for a Strong Network of International Decision-Makers" (Press Release of the Federal Ministry for Europe, Integration and Foreign Affairs). Retrieved 2nd of May, 2017, from https://www.bmeia.gv.at/en/the-ministry/press/announcements/2016/01/federal-minister-kurz-launching-austrian-leadership-programs-for-a-strong-network-of-international-decision-makers/

BMEIA (2017a). Auslandsservice-App (Foreign Service App Webpage). Retrieved 30th of April, 2017, from http://www.bmeia.gv.at/fileadmin/user_upload/Auslandsservice/index.html

BMEIA (2017b). Der höhere auswärtige Dienst (Information Page on the Diplomatic Service). Retrieved 2nd of May, 2017, from http://www.bmeia.gv.at/das-ministerium/karrieremoeglichkeiten/laufbahn-im-bmeia/hoeherer-auswaertiger-dienst/

BMEIA (2017c). Organigramm des Bundesministeriums für Europa, Integration und Äußeres (Organizational Chart of the Federal Ministry for Europe, Integration and Foreign Affairs). Retrieved 2nd of May, 2017, from https://www.bmeia.gv.at/fileadmin/user_upload/Zentrale/Ministerium/Organigramm_0117.pdf

BMEIA (2017d). Reiseregistrierung (Travel Registration Webpage). Retrieved 30th of April, 2017, from http://www.reiseregistrierung.at/

BMEIA (2017e). Verzeichnis der Österreichischen Vertretungsbehörden weltweit (List of Austrian Representations Worldwide). Retrieved 8th of October 2017, 2017, from http://www.bmeia.gv.at/botschaften-konsulate/suche-nach-oesterreichischen-vertretungen/

BMF (2014). *Bundesfinanzgesetz (Federal Finance Act)*. Federal Ministry of Finance. Retrieved from https://service.bmf.gv.at/BUDGET/Budgets/2014_2015/bfg2014/Bundesfinanzgesetz_2014.pdf

BMF (2015). *Bundesfinanzgesetz (Federal Finance Act)*. Federal Ministry of Finance. Retrieved from https://service.bmf.gv.at/BUDGET/Budgets/2014_2015/bfg2015/Bundesfinanzgesetz_2015.pdf

BMF (2016). *Bundesfinanzgesetz (Federal Finance Act)* Retrieved from https://service.bmf.gv.at/BUDGET/Budgets/2016/bfg/Bundesfinanzgesetz_2016.pdf

BMWFW (2011). Mitterlehner: Neue Modernisierungspartnerschaft mit Russland fixiert (Press Release of the Federal Ministry for Science, Research and Economy). Retrieved 2nd of May, 2017, from http://www.bmwfw.gv.at/Presse/Archiv/Archiv2011/Seiten/russischeKommission.aspx

BMWFW (2013). Mitterlehner: Wirtschaftsbeziehungen mit Russland auf neue Ebene heben (Press Release of the Federal Ministry of Science, Research and Economy). Retrieved 2nd of May, 2017, from http://www.bmwfw.gv.at/Presse/Archiv/Archiv2013/Seiten/MitterlehnerWirtschaftsbeziehungenmitRusslandaufneueEbeneheben.aspx

Böhler, I. (2007). "Wenn die Juden ein Volk sind, so ist es ein mieses Volk": Die Kreisky-Peter-Wiesenthal Affäre 1975. In M. Gehler & H. Sickinger (Eds.), *Politische Affären und Skandale in Österreich: Von Mayerling bis Waldheim* (pp. 502-531) Innsbruck/Wien/Bozen: Studien Verlag

Bratberg, Ø. (2007). Bilateral Diplomacy in an Integrated Europe: The Co-existence of Institutional Orders? *ARENA Working Paper (10)*: Arena Centre for European Studies, University of Oslo

Bruckmüller, E. (1994). *Österreichbewusstsein im Wandel: Identität und Selbstverständnis in den 90er Jahren*. Wien: Amalthea Signum Verlag

Bull, H. (1977). *The Anarchical Society: A Study of Order in World Politics*. London: Verso

Bulmer, S. J., & Radaelli, C. M. (2004). The Europeanisation of National Policy? *Queen's Papers on Europeanisation (1)*: Queen's University of Belfast

Bunzl, J. (1991). *Gewalt ohne Grenzen: Nahost-Terror und Österreich*. Wien: Braumüller

Bußjäger, P. (2012). Föderalismus in Österreich, Deutschland und der Schweiz. In P. Filzmaier, P. Plaikner, & K. A. Duffek (Eds.), *Bundesländer und Landtage: Föderalismus und politischer Wettbewerb, österreichische Besonderheiten und internationaler Vergleich* (pp. 37-53) Wien: Facultas

Caporaso, J. A. (2000). Changes in the Westphalian Order: Territory, Public Authority, and Sovereignty. *International Studies Review, 2*(2), 1-28

Carta, C., & Whitman, R. (2013). The United Kingdom and the European External Action Service. In R. Balfour & K. Raik (Eds.), *The European External Action Service and National Diplomacies* (pp. 137-148). EPC Issue Paper (73): European Policy Centre

Cede, F., & Prosl, C. (2015). *Anspruch und Wirklichkeit: Österreichs Außenpolitik seit 1945*. Innsbruck/Wien/Bozen: Studien Verlag

Checkel, J. T. (2005). International Institutions and Socialization in Europe: Introduction and Framework. *International Organization, 59*(4), 801-826

Christen, E., Fritz, O., Huber, P., & Streicher, G. (2014). *Makroökonomische Effekte des Handelskonflikts zwischen der EU und Russland*. Österreichisches Institut für Wirtschaftsforschung. Retrieved from http://www.bmwfw.gv.at/EnergieUnd Bergbau/Energieeffizienz/Documents/Endbericht%20EU-Russland%20Sanktionen %20WIFO%2010.12.2014.pdf

Comelli, M., & Matarazzo, R. (2011). Rehashed Commission Delegations or Real Embassies? EU Delegations Post-Lisbon. *IAI Working Papers (11/23)*: Instituto Affari Internazionali

Declaration of the Four Nations on General Security (1943). Retrieved 2nd of May, 2017, from http://www.ibiblio.org/pha/policy/1943/431000a.html

Der Derian, J. (1987). *On Diplomacy: A Genealogy of Western Estrangement*. Oxford: Basil Blackwell

Der Derian, J. (2009). Mediating Estrangement: A Theory for Diplomacy. In J. Der Derian (Ed.), *Critical Practices in International Theory: Selected Essays* (pp. 7-31). Abingdon/New York: Routledge

Der Standard (2007). Plassnik will Außenministerium umbenennen. Retrieved 2nd of May, 2017, from http://derstandard.at/2726727/Plassnik-will-Aussenministerium-umbenennen

Dialer, D., & Mast, F. (2012). EU-Lobbying der Regionen am Beispiel österreichischer Bundesländer. In P. Filzmaier, P. Plaikner, & K. A. Duffek (Eds.), *Bundesländer und Landtage: Föderalismus und politischer Wettbewerb, österreichische Besonderheiten und internationaler Vergleich* (pp. 74-90). Wien: Facultas

DiMaggio, P. J. (1997). Culture and Cognition. *Annual review of sociology, 23*, 263-287

DiMaggio, P. J., & Powell, W. W. (1991a). Introduction. In W. W. Powell & P. J. DiMaggio (Eds.), *The New Institutionalism in Organizational Analysis* (pp. 1-40). Chicago/London: University of Chicago Press

DiMaggio, P. J., & Powell, W. W. (1991b). The Iron Cage Revisited: Institutional Isomorphism and Collective Rationality in Organization Fields. In W. W. Powell & P. J. DiMaggio (Eds.), *The New Institutionalism in Organizational Analysis* (pp. 63-82). Chicago/London: University of Chicago Press

Diplomatische Akademie Wien (2018). *Mission Statement*. Retrieved 10th of February 2018, 2018, from https://www.da-vienna.ac.at/de/Die-Akademie/Diplomatische-Akademie-Wien/Mission-Statement

Dobbin, F. (1994). *Forging Industrial Policy: The United States, Britain and France in the Railway Age*. New York: Cambridge University Press

Doktor, C. (2007). *Die Aussen- und Sicherheitspolitik Österreichs und der Schweiz gegenüber der GASP der Europäischen Union: Eine diskurstheoretische Analyse*. Berlin/Münster/Wien/Zürich/London: LIT Verlag

Duke, S. (2012). Now We Are One... A Rough Start for the EEAS. *Eipascope*(1), 25-29

Duke, S. (2015). Diplomatic Training in the European Union. In D. Spence & J. Bátora (Eds.), *The European External Action Service: European Diplomacy Post-Westphalia* (pp. 403.418). Basingstoke, New York: Palgrave Macmillan

ECFR (2012). *European Foreign Policy Scorecard 2012*. London: European Council on Foreign Relations

ECFR (2013). *European Foreign Policy Scorecard 2013*. London: European Council on Foreign Relations

ECFR (2014). *European Foreign Policy Scorecard 2014*. London: European Council on Foreign Relations

ECFR (2015). *European Foreign Policy Scorecard 2015*. London: European Council on Foreign Relations

ECFR (2016). *European Foreign Policy Scorecard 2016*. London: European Council on Foreign Relations

EEAS (2016). European Diplomatic Programme. Retrieved 2nd of May, 2017, from https://eeas.europa.eu/headquarters/headquarters-homepage_en/2464/European%20Diplomatic%20Programme

EEAS (2017a). Delegation of the European Union to the former Yugoslav Republic of Macedonia: Chronology of Bilateral Relations. Retrieved 2nd of May, 2017, from http://eeas.europa.eu/delegations/the_former_yugoslav_republic_of_macedonia/eu_the_former_yugoslav_republic_of_macedonia/chronology/index_en.htm

EEAS (2017b). The EU's many International Roles. Retrieved 2nd of May, 2017, from http://www.eeas.europa.eu/what_we_do/index_en.htm

Egeberg, M. (2004). An Organisational Approach to European Integration: Outline of a Complementary Perspective. *European Journal of Political Research, 43*(2), 199-219

Eisenstadt, S. N. (1964). Institutionalization and Change. *American Sociological Review, 29*(2), 235-247

Embacher, H., & Reiter, M. (1998). *Gratwanderungen: Die Beziehungen zwischen Österreich und Israel im Schatten der Vergangenheit*. Wien: Picus

Enos-Attali, S. (2005). *Is Non-Alignment Still a Relevant Foreign and Security Policy Option for Small EU Member States? A Comparative Study of the Choices made by Austria, Ireland, Malta and Sweden with Respect to the Changing Global Security Environment.* Conference Paper Presented at the CEPSA Annual Conference 2005: Wien. Retrieved from http://politikwissenschaft.univie.ac.at/fileadmin/user_upload/inst_politikwiss/Veranstaltungen/CEPSA/enos-attali_sophie.pdf

European Commission (2014). *International Cooperation and Development: Fighting Poverty in a Changing World.* Brussels: Luxembourg Publications Office of the European Union

European Commission (2015a). *Commission Staff Working Document: Kosovo* 2015 Report.* Retrieved from http://ec.europa.eu/enlargement/pdf/key_documents/2015/20151110_report_kosovo.pdf

European Commission (2015b). *Commission Staff Working Document: Montenegro 2015 Report.* Retrieved from http://ec.europa.eu/enlargement/countries/detailed-country-information/montenegro/index_en.htm

European Commission (2015c). *Commission Staff Working Document: The Former Yugoslav Republic of Macedonia Report 2015.* Retrieved from http://ec.europa.eu/enlargement/pdf/key_documents/2015/20151110_report_the_former_yugoslav_republic_of_macedonia.pdf

European Council (2010). Council Decision of 26 July 2010: Establishing the Organisation and Functioning of the European External Action Service. *Official Journal of the European Union*(2010/427/EU), L 201/230-L 201/240

Ferguson, Y. H., & Mansbach, R. W. (1996). *Polities: Authority, Identities, and Change.* Columbia: University of South Carolina Press

Ferrero-Waldner, B. (2002). *Kurs setzen in einer veränderten Welt*: Holzhausen

Flick, U. (2012). *Qualitative Sozialforschung: Eine Einführung* (Fifth Ed.). Reinbek bei Hamburg: Rowohlt

Fossum, J. E. (2002). The Transformation of the Nation-State: Why Compare the EU and Canada? *ARENA Working Paper (28)*: Arena Centre for European Studies, University of Oslo

Froschauer, U., & Lueger, M. (2003). *Das qualitative Interview.* Wien: WUV

Gärtner, H., Höll, O., & Luif, P. (2005). Österreichische Außen- und Sicherheitspolitik. In G. E. Gustenau (Ed.), *Österreich als außen- und sicherheitspolitischer Akteur: Anspruch und Wirklichkeit* (pp. 10-16). Wien: Büro für Sicherheitspolitik des Bundesministeriums für Landesverteidigung

Gehler, M. (1995). "L'unique objectiv des Soviétiques est de viser l'Allemagne" Staatsvertrag und Neutralität 1955 als "Modell" für Deutschland? In T. Albrich, K.

Eisterer, M. Gehler, & R. Steininger (Eds.), *Österreich in den Fünfzigern* (pp. 259-298). Innsbruck/Wien: Studien Verlag

Gehler, M. (1996). *Verspielte Selbstbestimmung? Die Südtirolfrage 1945/46 in US-Geheimdienstberichten und österreichischen Akten: Eine Dokumentation.* Innsbruck: Universitätsverlag Wagner

Gehler, M. (2005a). *Österreichs Außenpolitik der Zweiten Republik: Von der alliierten Besatzung bis zum Europa des 21. Jahrhunderts* (Vol. 1). Innsbruck: Studien Verlag

Gehler, M. (2005b). *Österreichs Außenpolitik der Zweiten Republik: Von der alliierten Besatzung bis zum Europa des 21. Jahrhunderts* (Vol. 2). Innsbruck: Studien Verlag

Gehler, M. (2007a). "...eine grotesk überzogene Dämonisierung eines Mannes..." Die Waldheim-Affäre 1986 - 1992. In M. Gehler & H. Sickinger (Eds.), *Politische Affären und Skandale in Österreich: Von Mayerling bis Waldheim* (pp. 614-666). Innsbruck/Wien/Bozen: Studien Verlag

Gehler, M. (2007b). "...this nine days wonder?" Die "Figl-Fischerei" von 1947: Eine politische Affäre mit Nachspiel. In M. Gehler & H. Sickinger (Eds.), *Politische Affären und Skandale in Österreich: Von Mayerling bis Waldheim* (pp. 346-381). Innsbruck/Wien/Bozen: Studien Verlag

Gehler, M., & Bischof, G. (2006). Austrian Foreign Policy after World War II. In G. Bischof, A. Pelinka, & M. Gehler (Eds.), *Austrian Foreign Policy in Historical Context* (pp. 1-24). New Brunswick: Library of Congress

Gehmacher, E., Birk, F., & Ogris, G. (1986). Die Waldheim Wahl: Eine erste Analyse. *Journal für Sozialforschung, 3*(26), 319-331

Goetschel, L. (1998). The Foreign and Security Policy Interests of Small States in Today's Europe. In L. Goetschel (Ed.), *Small States Inside and Outside the European Union. Interests and Politics* (pp. 13-31). Boston: Kluwer Academic Publishers

Gromadzki, G. (2013). Poland and the European External Action Service. In R. Balfour & K. Raik (Eds.), *The European External Action Service and National Diplomacies* (pp. 63-73). EPC Issue Paper (73): European Policy Centre

Gross, L. (1948). The Peace of Westphalia: 1648-1948. *The American Journal of International Law, 42*(1), 20-41

Hagemann, S. (2010). Voting, Statements and Coalition-Building in the Council from 1999 to 2006. In D. Naurin & H. Wallace (Eds.), *Unveiling the Council of the European Union: Games Governments play in Brussels* (pp. 36-58). Basingstake/New York: Palgrave Macmillan

Hahn-Fuhr, I., & Worschech, S. (2014). External Democracy Promotion and Divided Civil Society: The Missing Link. In T. Beichelt, I. Hahn-Fuhr, F. Schimmelfennig, & S. Worschech (Eds.), *Civil Society and Democracy Promotion: Challenges to Democracy in the 21st Century* (pp. 11-41). Basingstoke/New York: Palgrave Macmillan

Heer, F. (1981). *Der Kampf um die österreichische Identität*. Wien: Böhlau

Held, D., McGrew, A. G., Goldblatt, D., & Perraton, J. (1999). *Global Transformations: Politics, Economics and Culture*. Cambridge: Polity Press

Hey, J. A. (2003). Introducing Small State Foreign Policy. In J. A. Hey (Ed.), *Small States in World Politics: Explaining Foreign Policy Behavior* (pp. 1-12). Colorado: Lynne Rienner Publishers

Hinteregger, G. (2008). *Im Auftrag Österreichs. Gelebte Außenpolitik von Kreisky bis Mock*. Wien: Amalthea Signum Verlag

Hocking, B. (2005a). Conclusion. In B. Hocking & D. Spence (Eds.), *Foreign Ministries in the European Union: Integrating Diplomats* (pp. 273-286). New York: Palgrave Macmillan

Hocking, B. (2005b). Introduction: Gatekeepers and Boundary-Spanners: Thinking about Foreign Ministries in the European Union. In B. Hocking & D. Spence (Eds.), *Foreign Ministries in the European Union: Integrating Diplomats* (pp. 1-17). Basingstoke/New York: Palgrave Macmillan

Hocking, B. (2013). The Ministry of Foreign Affairs and the National Diplomatic System. In P. Kerr & G. Wiseman (Eds.), *Diplomacy in a Globalizing World: Theories and Practices* (pp. 123-140). New York: Oxford University Press

Höll, O. (1994). The Foreign Policy of the Kreisky Era. In G. Bischof & A. Pelinka (Eds.), *The Kreisky Era in Austria* (pp. 32-77). New Brunswick: Transaction Publishers

Höll, O. (2001). Österreich unter Beobachtung: Ein Rück- und Ausblick. In ÖGAVN (Ed.), *Österreichisches Jahrbuch für Internationale Politik 2000* (pp. 23-33). Wien: Braumüller

Höll, O. (2002). Außen- und Sicherheitspolitik. In H. Neisser & S. Puntscher-Riekmann (Eds.), *Europäisierung der österreichischen Politik. Konsequenzen der EU-Mitgliedschaft* (pp. 369-395). Wien: WUV-Universitäts-Verlag

Höll, O. (2010a). Österreichs Rolle in der EU: Europäische Erwartungen und österreichische Realität. In J. Pucher & J. Frank (Eds.), *Strategie und Sicherheit 2010: Das strategische Profil der Europäischen Union* (pp. 365-374). Wien: Böhlau

Höll, O. (2010b). Wolfgang Schüssel and Austrian Foreign Policy. In G. Bischof & F. Plasser (Eds.), *The Schüssel Era in Austria*. New Orleans: New Orleans University Press

Höll, O. (2014). Die Österreichische Außen- und Sicherheitspolitik der 2. Republik. In P. Strobl (Ed.), *Österreich in der Zweiten Republik: Ein Land im Wandel* (pp. 71-88). Hamburg: Verlag Dr. Kovac

Höll, O., Pollak, J., & Puntscher-Riekmann, S. (2003). *Austria: Structural Domestic Change through European Integration*. Wien: Österreichische Akademie der Wissenschaften, Forschungsstelle für Institutionellen Wandel und Europäische Integration

Holsti, K. J. (2004). *Taming the Sovereigns: Institutional Change in International Politics*. New York: Cambridge University Press

Ishkanian, A. (2014). Engineered Civil Society: The Impact of 20 Years of Democracy Promotion on Civil Society Development in Former Soviet Countries. In T. Beichelt, I. Hahn-Fuhr, F. Schimmelfennig, & S. Worschech (Eds.), *Civil Society and Democracy Promotion: Challenges to Democracy in the 21st Century* (pp. 150-170). Basingstoke/New York: Palgrave Macmillan

Jones, R. A. (1983). *The British Diplomatic Service 1815-1914*. Waterloo: Wilfrid Laurier University Press

Jönsson, C., & Hall, M. (2005). *Essence of Diplomacy*. Basingstoke/New York: Palgrave Macmillan

Juncos, A., & Pomorska, K. (2006). Playing the Brussels Game: Strategic Socialisation in the CFSP Council Working Groups. *European Integration Online Papers, 10*(11)

Juncos, A., & Pomorska, K. (2015). Attitudes, Identities and the Emergence of an Esprit the Corps in the EEAS. In D. Spence & J. Bátora (Eds.), *The European External Action Service: European Diplomacy Post-Westphalia* (pp. 373-391). Basingstoke, New York: Palgrave Macmillan

Kaeding, M., & Selck, T. J. (2005). Mapping out Political Europe: Coalition Patterns in EU Decision-making. *International Political Science Review, 26*(3), 271-290

Karsh, E. (1988). *Neutrality and Small States*. Abingdon/New York: Routledge

Kernaghan, K. (2000). The Post-bureaucratic Organization and Public Service Values. *International Review of Administrative Sciences, 66*(91), 91-104

Keukeleire, S. (2003). The European Union as a Diplomatic Actor: Internal, Traditional, and Structural Diplomacy. *Diplomacy and Statecraft, 14*(3), 31-56

Kiss, L. J., Königova, L., & Luif, P. (2003). Die "Regionale Partnerschaft": Subregionale Zusammenarbeit in der Mitte Europas. *Österreichische Zeitschrift für Politikwissenschaft, 32*(1), 57-75

Kneucker, R. (1983). Institutionelle Aspekte der Außenpolitik. In R. Kicker, A. Khol, & H. Neuhold (Eds.), *Außenpolitik und Demokratie in Österreich: Strukturen - Strategien - Stellungnahmen* (pp. 31-110). Salzburg: Wolfgang Neugebauer Verlag

Knitel, H. G. (1986). Wien als Sitz internationaler Organisationen und als internationale Konferenzsstadt *Österreichisches Jahrbuch für Politik 1985* (pp. 471-494). Wien/München: Böhlau

Kofler, M. (2003). *Kennedy und Österreich: Neutralität im Kalten Krieg*. Innsbruck/Wien: Studien Verlag

Kramar, K. (2014). "Neutrales Land kann Gesprächskanal bieten" (Interview with Austrian Foreign Minister Sebastian Kurz). Retrieved 2nd of May, 2017, from http://kurier.at/politik/inland/pragmatismus-bei-putin-besuch/71.810.594#section-71877713

Kramer, H. (1988). "Wende" in der österreichischen Außenpolitik? Zur Außenpolitik der SPÖ-ÖVP-Koalition. *Österreichische Zeitschrift für Politikwissenschaft*(17), 117-131

Kramer, H. (2006). Strukturentwicklung der Außenpolitik (1945-2005). In H. Dachs (Ed.), *Politik in Österreich: das Handbuch* (pp. 807-837). Wien: Manz

Kramer, H. (2013). Österreichs Beitrag zur europäischen und globalen Sicherheit: Ein Plädoyer für mehr Selbstbewusstsein im Bekenntnis zu aktiver Neutralitäts- und Friedenspolitik. In T. Roithner, J. Frank, & E. Huber (Eds.), *Wieviel Sicherheit braucht der Friede? Zivile und militärische Näherungen zur österreichischen Sicherheitsstrategie* (pp. 89-100). Münster: LIT Verlag

Kramer, H. (2016). Austrian Foreign Policy 1995-2015. *Austrian Journal of Political Science, 45*(2), 49-57

Krasner, S. D. (1993). Westphalia and All That. In J. Goldstein & R. O. Keohane (Eds.), *Ideas and Foreign Policy* (pp. 235-264). New York: Cambridge Univ Press

Krasner, S. D. (1999). *Sovereignty: Organized Hypocrisy*: Princeton University Press

Krüger, M. (2003). Austria. In H. Ojanen (Ed.), *FIIA Report 2003: Neutrality and Non-alignment in Europe Today* (pp. 9-13). Helsinki: Finnish Institute of International Affairs

Krupa, M. (2013). Seid umschlungen! Zeit Online. Retrieved 2nd of May, 2017, from http://www.zeit.de/2013/01/Europa-Krise-Politik/seite-1

Lehnguth, C. (2013). *Waldheim und die Folgen: Der parteipolitische Umgang mit dem Nationalsozialismus in Österreich*. Frankurt am Main: Campus Verlag

Leitbetriebe Austria (2015). Integration ist Wachstumschance für heimischen Mittelstand. Retrieved 2nd of May, 2017, from http://www.leitbetriebe.at/integration-ist-wachstumschance-fur-heimischen-mittelstand/

Lewis, J. (2010). Strategic Bargaining, Norms and Deliberation. In D. Naurin & H. Wallace (Eds.), *Unveiling the Council of the European Union: Games Governments play in Brussels* (pp. 165-184). Basingstoke/New York: Palgrave Macmillan

Luif, P. (1982). Österreich zwischen den Blöcken: Bemerkungen zur Außenpolitik des neutralen Österreich. *Österreichische Zeitschrift für Politikwissenschaft, 11*(2), 209-220

Luif, P. (1995). *On the Road to Brussels. The Political Dimension of Austria's, Finland's, and Sweden's Accession to the European Union.* . Wien: Braumüller

Luif, P. (2000). Österreich und die europäische Integration 1984-1995. In M. Gehler & R. Steininger (Eds.), *Die Neutralen und die europäische Integration 1945-1995* (pp. 680-701). Wien: Böhlau

Luif, P. (2003a). Austria: The Burdens of History. In J. A. K. Hey (Ed.), *Small States in World Politics: Explaining Foreign Policy Behavior* (pp. 95-116). Colorado: Lynne Rienner Publishers

Luif, P. (2003b). The Changing Role of the Non-allied Countries in the European Union's Common Foreign and Security Policy. In M. Gehler, A. Pelinka, & G. Bischof (Eds.), *Österreich in der Europäischen Union: Bilanz seiner Mitgliedschaft* (pp. 275-296). Wien/Köln/Weimar: Böhlau

Luif, P. (2006). Österreich und die Europäische Union. In H. Dachs, P. Gerlich, H. Gottweis, H. Kramer, V. Lauber, W. C. Müller, & E. Tálos (Eds.), *Politik in Österreich: Das Handbuch* (pp. 862-883). Wien: Manz

Luif, P. (2007). Der lange Weg nach Brüssel. In P. Luif (Ed.), *Österreich, Schweden, Finnland: Zehn Jahre Mitgliedschaft in der Europäischen Union* (pp. 61-84). Wien/Köln/Weimar: Böhlau

March, J. G., & Olsen, J. P. (1989). *Rediscovering Institutions: The Organizational Basis of Politics*. New York: Free Press

March, J. G., & Olsen, J. P. (1998). The Institutional Dynamics of International Political Orders. *International Organization, 52*(4), 943-969

March, J. G., & Olsen, J. P. (2004). The Logic of Appropriateness *ARENA Working Paper (4)*: Arena Centre for European Studies, University of Oslo

Marcussen, M., Risse, T., Engelmann-Martin, D., Knopf, H. J., & Roscher, K. (1999). Constructing Europe? The Evolution of French, British and German Nation State Identities. *Journal of European Public Policy, 6*(4), 614-633

Mattila, M. (2010). Voting and Coalitions in the Council after the Enlargement. In D. Naurin & H. Wallace (Eds.), *Unveiling the Council of the European Union: Games Governments play in Brussels* (pp. 23-35). Basingstoke/New York: Palgrave Macmillan

Mattingly, G. (1955). *Renaissance Diplomacy*. Baltimore: Penguin Books

Maurer, H. (2016). Austrian Diplomacy in a Changing Global and European Context: Between Innovation, Adaptation and Resilience. *Austrian Journal of Political Science, 45*(2), 35-47

Maurer, H., & Raik, K. (2014). Pioneers of a European Diplomatic System: EU Delegations in Moscow and Washington *FIIA Analysis* (Vol. 1): The Finnish Institute of International Affairs

Melissen, J. (2005). The New Public Diplomacy: Between Theory and Practice. In J. Melissen (Ed.), *The New Public Diplomacy: Soft Power in International Relations* (pp. 3-27). Basingstoke/New York: Palgrave Macmillan

Meyer, J. W., & Scott, W. R. (1992). Centralisation and the Legitimacy Problems of Local Government. In J. W. Meyer & R. W. Scott (Eds.), *Organizational Environments: Ritual and Rationality* (pp. 199-215). Newbury Park: Sage

Moser, M. (2015a). Der Gentest. *NZZ Österreich*. Retrieved 30th of April, 2017, from https://nzz.at/phenomenon/der-gentest/

Moser, M. (2015b). Extrapunkte für Geeignete. *NZZ Österreich*. Retrieved 30th of April, 2017, from https://nzz.at/phenomenon/extrapunkte-fuer-geeignete/

Murdoch, Z., & Trondal, J. (2015). The Advance of a European Executive Order in Foreign Policy? Recruitment Practices in the European External Action Service. In D. Spence & J. Bátora (Eds.), *The European External Action Service: European Diplomacy Post-Westphalia* (pp. 105-122). Basingstoke, New York: Palgrave Macmillan

Naurin, D., & Wallace, H. (2010). Introduction: From Rags to Riches. In D. Naurin & H. Wallace (Eds.), *Unveiling the Council of the European Union: Games Governments play in Brussels* (pp. 1-20). Basingstoke/New York: Palgrave Macmillan

Neuhold, H. (1992). Die dauernde Neutralität Österreichs in einem sich wandelnden internationalen System. In H. Neuhold & P. Luif (Eds.), *Das außenpolitische Bewußtsein der Österreicher: Aktuelle internationale Probleme im Spiegel der Meinungsforschung* (pp. 87-108). Wien: Braumüller

Neuhold, H. (2003). Comments on the Austrian Positions. In H. Ojanen (Ed.), *FIIA Report 2003: Neutrality and Non-alignment in Europe Today* (pp. 14-18). Helsinki: Finnish Institute of International Affairs

Neuhold, H. (2005). Austria. In B. Hocking & D. Spence (Eds.), *Foreign Ministries in the European Union: Integrating Diplomats*. Basingstoke/New York: Palgrave Macmillan

Neumann, I. B. (2003). The English School on Diplomacy: Scholarly Promise Unfulfilled. *International Relations, 17*(3), 341-369

Neumann, I. B. (2005). To be a Diplomat. *International Studies Perspectives, 6*(1), 72-93

Nicolson, H. G. (1988). *Diplomacy*. London: Oxford University Press

Nowotny, E. (2006). Diplomats: Symbols of Sovereignty become Managers of Interdependence: The Transformation of the Austrian Diplomatic Service. In G. Bischof, A. Pelinka, & M. Gehler (Eds.), *Austrian Foreign Policy in Historical Context* (pp. 25-38). New Brunswick: Transaction Publishers

Nowotny, T. (2011). *Diplomacy and Global Governance: The Diplomatic Service in an Age of Worldwide Interdependence*. New Brunswick: Transaction Publishers

Öhlinger, T. (2002). Die Europäisierung der österreichischen Verfassung. In H. Neisser & S. Puntscher-Riekmann (Eds.), *Europäisierung der österreichischen Politik: Konsequenzen der EU-Mitgliedschaft* (pp. 81-100). Wien: WUV

Olsen, J. P. (1996). Europeanization and Nation-State Dynamics. In S. Gustavsson & L. Lewin (Eds.), *The Future of the Nation State: Essays on Cultural Pluralism and Political Integration* (pp. 245-285). Abingdon/Stockholm/New York: Routledge/Nerenius & Santárus Publishers

Olsen, J. P. (2002). The Many Faces of Europeanization. *Journal of Common Market Studies, 40*(5), 921-952

Onestini, C. (2015). A Hybrid Service: Organising Efficient EU Foreign Policy. In D. Spence & J. Bátora (Eds.), *The European External Action Service: European Diplomacy Post-Westphalia* (pp. 65-86). Basingstoke, New York: Palgrave Macmillan

Osiander, A. (2001). Sovereignty, International Relations, and the Westphalian Myth. *International Organization, 55*(2), 251-287

Österreichisches Parlament (1991). *Stenographisches Protokoll der 44. Sitzung des Nationalrates der Republik Österreich (Protocol of the 44th Parliament Session)*. Retrieved from http://www.parlament.gv.at/PAKT/VHG/XVIII/NRSITZ/NRSITZ_00044/imfname_142034.pdf

ÖVP/FPÖ (2017). Zusammen. Für unser Österreich: Regierungsprogramm 2017-2022. Retrieved from https://www.oevp.at/Programme-Statuten-Logos

Pahr, W. (2002). Österreich in der Welt. In R. Kriechbaumer, O. Rathkolb, & O. M. Maschke (Eds.), *Mit anderen Augen gesehen: Internationale Perzeptionen Österreichs 1955-1990* (pp. 1-16). Wien/Köln/Weimar: Böhlau

Panke, D. (2010). Small States in the European Union: Structural Disadvantages in EU Policy-making and Counter-Strategies. *Journal of European Public Policy, 17*(6), 799-817

Paschke, K. T. (2001). Report on the Future of Bilateral Diplomacy in Europe: Report on the Special Inspection of 14 German Embassies in the Countries of the European Union. *Favorita Papers (2)* (pp. 7-30): Vienna School of International Studies

Pelinka, A. (2002). Koalitionen in Österreich: Keine westeuropäische Normalität. In S. Kropp, S. S. Schüttemeyer, & R. Sturm (Eds.), *Koalitionen in West- und Osteuropa* (pp. 69-87). Opladen: Leske + Budrich

Pelinka, A., & Rosenberger, S. (2003). *Österreichische Politik: Grundlagen-Strukturen-Trends*. Wien: Facultas

Peters, B. G. (1998). Managing Horizontal Government: The Politics of Co-ordination. *Public Administration, 76*(2), 295-311

Pleinert, O. (2002). Israels Blick auf Österreich. In O. Rathkolb, O. M. Maschke, & S. A. Lütgenau (Eds.), *Mit anderen Augen gesehen: Internationale Perzeptionen Österreichs 1955-1990* (pp. 761-802). Wien/Köln/Weimar: Böhlau

Pospisil, J., & Khittel, S. (2008). Sicherheitspolitische Entwicklungszusammenarbeit von Kleinstaaten: Eine vergleichende Analyse der Praxis von Österreich, der Schweiz, Schweden und den Niederlanden anhand von ausgewählten Fallbeispielen. *ÖFSE Forum* 37

Pouliot, V. (2010). *International Security in Practice: The Politics of NATO-Russia Diplomacy*. Cambridge: Cambridge University Press

Prior, T., & Ultsch, C. (2017). Koalitionsverhandlungen: Kurz zieht die EU-Agenden an sich. In Die Presse. Retrieved 16th of December 2017, from https://diepresse.com/home/ausland/

eu/5337340/Koalitionsverhandlungen_Kurz-zieht-die-EUAgenden-an-sich

Raik, K. (2013). Estonia and the European External Action Service. In R. Balfour & K. Raik (Eds.), *The European External Action Service and National Diplomacies* (pp. 75-84). EPC Issue Paper (73): European Policy Centre

Rana, K. S. (2011). *21st Century Diplomacy: A Practitioner's Guide*. London/New York: The Continuum International Publishing Group

Rathkolb, O. (1998). "Europa mit der Seele suchen..." Bruno Kreisky's andere Europa Visionen. In Stiftung Bruno Kreisky Archiv/Historisches Museum der Stadt Wien (Ed.), *Bruno Kreisky:Seine Zeit und mehr* (pp. 87-104). Wien

Rathkolb, O. (2004). Die neue "Konsularakademie" 1964: Diplomatische Akademie, ein "Lieblingsprojekt" Außenminister Kreiskys. In O. Rathkolb (Ed.), *250 Jahre: Von der Orientalischen zur Diplomatischen Akademie in Wien* (pp. 197-205). Innsbruck/Wien/München/Bozen: Studien Verlag

Rathkolb, O. (2011). *Die paradoxe Republik: Österreich 1945 bis 2010*. Wien: Haymon Taschenbuch

Rauchensteiner, M. (1981). *Spätherbst 1956: Die Neutralität auf dem Prüfstand.* Wien: Bundesverlag

Rechnungshof (2014). *Struktur österreichischer Vertretungen innerhalb der EU (Report of the Austrian Court of Audit on the Structure of Austrian Representations inside the EU).* Retrieved from_http://www.rechnungshof.gv.at/berichte/ansicht/detail/struktur-oesterreichischer-vertretungen-innerhalb-der-eu.html

Reisacher, M. (2010). *Die Konstruktion des "Staats, den keiner wollte".* (Master Thesis), University of Vienna, Vienna. Retrieved from http://othes.univie.ac.at/10190/1/2010-06-07_0252520.pdf

Riordan, S. (2004). *The New Diplomacy.* Cambridge: Polity

Röhrlich, E. (2009). *Kreiskys Außenpolitik: Zwischen österreichischer Identität und internationalem Programm.* Wien: Vienna University Press

Rosenbaum, E., & Hoffer, W. (1993). *Betrayal: The Untold Story of the Kurt Waldheim Investigation and Cover-Up.* New York: St. Martin's Press

Ruggie, J. G. (1983). Continuity and Transformation in the World Polity: Toward a Neorealist Synthesis. *World Politics, 35*(2), 261-285

Ruggie, J. G. (1993). Territoriality and Beyond: Problematizing Modernity in International Relations. *International Organization, 47*(1), 139-174

Salzburger Nachrichten (2015). Außenministerium wird "redimensioniert". Retrieved 8th of October, 2017, from_http://www.salzburg.com/nachrichten/oesterreich/politik/sn/artikel/aussenministerium-wird-redimensioniert-155586/

Schattovits, H. A. (1986). *Aufgabenplanung: Ansätze für rationale Verwaltungsreform.* Wien/Köln/Graz: Böhlau

Schilling, H. (1998). Der Westfälische Friede und das neuzeitliche Profil Europas. In H. Durchhardt (Ed.), *Der Westfälische Friede: Diplomatie, politische Zäsur, kulturelles Umfeld, Rezeptionsgeschichte* (pp. 1-32). München: Oldenbourg Verlag

Schimmelfennig, F. (2014). Democracy Promotion and Civil Society in Eastern Europe: Conclusions. In T. Beichelt, I. Hahn-Fuhr, F. Schimmelfennig, & S. Worschech (Eds.), *Civil Society and Democracy Promotion: Challenges to Democracy in the 21st Century* (pp. 217-233). Basingstoke/New York: Palgrave Macmillan

Schlesinger, T. O. (1972). *Austrian Neutrality in Postwar Europe: The Domestic Roots of a Foreign Policy.* Wien: Braumüller

Schneider, H. (1990). *Alleingang nach Brüssel: Österreichs EG-Politik.* Bonn: Europa Union Verlag

Schütz, A. (1964). The Social World as Taken for Granted and its Structurization. In A. Brodersen (Ed.), *Collected Papers II: Studies in Social Theory* (pp. 229-238). The Hague: Martinus Nijhoff

Scott, W. R. (2014). *Institutions and Organizations: Ideas, Interests, and Identities* (Fourth ed.). Los Angeles: Sage

Seabrooke, L. (2011). Economists and Diplomacy. *International Journal, 66*(3), 629-644

Serrano de Haro, P. A. (2012). Participation of the EU in the Work of the UN: General Assembly Resolution 65/276. *CLEER Working Papers (4)*: CLEER Centre for the Law of EU External Relations

Sharp, P. (1999). For Diplomacy: Representation and the Study of International Relations. *International Studies Review, 1*(1), 33-57

Sharp, P. (2003). Herbert Butterfield, the English School and the Civilizing Virtues of Diplomacy. *International Affairs, 73*(4), 855-878

Sharp, P. (2005). Revolutionary States, Outlaw Regimes and the Techniques of Public Diplomacy. In J. Melissen (Ed.), *The New Public Diplomacy: Soft Power in International Relations* (pp. 106-123). Basingstoke/New York: Palgrave Macmillan

Sharp, P. (2009). *Diplomatic Theory of International Relations* (Vol. 111). New York: Cambridge University Press

Sharp, P. (2013). Diplomacy in International Relations Theory and Other Disciplinary Perspectives. In P. Kerr & G. Wiseman (Eds.), *Diplomacy in a Globalizing World* (pp. 51-67). Oxford/New York: Oxford University Press

Skuhra, A. (1995). Österreich im Sicherheitsrat der Vereinten Nationen 1991/92. *Österreichische Zeitschrift für Politikwissenschaft,*(24), 399-420

Skuhra, A. (2006). Österreichische Sicherheitspolitik. In H. Dachs, P. Gerlich, H. Gottweis, H. Kramer, V. Lauber, W. C. Müller, & E. Tálos (Eds.), *Politik in Österreich: Das Handbuch* (pp. 838-861). Wien: Manz

Sonnleitner, S. (2015). Austrian Bilateral Diplomacy in the Context of EU Membership: Case Study on the Austrian Ministry of Foreign Affairs. *EUFORPOL Working Paper Series (7)*: Institute of European Studies and International Relations, Comenius University Bratislava

SORA/ISA (2013). *Analyse Volksbefragung Wehrpflicht 2013 (Analysis of the Referendum on Compulsory Military Service 2013)*. Institut für Strategieanalysen and Institute for Social Research and Consulting. Retrieved from http://www.sora.at/fileadmin/downloads/wahlen/2013_Volksbefragung_Wahlanalyse.pdf

Spence, D. (2005). The Evolving Role of Foreign Ministries in the Conduct of European Union Affairs. In B. Hocking & D. Spence (Eds.), *Foreign Ministries in the European Union: Integrating Diplomats* (pp. 18-36). Basingstoke/New York: Palgrave Macmillan

Spence, D. (2012). The Early Days of the European External Action Service: A Practioner's View. *The Hague Journal of Diplomacy, 7*(1), 115-134

Spence, D. (2015). The EEAS and Its Epistemic Communities: The Challenges of Diplomatic Hybridism. In D. Spence & J. Bátora (Eds.), *The European External Action Service: European Diplomacy Post-Westphalia* (pp. 43-64). Basingstoke, New York: Palgrave Macmillan

Spruyt, H. (1994). Institutional Selection in International Relations: State Anarchy as Order. *International Organization, 48*(4), 527-557

Stadlmayer, V. (2002) *Kein Kleingeld im Länderschacher: Südtirol, Triest und Alcide Degasperi 1945/1946* (Vol. 320). Innsbruck: Universitätsverlag Wagner

Stangl, A. (2014). Mythen und Narrative: "Der Staat wider Willen" und "Der Staat, den keiner wollte". *Erster Weltkrieg und das Ende der Habsburgermonarchie.* Retrieved 2nd of May, 2017, from http://ww1.habsburger.net/de/kapitel/mythen-und-narrative-der-staat-wider-willen-und-der-staat-den-keiner-wollte

Statistik Austria (2015). Die wichtigsten Handelspartner Österreichs 2015 (Most Important Trading Partners of Austria 2015). Retrieved 30th of April, 2017, from http://www.statistik.at/web_de/services/wirtschaftsatlas_oesterreich/aussenhandel/index.html

Statistik Austria (2016). *Auslandsösterreicherinnen und Auslandsösterreicher 2016 (Number of Austrians Living Abraod 2016).* Retrieved from http://www.statistik.at/web_de/statistiken/menschen_und_gesellschaft/bevoelkerung/internationale_uebersich/index.html

Stourzh, G. (2004). Eine Besprechung in der Armbrustergasse. In O. Rathkolb (Ed.), *250 Jahre: Von der Orientalischen zur Diplomatischen Akademie in Wien* (pp. 183-196). Innsbruck/Wien/München/Bozen: Studien Verlag

Stourzh, G. (2005). *Um Einheit und Freiheit: Staatsvertrag, Neutralität und das Ende der Ost-West-Besetzung Österreichs 1945-1955.* Wien: Böhlau

Suchmann, M. C. (1995). Managing Legitimacy: Strategic and Institutional Approaches. *Academy of Management Review, 20*, 571-610

Tálos, E. (2008). *Sozialpartnerschaft: Ein zentraler politischer Gestaltungsfaktor in der Zweiten Republik.* Innsbruck/Wien/Bozen: Studien Verlag

Terpan, F. (2013). In Search of Leadership: French Expectations of the European External Action Service. In R. Balfour & K. Raik (Eds.), *The European External*

Action Service and National Diplomacies (pp. 129-136). EPC Issue Paper (73): European Policy Centre

Teschke, B. (2003). *The Myth of 1648: Class, Geopolitics, and the Making of Modern International Relations*. London/New York: Verso

Teschke, B. (2006). Debating 'The Myth of 1648': State Formation, the Interstate System and the Emergence of Capitalism in Europe—A Rejoinder. *International Politics, 43*(5), 531-573

Thalberg, H. (1983). Die Nahost-Politik. In E. Bielka, P. Jankowitsch, & H. Thalberg (Eds.), *Die Ära Kreisky: Schwerpunkte der österreichischen Außenpolitik* (pp. 293-322). Wien: Europa Verlag

Thorhallsson, B. (2006). The Size of States in the European Union: Theoretical and Conceptual Perspectives. *European Integration, 28*(1), 7-31

Thornton, P. H., Ocasio, W., & Lounsbury, M. (2012). *The Institutional Logics Perspective: A new Approach to Culture, Structure, and Process*. Oxford/New York: Oxford University Press

Trettler, H. (2007). Der umstrittene Handschlag: Die Affäre Frischenschlager - Reder. In M. Gehler & H. Sickinger (Eds.), *Politische Affären und Skandale in Österreich: Von Mayerling bis Waldheim* (pp. 592-613). Innsbruck/Wien/Bozen: Studien Verlag

Tulmets, E. (2014). *East Central European Foreign Policy Identity in Perspective: Back to Europe and the EU's Neighbourhood*. Basingstoke/New York: Palgrave Macmillan

Uilenreef, A. D. (2013). Reporting and Representation: Intra EU-Diplomacy and Dutch Bilateral Embassies. *The Hague Journal of Diplomacy, 8*(2), 115-137

van Schaik, L. (2013). The Glass is Half Full: The European External Action Service through Dutch Eyes. In R. Balfour & K. Raik (Eds.), *The European External Action Service and National Diplomacies* (pp. 97-106). EPC Issue Paper (73): European Policy Centre

Walgenbach, P., & Meyer, R. E. (2008). *Neoinstitutionalistische Organisationstheorie*. Stuttgart: Kohlhammer

Watson, A. (1984). *Diplomacy: The Dialogue Between States*. London: Routledge

Weber, M. (2006). *Wirtschaft und Gesellschaft*. Paderborn: Voltmedia

Wight, M. (1977). *Sytems of States*. Leicester: Leicester University Press

Wintersteiner, W. (2013). Bescheidener Vorschlag zum Umbau des Verteidigungsministeriums in ein Ministerium für Frieden und Sicherheit: Argumente für eine friedenspolitisch basierte Außenpolitik Österreichs. In T. Roithner, J. Frank, & E.

Huber (Eds.), *Wieviel Sicherheit braucht der Friede? Zivile und militärische Näherungen zur österreichischen Sicherheitsstrategie*. Münster: LIT Verlag

Wistrich, R. S. (1992). The Kreisky Phenomenon: A Reassessment. In R. S. Wistrich (Ed.), *Austrians and Jews in the Twentieth Century: From Franz Joseph to Waldheim* (pp. 234-252). New York: St. Martin's Press

Wittmann, H. (1983). Die Rolle des Parlaments und der Parteien in der Außenpolitik. In R. Kicker, A. Khol, & H. Neuhold (Eds.), *Aussenpolitik und Demokratie in Österreich: Strukturen, Strategien, Stellungnahmen: ein Handbuch* (pp. 111-170). Salzburg: Wolfgang Neugebauer Verlag

WKO (2015). Außenwirtschafts Center (Foreign Trade Centre). Retrieved 23rd of March, 2015, from_https://www.wko.at/Content.Node/service/aussenwirtschaft/AussenwirtschaftsCenter.html

Wodak, R., De Cillia, R., Reisigl, M., & Liebhart, K. (2009). *The Discursive Construction of National Identity*. Edinburgh: Edinburgh University Press

Wright, T. (2013). Bilateral and Multilateral Diplomacy in Normal Times and in Crises. In P. Kerr & G. Wiseman (Eds.), *Diplomacy in a Globalizing World: Theories and Practices* (pp. 175-191). Oxford/New York: Oxford University Press

Yale University (2016). Environmental Performance Index (Vol. 2016)

Yin, R. K. (2009). *Case Study Research: Design and Methods* (Fourth ed.). Thousand Oaks: Sage Publications

Zirnig, D. (2013, 17th of December). Transcript of an Interview with President Heinz Fischer in the TV News Magazine ZIB2 on ORF 2, 16th of December 2013. Retrieved 29th of October, 2015, from http://neuwal.com/index.php/2013/12/17/ich-glaube-dass-dieses-programm-und-diese-mannschaft-einen-vertrauensvorschuss-verdient-heinz-fischer-in-der-zib2-bei-armin-wolf-transkript/

Empirical Sources

Interview-Set 1 – Representatives of Embassies and the MFA
Embassies inside the EU
Interview 1: representative of an inner-EU bilateral embassy, February 2014
Interview 2: representative of an inner-EU bilateral embassy, February 2014
Interview 3: representative of an inner-EU bilateral embassy, July 2014
Interview 4: representative of an inner-EU bilateral embassy, July 2014
Interview 5: representative of an inner-EU bilateral embassy, September 2014
Interview 6: representative of an inner-EU bilateral embassy, September 2014
Embassies in Third Countries
Interview 7: representative of a bilateral embassy in a third country, March 2014
Interview 8: representative of a bilateral embassy in a third country, July 2014
Interview 9: representative of a bilateral embassy in a third country, September 2014
Interview 10: representative of a bilateral embassy in a third country, September 2014
Interview 11: representative of a bilateral embassy in a third country, September 2014
Interview 12: representative of a bilateral embassy in a third country, March 2015
MFA
Interview 13: EU-based representative of the Austrian MFA, February 2014
Interview 14: EU-based representative of the Austrian MFA, February 2014
Interview 15: representative of the Austrian MFA in Vienna, March 2015
Interview 16: representative of the Austrian MFA in Vienna, March 2015
Interview 17: representative of the Austrian MFA in Vienna, March 2015
Interview-Set 2 – Three Generations of Diplomats
Target Group 1
Interview 18: former representative of the Austrian MFA (retired), November 2014
Interview 19: former representative of the Austrian MFA (retired), March 2015
Interview 20: former representative of the Austrian MFA (retired), March 2015
Interview 21: former representative of the Austrian MFA (retired), March 2015
Target Group 2
Interview 22: representative of the Austrian MFA (senior diplomat), January 2015
Interview 23: representative of the Austrian MFA (senior diplomat), March 2015
Interview 24: representative of the Austrian MFA (senior diplomat), March 2015
Interview 25: representative of the Austrian MFA (senior diplomat), May 2015
Target Group 3
Interview 26: representative of the Austrian MFA (junior diplomat), March 2015

Interview 27: representative of the Austrian MFA (junior diplomat), March 2015
Interview 28: representative of the Austrian MFA (junior diplomat), March 2015
Interview 29: representative of the Austrian MFA (junior diplomat), March 2015